658.403
AP AB
1 0 2711.

This book is to be returned on
the last date stamped below

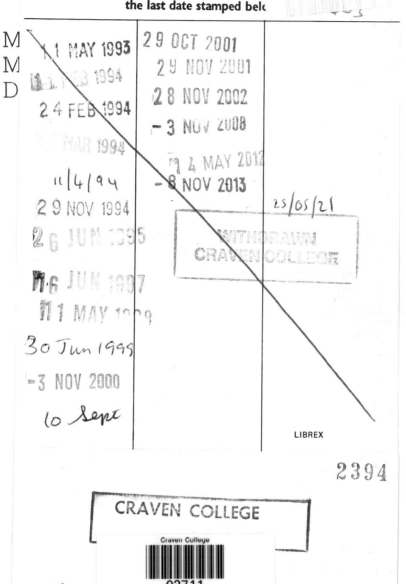

M
M
D

1 1 MAY 1993    2 9 OCT 2001

1994    2 9 NOV 2001

2 4 FEB 1994    2 8 NOV 2002

MAR 1994    - 3 NOV 2008

11/4/94    4 MAY 2012

2 9 NOV 1994    - 8 NOV 2013

2 6 JUN 1995    25/05/21

WITHDRAWN
CRAVEN COLLEGE

1 6 JUN 1997

1 1 MAY 1998

30 Jun 1999

- 3 NOV 2000

10 Sept

LIBREX

2394

CRAVEN COLLEGE

Craven College

02711

# MAKING MANAGEMENT DECISIONS

## SECOND EDITION

## STEVE COOKE
Sheffield Business School

## NIGEL SLACK
University of Warwick

## PRENTICE HALL
NEW YORK   LONDON   TORONTO   SYDNEY   TOKYO   SINGAPORE

First published 1984
This second edition published 1991 by
Prentice Hall International (UK) Ltd
66 Wood Lane End, Hemel Hempstead
Hertfordshire HP2 4RG
A division of
Simon & Schuster International Group

© Prentice Hall International (UK) Ltd, 1991

All rights reserved. No part of this publication may be
reproduced, stored in a retrieval system, or transmitted,
in any form, or by any means, electronic, mechanical,
photocopying, recording or otherwise, without prior
permission, in writing, from the publisher.
For permission within the United States of America
contact Prentice Hall Inc., Englewood Cliffs, NJ 07632.

Typeset in 11/12 pt Compugraphic Times
by MHL Typesetting Ltd, Coventry

Printed and bound in Great Britain
by Page Bros, Norwich

---

Library of Congress Cataloging-in-Publication Data

Cooke, Steve.
 Making management decisions/Steve Cooke and Nigel Slack. — 2nd
ed.
  p. cm.
 Includes bibliographical references and index.
 ISBN 0-13-543406-8
 1. Decision-making. I. Slack, Nigel. II. Title.
 HD30.23.C665 1991
 658.4'03 — dc20                                              90-20450
                                                                  CIP

---

British Library Cataloguing in Publication Data

Cooke, Steve
 Making management decisions. — 2nd ed
 1. Management. Decision making & problem solving
 I. Title II. Slack, Nigel
 658. 403

 ISBN 0-13-543406-8

---

2 3 4 5   95 94 93 92

To builders and shapers
and, of course,
to impress Angela further

CRAVEN COLLEGE

# Contents

CRAVEN COLLEGE

# Part II  The decision makers

## 2  Individual decision behaviour ... 43

## 3  The social context ... 63

# Part IV  Decision practice

## 8  Getting objectives straight ... 223

## 9  Understanding the problem ... 238

## 10  Generating the options ... 258

# Preface

## From the Preface to the First Edition

Making decisions and bearing the responsibility for them is one of the cornerstones of the manager's job. Quite simply, if managers did not make decisions they would not be managers! This fundamental importance of decision making is reflected in the attention shown to it by several academic disciplines. Philosophy, economics, mathematics and the social sciences have all contributed to better the understanding of how decisions are made, or ought to be made.

Among all this interest two academic areas stand out as offering particularly helpful contributions to the practical business of making better decisions. These areas are the *behavioural sciences*, which help us to understand how we and others behave when faced with a decision, and the applied mathematics of *operational research*, which provides potentially powerful tools for the modelling and analysis of complex decisions. Yet the full contribution of these two academic areas is only realized if they are focused through the reality of practical management experience. After all, decision making is an extremely practical business — in making a decision there must be the commitment actually to do something.

To understand management decision making and so hopefully make better decisions, one must be able to recognize different types of decision, understand the contribution of the behavioural and quantitative sciences and have a knowledge of the practical steps to be taken in making decisions.

## The Second Edition

The material for the first edition was originally developed from our experience of running a post-graduate management programme. Since then we have had the opportunity to test out our model and to think through and develop our ideas further.

This has resulted in a number of changes in the second edition. Our basic decision model is simplified in terms of the number of steps it contains, and the idea of the cyclical process is emphasized rather more. We have also introduced the idea of decision making as being a process of expansion and contraction: expansion in those areas where exploration is required, contraction where the need is for initiation of events and of action.

We have also incorporated within Parts II and III suggestions for establishing the support processes necessary (in our view) for high-quality decision making, concentrating in the final part on working through the major stages of objective setting, understanding the problem, generating options, evaluation and choice.

Finally, it might be fair to say that we have chosen to be more prescriptive about our view of good practice where this has seemed to be appropriate. A consequence of this approach is that the statements at the end of each chapter shift from being a rather traditional 'summary' in Part I to 'practical prescriptions' in the remainder of the book.

# Acknowledgements

Help and advice is accumulated over a long period of time. Our thanks go to our colleagues and our students for their advice, criticism and feedback gathered during the past several years. As always, any errors, omissions or misrepresentation of their wise words are entirely our own responsibility.

In today's world of word-processing, much of the burden of the preparation of this edition has fallen on those at home. To our families go our thanks and appreciation.

# PART I

## Decisions and management

Management life, like our everyday life, involves a whole series of decisions. They may be trivial or important, repetitive or novel, expected or unforeseen, but all are part of how managers spend their time. Because of the importance of decision making to managers, we must begin this book by coming to understand exactly what is meant by 'management decisions'. Not surprisingly, two concepts which are crucial in understanding management decisions are those of 'managers and management activity' and 'decisions and decision making'. Part I of this book introduces these issues, and examines the different types of decision which managers may have to face.

CHAPTER 1 — DECISION MAKING IN MANAGEMENT — introduces these concepts by treating decisions as a cyclical process — a sequence of steps or activities through which decision makers work — and second as a collection of elements, the things which are present and can be recognized in all decisions. The idea of expansion and contraction is introduced. We place decision making in a management context by looking at the nature of management activity and identifying its central role.

We then develop a typology, classifying management decisions as to whether they are strategic or operational, unstructured or structured, and dependent or independent of other decisions. The effect of the type of decision on its elements is also illustrated. The influence of an organization's environment is then examined, especially in the way it determines the perceived uncertainty of a decision and the time available to make the decision. Finally, the issue of managerial discretion is discussed.

# 1 Decision making in management

## Introduction

Popular images of management usually place decision making at the centre of management life. The media, and especially television, present the business tycoon and the top manager as a thrusting and dynamic character, almost totally involved in 'making decisions' and 'taking decisive action'. Up to a point, such a portrayal reflects the wider perception of what management is all about. The ability, and particularly the right, to make decisions clearly holds considerable status and is very attractive in the minds of many people. Good managers, it is said, are those who make good decisions. Indeed, it could be that the idea of reaching a position of decision-making power forms one of the most powerful motivators for many entering management who want to 'get to the top'. But is this image, however attractive, a fair representation of what happens in reality? What exactly do we mean by decision making anyway? Do managers actually spend much of their time in making decisions and, when they do, what sort of decisions do they make?

### Good and Bad Decisions

If one of the characteristics of a good manager is the ability to make good decisions, then it seems reasonable to start by trying to identify what a 'good decision' is. After all, we make decisions every day of our lives, most of them trivial, but some of them important, so we should have some basis on which to judge our decisions. It may be that we cannot truly judge how good a decision was without the benefit of perfect hindsight. If, after the consequences of a decision have become obvious, we can say, 'Looking back, the course of action we decided upon was the best available under the circumstances', then the decision can be judged a good one. Alternatively, if we believe that a different choice would have resulted in a better outcome, then the decision can be judged as (if not a bad one) not the best.

The other way of judging decisions involves judging *how* the decision was made.

Using this approach, a good decision is one where the decision maker fully understands the background, objectives, alternative courses of action, and range of possible consequences of a decision. The choice between the alternative courses of action is then made in a rational manner, consistent with the objectives of the decision. Conversely, a bad decision is one which is made in an irrational, careless or frivolous manner.

The paradox in this approach is that a frivolous or even a totally random decision can, by chance, produce a better outcome than the most thorough and conscientious decision! Yet we do believe that there must be a real connection between both methods. In the long run, decisions made in an informed and coherent manner will be more likely to produce satisfactory outcomes than those made without a full understanding of the decision, and of decision making in general.

## The Process of Decision Making

Since one criterion of a good decision is the way it is made, we should examine the process in some detail. The first important point is that, unless we restrict our definition of decision making to the moment of choice itself, it is not a sudden transaction but rather a process which occurs over a period of time. It involves carrying out certain steps in a particular order. These steps and their sequence we shall call the decision-making process.

### Decision Making or Problem Solving?

Before describing the steps in the decision-making process we must say how we see the two interrelated topics of decision making and problem solving fitting together. It is partly a semantic problem. Although both terms are frequently used by management writers, there is some considerable difference and confusion in the literature as to what each term means. Lang et al.,[1] in a review of managerial problem-solving models, summarize this confusion:

> some writers envisage problem solving as a broad process that includes decision making ... Other authors depict the opposite — problem solving as an element in the decision-making process ... A third set of authors treat decision making and problem solving as synonymous and use both terms to describe a general process of information gathering, analysis, and choice behaviour.

In this book we subscribe to the first position — decision making is *part* of the larger process of problem solving. We see decision making as focusing around the central problem of choice between alternative courses of action. Problem solving is a broader process which includes the recognition that problems exist, the interpretation and diagnosis of that problem, and the later implementation of whatever solution is thought to be appropriate. Figure 1.1 illustrates the steps

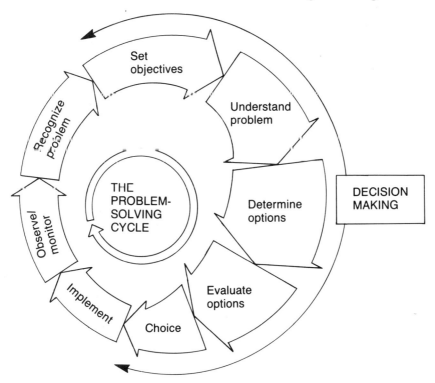

**Figure 1.1** The whole problem-solving cycle involves several stages. Decision making is part of the cycle

involved in this whole process of problem solving and delineates those which we regard as decision making proper and which are largely the concern of this book. However, it is useful to place decision making in its broader context, and so we will describe each of the steps in the total decision-making/problem-solving sequence.

## Steps in the Decision-Making/Problem-Solving Process

### Observe

The decision-making/problem-solving process starts with an individual manager noticing either that something is amiss or that some likely decision opportunity exists in the organization or its environment. This awareness of a potential decision need not necessarily be founded on hard evidence; it could be based on little more than intuition, a general feeling that all is not well. Following the awareness is a period of gestation or reflection which has been likened to *incubation*.[2]

*Recognize Problem*

Eventually, after reflection, or because of the accumulation of evidence, the point is reached where the individual manager is sufficiently convinced that the need for a decision is real. By this time the evidence may be clearly demonstrable, possibly in the form of the deviation of a performance measure from some desired state: for example, high work-in-progress or low sales.

*Set Objectives*

During this phase it is necessary to consider what it is hoped the decision will achieve or what goals it should work towards. Such goals are best described in terms of the behaviour of whatever part of the organization prompted an awareness of the problem in the first place. Frequently, decisions have to work towards several objectives and, in this case, the relative importance of each needs to be understood and to be made explicit.

Objectives are usually concerned with closing the gap between what has been observed and what is regarded as the desired state of the problem area. However, the desired state must be a function of whatever are the overall objectives of the organization. So this phase sometimes involves interpreting, and making operational, a company's overall goals and objectives (Chapter 8 deals with decision objectives in some detail). It also involves setting the boundaries to the decision area.

*Understand Problem*

Faced with a set of stimuli which are interpreted as indicating that a problem exists, there is a need for the manager to diagnose the true nature of the problem. This stage is particularly important. Faulty diagnosis — formulating the wrong problem — will seriously affect the rest of the process. The right answer to the wrong problem is as little use as the wrong answer to the right problem.

Where decisions are well 'structured' and understood, diagnosis can be simple. Many problems, however, are seen in different ways by different people, and this means that reaching agreement over the nature of the problem can sometimes become a difficult decision process. The end point of this stage is an agreed interpretation of a problem into its operational form. It often involves clarifying details of the problem and sometimes formalizing it by making a written statement or request for a decision. Chapter 9 deals with this stage.

*Determine the Options*

The length and importance of this phase will depend on how the decision has been defined earlier. If the decision boundaries have been defined narrowly, then the options might be already given (for example, 'Should we take a course of action or not?').

If the decision has been defined more broadly, the process of determining options is essentially a creative one. Solutions which are regarded as having, at least on the face of it, some potential for solving the problem are formally put into the decision arena. In fact, in practice, it can be difficult to separate this phase from the following evaluative phase, since it may include some crude screening of the options which are regarded as poor. But as we shall see in Chapter 10 this 'pre-evaluation' can seriously hinder creative decision making.

## Evaluate Options

The evaluation phase involves determining the extent to which each of the decision options meets the decision objectives. Here, the consequences of each decision option are spelt out in some detail and, if a mathematical model is being used in the decision process, it is now that it is most likely to be of use. Chapter 11 deals with the evaluation phase.

## Choice

This is the point in the decision process towards which all the other stages have been working. It is here that one of the decision options is chosen as being the most likely, if implemented, to prove satisfactory. The procedure for selection will depend largely on the size and constitution of the decision-making body. A single decision maker will exercise preference based on his or her value system and interests. A multi-decision-maker decision body could interact to resolve the choice by any combination of debate, consultation, delegation or political process. Part II covers the theoretical foundations of how single and multiple decision bodies behave, and Chapter 12 in Part IV looks in more detail at the choice stage itself.

## Implement

This phase involves making whatever changes the selected option requires. The effectiveness of the implementation phase will depend on the skill and ability of the manager charged with the task and also on the 'implementability' of the option itself. In fact the ease with which an option can be implemented is often regarded as an attribute of the option which will be taken into account during the evaluation phase.

## Monitor

When the chosen option has been implemented, it should be monitored to see how effective it is at solving or reducing the original problem. If the monitoring shows that the decision has effectively solved the problem, then this phase marks the end of the process. If, however, the resulting state of the organization is not regarded as satisfactory, then this phase becomes equivalent to the original observation phase, and the whole process starts afresh.

## Recycling in the Decision-Making Process

Although Box 1.1 illustrates what might be regarded as a logical sequence of activities within the decision-making process, it is not wholly representative of

---

## *Box 1.1*

## An Example of a Problem-Solving/Decision-Making Process

### Observe

A company makes specialized quality-testing equipment for the food-processing industry. Its general manager has noticed that the number of late deliveries to customers seems to be increasing.

### Recognition

After a time, the general manager receives a personal complaint from a customer who has suffered a second late delivery. The customer is an important one, and the manager feels the problem can no longer be ignored.

### Set Objectives

The general manager sees the problem as one of 'reducing the number of late deliveries'.

### Understanding the Problem

The general manager calls the manufacturing manager in to discuss the problem. The manufacturing manager argues that the salespeople are quoting unrealistic delivery promises and, when they get large new orders, are not giving enough notice to manufacturing to enable them to plan production effectively.

Faced with this explanation, the general manager defends the sales staff by saying that the nature of the market means that the company must be very competitive on delivery and must also react very quickly to get new business. The result is that they cannot give manufacturing such notice of likely new orders. The marketing manager maintains that the real problem is one of capacity — that the manufacturing manager is trying to keep unit costs down by underinvesting in productive capacity and therefore does not have sufficient flexibility to meet delivery times.

The general manager decides that the problem is essentially one of communication as neither of his subordinates seems to be in possession of pertinent information when making decisions. He then writes a memo to the marketing and manufacturing managers, asking them jointly to determine the best way to improve each other's awareness of current activities, especially the status of all potential customer orders and of shop-floor loading details.

## Determine Options

After consideration, these are listed as:

1. Install an entirely new real-time computer-based information system.
2. Require all salespeople to check with production control before making delivery promises.
3. Have weekly Friday afternoon management meetings.
4. Require all salespeople to fill in weekly 'potential customer' reports which indicate the likelihood of receiving orders from those customers in the near future.

Any combination of the above options is feasible.

## Evaluate Options

Each option is evaluated in terms of the quantity and quality of information it would produce for each department, and the cost in time and money of implementation. Neither the benefits nor the costs of each option are expressed entirely in quantitative terms.

## Select Option

The group decides that option 1 is likely to be too expensive and that option 4 is unlikely to produce much in the way of useful information. They therefore decide that options 2 and 3 should be implemented.

Both managers, together with their deputies, reserve the first two hours on Friday afternoon for regular management meetings. The marketing manager instructs all sales personnel to check with a nominated individual in the production control department before quoting delivery dates.

## Monitor

After six months of the new system, the position has improved but the general manager is still not totally satisfied. In consultation with the other two managers, the problem is redefined to include aspects of the organization of manufacturing, and the process starts over again.

actual management decision making! In practice, the stages in decision making are rarely so clearly defined or recognized as distinct stages by managers. But more importantly, decision making is not so *orderly* as our model implies. The process does not necessarily progress from one phase to the next without any backtracking or recycling. Real decision behaviour can exhibit frequent backtracks and jumps-forward before an option is finally selected. Thus the decision-making process may be not smooth but a jerky and hesitant progression involving, at times, one step forward and two steps backwards.

Recycles or backtracks in the decision process can occur for several different reasons, but two frequently observed causes are comprehension recycles and failure recycles:[3]

- *Comprehension recycles* are where the decision maker backtracks in order to understand the complexity of the decision better.

- *Failure recycles* are where some stage in the decision process has not succeeded in what it set out to do, and so an earlier stage in the decision process must be modified.

So our conceptual model of the decision-making/problem-solving process should more properly include a recycling route, as in Figure 1.2.

## The Elements of a Decision

So far we have described decision making as a process — a series of linked activities. But the process model of management decision does not bring out the key elements contained within a decision, and until we have identified these key elements it is difficult to understand a decision fully or to discriminate between the different types of management decision.

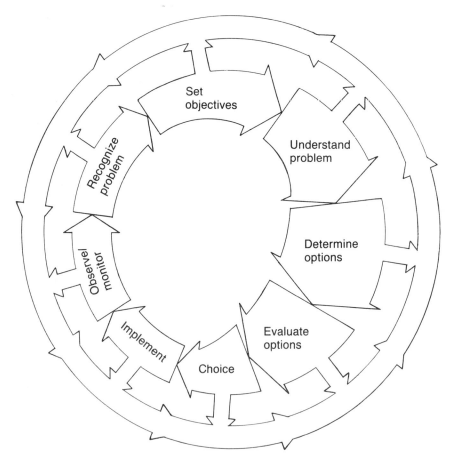

**Figure 1.2** Recycling often occurs in the problem-solving cycle

## Element 1: The Decision Body

By this rather formal term we simply mean the individual or set of individuals who make the decision. We assume that, since decision making involves some commitment to action, the decision body has a reasonable chance of taking the decision through to implementation. The most straightforward decision body to understand is the single decision maker. Where only one decision maker is involved it is that individual's task to carry through the decision making process. When more than one decision maker carries responsibility for the decision, the decision is said to have a 'multi-decision-maker' decision body. The committee is a typical example of a multi-decision-maker decision body (although committees are often there for other purposes as well as decision making). Individual members of committees often are representatives or delegates of parts of the organization and are expected to represent their departmental interests as well as contributing their own views.

In fact, there are very few decisions which can be reached by a single decision maker with total disregard for others' views. Even where the formal procedures of an organization dictate that an individual has the responsibility for making the decision, the views of interested parties will usually need to be sought and the tacit agreement or acquiescence of other individuals and groups obtained. When other managers' views need to be taken into consideration, then they can be considered to be part of the decision body itself. Clearly the implication is that all members of the decision body do not have the same degree of influence on a decision.

It is through the decision body that the organization's objectives are interpreted and translated into operational criteria. This means that the individuals within the decision body not only make the choice itself, but can also play an important part in deciding to what end the decision should be contributing. Furthermore, the decision body can, in effect, control which options are considered, what information is considered as relevant and how each option is evaluated. Because of this, the decision body is the *single most important element* in any decision. The behaviour of decision bodies is looked at in Chapters 2, 3 and 4.

## Element 2: The Decision Options

Decision options are the alternative courses of action between which the decision body must choose. Options lie at the heart of decision making because, unless there is more than one way to proceed, then there is no choice to be made and therefore no decision. The number of options in a decision can be anything between two and infinity. In this sense the simplest decision is that which involves taking a course of action or doing nothing — the yes/no decision. For example, suppose a company is deciding whether or not to subscribe to a new market information service. The decision options are either yes, we will subscribe, or no, we will not subscribe. The decision could then be evaluated by comparing the cost of the service with some estimate of the likely benefit of having the extra market information.

One type of decision where the options are always infinite is the case where the decision variable is continuous. For example, suppose the decision is, 'How much grit should we buy for this winter's road gritting?'. Then theoretically the decision options are infinite and range from zero to an infinite quantity of grit. Of course, we would normally limit the range of options in some way. In the case of buying grit, a sensible lower limit might be the minimum amount ever previously used, and a sensible upper limit the maximum amount ever previously used plus a safety factor. Even then, there are theoretically an infinite number of levels between these two limits; one course would be to take a number of representative levels between them.

As well as the number of options to be considered, the other major characteristic of decision options concerns how discernible they are at the start of the decision process. Some decisions have options which are obvious when the decision is defined: subscribe to the market information service or do not subscribe, for example. In other decisions, the precise nature of the options is not immediately apparent. For example, if the decision is to 'Decide how to improve the quality of market information', then not all the final options which could be considered will be evident without some further thought.

In fact, the options within a decision can turn out to be a mixture taken from a continuum which goes between 'totally defined at the beginning of the decision process' and 'completely novel and developed specifically for the decision in question'. For example, Minzberg *et al.*[4] classify decision options by whether they are:

- Given — fully developed at the start of the decision process.

- Found ready made — fully developed in the environment of the decision and discovered during the decision process.

- Custom made — developed especially for the decision in question.

- Modified — ready-made options with some customized features.

## Element 3: The Uncontrollable Factors

Uncontrollable factors are those parts of the decision which, although having an influence on the final outcome, cannot be controlled directly by the decision body. For example, if we are deciding how much production capacity to allocate to a new product, one of the factors which will influence our decision is the likely demand for the new product. While we cannot control the level of demand for a product directly, it is obviously too important an issue to ignore. One way of coping with this is to treat demand as a 'state of nature': that is, a state which the environment takes after, and independent of, the decision itself.

When there is only one uncontrollable factor, the total possible states of nature will correspond to all the states which that particular uncontrollable factor can take. When more than one uncontrollable factor is involved there could be a state of nature corresponding to every possible combination of the levels which the uncontrollable factors can take. So, for example, if 'total demand' and 'raw material cost' are the two uncontrollable factors in a decision, and if we choose to define three possible demand levels and four levels for raw material cost, then there are twelve possible states of nature in the decision.

When considering the uncontrollable factors within a decision, it is useful to take the three following steps:

1. Identify the factors which will influence the final consequence of a decision.

2. Identify the states or levels which each uncontrollable factor could take.

3. Attempt to predict the likelihood of these states or levels occurring for each of the uncontrollable factors.

So, in the production capacity decision the sequence might be:

1. Identify the factors. (For example, the major uncontrollable factors are (a) the level of demand for the product, and (b) the raw material cost of the product.)

2. Set the different levels. (For example, the level of demand will be between 5000 and 7000 units a year or between 7000 and 9000 units a year. The raw material cost will be between £25 and £30 per unit.)

3. Predict the likelihood. (For example, the probability of demand being between 5000 and 7000 units is 50 per cent, etc.)

## Element 4: The Consequences

For each combination of a decision option and the state of nature, there will be a consequence. Thus, if we have $N$ alternative options and $M$ mutually exclusive states of nature there will be $N \times M$ possible consequences. Figure 1.3 illustrates this as a matrix in which the two dimensions are the decision options and the alternative scenarios or states of nature. Each square of the matrix can then represent a possible consequence of the decision. This matrix formulation of simple decisions is useful, and we shall return to it in Chapter 6.

We can examine the possible consequences of a decision at a number of levels. For example, Mack[5] distinguishes between three levels of consequence:

1. *Primary consequences*, which are the straightforward statements of the operational results of an event.

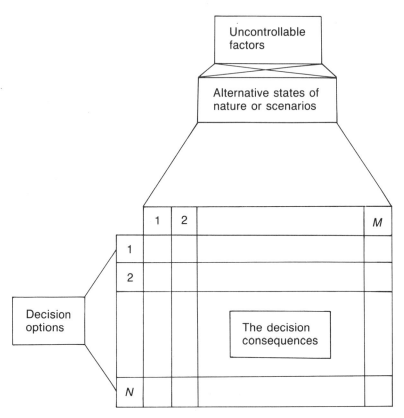

**Figure 1.3** The decision matrix

2. *Surrogate consequences*, which are the interpretation of the event expressed in whatever measures we are using to describe the outcomes.

3. *Evaluated consequences*, which are a measure of the worth or utility of the outcome to the decision body. This latter set of consequences will be a reflection of the decision body's preference or value structure.

Thus, in the capacity decision described previously we could have one particular consequence described at each level by the following statements:

1. *Primary consequence:* 'The annual demand is 8000 units and we have a plant capacity of 7000 units. Raw material cost is £24.'

2. *Surrogate consequence:* 'Profits from the product are running at £50 000 per month and the backlog of orders is high and increasing.'

3. *Evaluated consequence:* 'We are generally satisfied with the outcome in so much as we are getting revenue in at a time when the company badly needs the cash. However, we are worried about the impact on our customers of

the increasing backlog, and we would be willing to trade off some contribution to reduce the backlog.'

Notice how, as we move from primary to evaluated levels, the influence of the decision body becomes more important. A different decision body with different values might have put a quite different interpretation on the outcome at the evaluated level. It might also have chosen a different set of measures at the surrogate level. Notice also how, at each level, we need to describe more than one attribute of the consequence. So, at the primary level, stating the demand level alone would be inadequate; we need to describe demand and capacity and material cost. Similarly, at the evaluated level, we are dealing with two attributes — profits and backlog — although some attempt is being made to bring them together by implying some trade-off between the two. In fact, there is great pressure at the evaluated level to try and express each consequence of a decision in terms of a single composite unit. It would, after all, make evaluation considerably easier. However, as we shall see in Chapter 7, a meaningful overall measure of the value of a decision consequence is difficult to achieve.

## Managers and Decision Making

Although a great deal has been written on the role of the manager, little of it has examined what managers actually do in practice. In common with most writing on management (and indeed with much in this book), authors concerned with managerial jobs tend to offer ideas about what managers *ought* to do, rather than describe what actually happens. The key to understanding the part that decision making plays in a manager's job is to examine what it is that managers do in reality, and exactly how they spend their time. In order to achieve this insight, the first step we must take is to decide what we mean by the term 'manager'.

### What is a Manager?

The concept of 'managing' can be used in at least two very different ways. When we ask someone 'How are you managing?' we usually mean it in the sense of 'Can you cope?' or 'Are you keeping your head above water?' Used in this way, the notion of managing has almost a defensive quality about it. The accent is on mere survival, on riding out the storm and keeping losses, damage or injury to a minimum. There is certainly an element of this kind of management in almost all organizational activity, especially in harsh economic climates. But when we talk about management in organizational terms, we mean something rather more than this.

For example, consider the following quotation:

In general, our understanding of modern management is enhanced if we remember the fundamental managing process: 'managers' perform basic 'management functions' (of planning, organising, staffing, influencing and controlling), which are facilitated by the fundamental 'linking processes' of decision making and communicating, to achieve the basic managerial purpose of organisational effectiveness.[6]

This statement of what managers do (or at least ought to do) contains no suggestion of defensiveness. On the contrary, the impression is one of very positive activity. A range of managerial functions is identified, given means, and an end. (Note that this view of what managers do places considerable emphasis on decision making as a major means of achieving those ends.) So, by identifying these roles within the organization where such functions are located, we can determine who, by this definition, are actually managers, as distinct from those who carry the title of manager.

Mintzberg[7] sees a manager as the person in charge of an organization or one of its component parts. He or she is given formal authority over that unit, and holds responsibility for its efficient production of goods or services, and for the controlled adaptation to changes in its environment. The manager is also concerned with issues of effectiveness, of meeting goals and objectives. In this sense, there is no reason to exclude first-level supervisors from being considered as managers, provided that they meet the requirements of responsibility for production and for adapting to the environment. We should note that the scope of the 'environment' will change with hierarchical level. The environment for a junior manager or foreman will include other parts of the formal organization, as well as the world outside.

## The Range of Managerial Activity

In medium and large organizations, management structure usually involves some separation or delegation of function. Managers are appointed to deal with a particular process or range of operations (Box 1.2). Many managers find themselves with responsibility for a sub-unit within the overall framework of the larger organization. For example, we often find a specialist manager in charge of production. Under him or her there may be shift managers, quality control managers and a number of other specialized management positions. The same process of specialization occurs in other functional areas such as sales and finance. The result is an increase in the number of levels in the management hierarchy, and a widening of the differences between management jobs within the organization.

Faced with the problem of co-ordinating the activities of specialized sub-units, those running large organizations need to develop structures or mechanisms which will allow those units to operate effectively and in the interests of the organization as a whole. So we find specialist management roles (Box 1.3) which are concerned with monitoring, evaluating and co-ordinating (the information managers), and those which exist to provide specialist services and support both to line and senior management (the staff managers).

## Box 1.2

# What Do Managers Do?

Mintzberg[8] has developed a set of ten roles which, he contends, are common to the jobs of all managers. These are divided into three groups:

### The Interpersonal Roles

Managers are given positions of formal authority and status within their organizations. These positions generate three interpersonal roles:

- *Figurehead*. The status of manager obliges the occupant to carry out a number of social, symbolic and legal duties.

- *Leader*. The manager provides direction, guidance and motivation for subordinates. This role includes responsibility for staffing and for training and developing subordinates. Leadership is among the most widely acknowledged of all management roles.

- *Liaison*. Part of the manager's job is to build and maintain links and contacts with groups and individuals outside of the work unit for which he or she is directly responsible. This role helps in linking the organization or parts of the organization with its environment.

### The Informational Roles

Managers find themselves in a rather special focal position in respect of organizational information, both as collectors and as disseminators inside and outside the organization:

- *Monitor*. The manager seeks information in order to identify problems and opportunities, trends and ideas. The monitoring role is necessary in understanding what is going on inside and outside the organization.

- *Disseminator*. The manager is able both to pass information into the organization from outside, and to pass information generated internally to subordinates. Such information can be 'factual' or 'preferential' (what 'ought' to be).

- *Spokesperson*. While the disseminator role is concerned with information inside the organization, the role of spokesperson is concerned with transmitting information outwards into the environment. The manager may be called upon to speak on behalf of the organization as an expert, or as a lobbyist.

### The Decision Roles

The remaining roles are seen as perhaps the most crucial part of the manager's work, justifying the high status and rewards attached to top management jobs:

- *Entrepreneur*. Here the manager sponsors and initiates planned and controlled changes within the organization or work unit. This implies a pro-active approach, planning ahead and seizing opportunities which improve the organization, its efficiency and its performance. The entrepreneurial role will depend heavily on effective monitoring inside and outside the organization.

- *Disturbance Handler*. This role involves coping with the 'involuntary' problems faced by organizations. Unexpected disturbances may occur where, although the change is planned, the full consequences may not be known. They can, of course, also occur as a result of bad management, through insensitive handling of interpersonal and informational roles. In such circumstances, management becomes a 'coping' activity.

- *Resource Allocator.* Managers exercise considerable decision-making authority in allocating scarce resources to others. A manager can allocate resources in three ways: by scheduling time, by programming work and by authorizing planned activities, so determining in a very significant way which of the organizational decisions and activities get implemented or have successful outcomes.

- *Negotiator.* Managers sometimes have to negotiate on behalf of their organization or unit with others from outside, perhaps for the acquisition of needed resources, or to agree commitment of some kind on behalf of the organization. Managers are key figures in negotiated decision making because of their other roles of figurehead, spokesperson and, particularly, resource allocator.

The ten roles form an integrated package. Poor performance in one role produces a knock-on effect, reducing performance in other roles.

## Box 1.3

The responsibilities of each functional area will themselves shape the nature of its management activity. So the requirements of, for example, the marketing, operations, finance and personnel functions can imply different sets of managerial roles.

Marketing managers are required to sell the company's products or services by representing the company to its customers; this implies figurehead and liaison roles. Marketing is also responsible for the long-term development of the company's products and services, which is largely a monitor role. Operations managers are concerned with managing the fixed resources of an organization, coping with emergencies and making sure that what should happen does indeed happen. Their managerial roles, therefore, tend to be those of disturbance handler and negotiator. The finance function has several sets of responsibilities, and the managerial roles differ for each. The finance manager must act as the organization's bookkeeper and also be an evaluator who judges the financial merits of possible courses of action; in this capacity he or she acts as a resource allocator. In addition the finance manager must sometimes act as a 'funds finder' for the organization, which can involve liaison and negotiator roles. The personnel function also has more than the one set of responsibilities. The personnel manager must develop the effectiveness of the people who work for the organization, thus taking on leader and liaison roles. He or she must also deal with the day-to-day problems of the employees of the organization in the manner of a disturbance handler. Finally, a personnel manager often acts as the management's representative to the workforce, for example in pay talks, and as such acts as negotiator.

## Management Level

In the same way that the importance of work roles varies with management function, we might expect variation according to the level which managers occupy in the organizational hierarchy. However, Mintzberg[9] holds that there is essentially no difference in kind between the jobs of top managers and of those at lower levels. He argues that the real difference is in orientation, and in the ends to which managerial activities are directed. Lower-level managers are likely to be concerned more with maintaining a steady work flow within the unit or area for which they are held to be responsible. Work is likely to be focused around current issues and immediate problems. In addition, managers at lower levels in the organization are likely to be more specialized: that is, to be concerned with a much narrower range of issues than managers higher up in the organization. Given such an immediate emphasis on daily promotion and work flow, the two decision roles of disturbance handler and negotiator are going to be particularly important.

Senior managers, on the other hand, are likely to spend proportionately more of their time on strategic issues that relate the organization to its environment. They will be concerned with the longer term, rather than the day-to-day issues of the operational manager. As a result, senior managers and executives will play more of an entrepreneurial role than managers at lower levels. Adaptation and 'opportunity management' are, of course, part of any manager's job, but they become more important the higher one goes up the managerial ladder. In addition, representing an organization in the outside world means that the roles of spokesperson and figurehead will also be prominent.

## Managerial Activity and Discretion

Any formal statement of a manager's functional responsibility will not determine the total range of activities which constitute the job. Take two individuals and place them in exactly the same managerial job, and they are likely to spend their time doing different things. There must be few, if any, management jobs, where some degree of discretion does not exist, either in what work is done or in how it is done. Stewart[10] describes this discretion as choices — being 'the activities which a jobholder can do but does not have to do. They are the opportunities for one jobholder to do different work from another, and do it in different ways'. Stewart's framework for understanding choices in managerial jobs involves two further elements — demands and constraints. Demands are 'what anyone in the job has to do'. Constraints are 'the factors internal or external to the organisation that limit what the jobholder can do'.

Jobs which have wide-ranging demands but are tightly constrained will have less discretion than jobs where demands are relatively few and constraints relaxed. So, for example, a line production manager in a food-processing plant might be required to be physically present, supervising the operations of the plant, for a large part of the working day. At the same time, the fixed production process and rigid production schedules might strictly limit any available flexibility. This particular combination of high job demands and tight constraints means that the manager has relatively little discretion on what type of activities are involved in the job.

Compare this, for example, to a product development manager in a higher-technology industry, who is given responsibility for fostering new product ideas and developing them for manufacture. The demands of this job in terms of the amount of activity strictly required of the job will probably be fairly small, and the constraints on what he or she can do relatively relaxed. The area of choice as to what is involved in the job is therefore much greater than in the case of the previously described production manager. Nevertheless, both jobs do contain some discretion for the manager to choose to be involved in one activity rather than another, even though the degree of this discretion will differ. Figure 1.4 illustrates Stewart's framework.

## The Place of Decision Making in Management

We can see, then, that the work content of any manager's job can vary according to such factors as size of organization, level in the hierarchy and the particular job function. Whilst all managers may indeed carry out all ten of Mintzberg's work roles, some of those roles will be very much more important than others for any individual manager. Equally, the type and nature of decision made will vary according to the position of the decision maker within his or her organization. Nonetheless, decision making is a key activity for management. Harrison is quite clear that management *is* decision making: 'it is instructive to recall the notion, that management is synonymous with decision making'.[11] If we hold to Harrison's position, then we imply that a lot of what managers actually do is not 'true' management. Drucker is closer to our own position when he argues strongly that

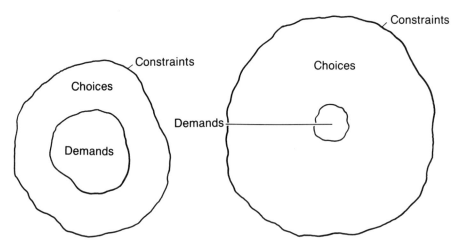

**Figure 1.4** The demands, constraints, choices model. (Reproduced by permission of Rosemary Stewart. From *Choices for the Manager: A guide to managerial work and behaviour*, McGraw-Hill, 1982)

decision making is the *key* executive task: 'Decision making is only one of the tasks of an executive. It usually takes but a small fraction of his time. But to make decisions is the "specific" executive task.'[12]

In reality, managers do lots of things that cannot in any real sense be connected with making decisions. This surely does not mean that these activities are any less 'managerial'. In many cases such activities are an essential part of a manager's job, and to exclude them from any definition of management cannot be sensible. Decision making, rather than being synonymous with management, is both essential and central to it.

## Types of Management Decision

All management decisions are not the same. We know that, in practice, those occupying different positions within the organization, and therefore performing a different set of management tasks, are confronted with very different types of decision. For example, a personnel manager, whose major task is to manage a programme on ongoing and regular recruitment, will face very different decisions from one whose job it is to advise the company's top management on a large-scale and traumatic redundancy programme. So we need some kind of classification of decision types, in order that we can differentiate one decision from another.

One method by which we might categorize decisions is by ascertaining which part of the organization has responsibility for the decision. By doing this, we would develop a kind of 'organization tree' of decisions which would correspond closely to the company's organizational structure. The problem with doing this is that it would involve us in the specific management content of, for example, quality controllers, brand managers, personnel managers and all the other people who have responsibility for specific areas of the organization's activity. Instead of this, we need to identify the general dimensions of decisions, which portray their essential character without resort to their specific substance.

Three dimensions are particularly useful in differentiating management decisions:

1. How much of the organization the decision encompasses, i.e. whether the decision is *strategic* or *operational*.

2. How well defined the decision is, i.e. whether the decision is *structured* or *unstructured*.

3. How connected the decision is with others, i.e. whether the decision is *dependent* or *independent*.

### Strategic and Operational Decisions

A manager who is in charge of a small manufacturing unit might, over a period of time, make several decisions. These will include such things as:

1. Should a machine which is starting to give trouble be replaced, or should the maintenance people patch it up?

2. Should a further experienced worker be taken on, or should a younger person be hired to train up?

3. Should order A or order B be given priority in this week's schedule?

The second manager's set of decisions is strategic in nature. They involve the future of the whole organization, and are important, probably long term in their effects and cannot be made in a 'routine' manner. Because of the rate of environmental change suffered by most organizations, together with developments in the technology and resources that managers have available to them, strategic decisions are usually one-offs, characterized by a high degree of risk and/or uncertainty.

So, in the way we use the term, strategic decisions differ from operational decisions in that they:

● Relate the organization to its environment.

● Involve a large part of the organization.

The term 'strategic' then depends on how we choose to define 'the organization'. The first manager in our example, who is in charge of the small manufacturing unit, can make decisions which are strategic in terms of the unit, if not the whole company. So, for example, if the manager decides to change the working pattern of the unit from a two-shift to a three-shift day, then that decision is strategic for the unit. It changes the unit's position in its environment and affects the whole unit. In this case, though, the environment of the unit includes the rest of the organization; and the decision, although strategic in terms of the unit, is operational in terms of the whole organization.

## *The Trend Towards Strategic Decisions*

The danger of separating out operational roles from strategic ones in too rigid a way is all too evident: 'what appear to be routine manufacturing decisions frequently come to limit the corporation's strategic option, binding it ... to a non-competitive posture which may take years to turn around'.[13]

Recently, and in response to the need to establish smaller, more responsive operating units within a rapidly changing environment, there have been moves to push down decision-making authority within organizations and to give significant sub-units much more responsibility for their actions and for control over assigned or delegated resources. The consequence has been that in many organizations staff are taking on genuine management roles, and strategic decisions are being influenced, and indeed taken, much lower down in the organization than previously. The distinction between strategic and operational decisions is much less easy to maintain in times of rapid change and uncertainty than it is under stable conditions.

Francis Aguilar[14] sees managers as being both investors and controllers when he sets out the key management tasks as being:

1. To create a *shared vision* of where the department is going.

2. To *develop* the organization's capabilities and resources, including those of the staff working in it.

3. To ensure that the *right things get done*.

4. To improve the quality of *strategic thinking* within the organization.

## Unstructured and Structured Decisions

Some decisions are clear, well defined, distinct and unambiguous. Other decisions are ill-understood, fuzzy and difficult to tackle. These are the differences between structured and unstructured decisions, and from the purely practical viewpoint the dimension is perhaps the most important in determining the ease with which a decision can be made.

The first decision in Box 1.4 is structured. It is structured in the sense that it is well defined. The decision maker knows the extent of the decision, and the options between which a choice has to be made are clear. Neither is the decision novel: evaluation criteria have been previously thought through and are explicit and

---

## *Box 1.4*

### A Structured Decision

'I have to choose a new packaging machine for our existing products. There are only two types of machine on the market, both of which are fairly similar to our existing machine, which can no longer keep up with production requirements. Both types have been on the market for some years and are considered reliable by the industry. I will choose the machine which gives the best after-tax discounted return, calculated over a five-year period. This will involve collecting details of each machine, such as purchase price and running costs, from the manufacturers, and using this information in a predetermined formula which our accounts department issues for all such decisions. I will then place an order for the chosen machine and inform the departmental foreman as to when it should arrive.'

### An Unstructured Decision

'I need to decide what our product range should look like in two years' time. The reports coming back from our salespeople indicate that some of the products are beginning to be less attractive than our competitors' products. Whether we can merely update some of our existing products, or alternatively go for a totally new product range, I do not know. Since the decision will affect several other areas of the company, I will have to consult and take advice from managers in other functional areas. I suppose that any decision will have to be broadly in line with what they feel is feasible. The new product range will have to provide the basis for the long-term security of the company, without requiring a level of immediate funding which will threaten the company's short-term survival.'

---

unambiguous. A decision maker, therefore, has a well understood and agreed procedure to follow in order to reach a choice. In other words, the decision is 'programmable'.[15]

The second decision is unstructured. The decision body is not clearly defined, in terms of either who is involved in the decision or what their objectives might be. The options to be considered are not immediately apparent because the decision is unlikely to have occurred before in this form or under these exact circumstances. Also, because of the novelty of the decision, the decision maker does not have a clear view of how to tackle the decision. In fact, different managers will probably have different views, both on the decision itself and on how to tackle it. Thus, even agreement on the best way to proceed with the decision could prove difficult to reach.

## Dependent and Independent Decisions

The third important way to categorize decisions is in terms of their degree of dependency on other decisions. The degree of dependency of a decision can be measured on two scales: a scale representing influence of past and possible future decisions, and a scale representing the degree of influence across other areas of the organization. Figure 1.5 shows these types of dependency diagrammatically.

The first scale concerns past and future decisions. Many decisions are influenced by other decisions that have been taken in the past. Sometimes past decisions have determined the resource constraints within which we can work on the present decision. Sometimes past decisions have contributed to a slowly developing set of policies which in effect constrain what is considered to be appropriate and feasible. Sometimes the degree of previous support for a decision can be such that

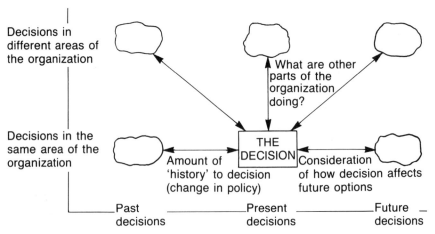

**Figure 1.5** Possible relationships between the decision and other decisions

any change can prove embarrassing. For example, the decision on when to call a halt to a project which is not proving particularly successful, but which has consumed large amounts of resources, can be very difficult. Although, rationally, a decision should not be influenced by how much expenditure has preceded it, real decision behaviour is very much affected by the degree and nature of the history to the decision. There are plenty of examples of 'good money being thrown after bad'.

A decision can also be affected by considerations of future decisions. The degree to which an option commits us to a future course of action or prohibits us taking particular courses of action may be legitimately included as one of the important consequences of a decision. For example, suppose a small independent airline operator runs a fleet of executive jets. These aircraft can take up to four passengers and are chartered out complete with pilots for short periods, sometimes for single trips. Business has been growing rapidly and is expected to grow for the next two years. After that, there could be a slight decline in business, as more competitors enter the market. Further aircraft have to be bought immediately to cope with the expected demand over the next two years. The decision is whether to purchase the same type of aircraft as are presently being used (ideal for the present market) or, alternatively, to purchase slightly larger aircraft which could carry up to ten passengers. This latter type of aircraft, although not ideal for current business, would have far greater flexibility and would match probable future purchases. If the market did turn down, as expected, then they could be used for other types of work. When making this decision the chief executive of the airline will be considering not only the present position, but also how the present decision could constrain future decisions.

The other scale concerns the degree to which a decision is isolated organizationally. Some decisions are relatively limited in their effect on the rest of the organization, while others have broad-ranging consequences. For example, suppose a production manager is replacing a particular machine. If the new machine is capable of producing in exactly the same way as the old one but at a lower cost, then the decision is a relatively self-contained one. But suppose the new machine is only capable of lower unit cost with a longer production run, or has quality potential which could be exploited by the marketing department, or has a different set of operator skill requirements. Then the decision is very much more dependent on how other areas within the organization regard the possible consequences of the decision, and on the decisions taken by those other areas.

## Decision Types and Decision Elements

Each of our three dimensions represents a continuum rather than a straightforward dichotomy, and decisions may be placed anywhere on each continuum. This means that there are, theoretically, an infinite number of decision types. However, in order to examine the way in which the elements of decisions vary with decision type, we can make a generalization which greatly simplifies the task. This is that strategic decisions tend to be unstructured and dependent, whereas operational decisions tend to be structured and independent. This crude generalization is borne out when we see the characteristics of each decision element for the two categories of decision as shown in Figure 1.6.

Interpreting this figure needs some care. We are not trying to say that all operational decisions are also structured and independent, and that all strategic decisions are also unstructured and dependent, but there does tend to be some connection between the three dimensions. There are, for example, far more strategic decisions which are dependent than there are strategic decisions which are independent. There are more unstructured strategic decisions than structured strategic decisions, and so on. Nor are we implying that the nature of the decision elements will always vary with decision type as Figure 1.6 indicates. So, for instance, while the decision options of a strategic decision are less likely to be immediately apparent than in an operational decision, a decision which is strategic and unstructured and dependent is very unlikely to have decision options which are immediately apparent.

## The Decision Environment

A great deal of managerial decision making takes place at or across the boundaries of the organization, and yet concern with the environment within which organizations operate is a relatively recent phenomenon. Classical ideas about organizations tended to look inwards, focusing on the search for the 'perfect organization' where successful operation is achieved through good organization and proper work methods; where 'efficiency' of internal operation is seen as the way to overall effectiveness. If the correct principles of management are adhered to, then the organization will always gain best advantage, whatever is going on in the outside world.

More modern views would see the organization as an 'open system', taking resources from and giving products and services back to the wider environment, adapting and reacting to changing opportunities, threats and challenges in that environment. Most managers are only too well aware, particularly after the upheavals of the last decade or so, that no business or organization can remain in ignorance of, or unresponsive to, what is going on in its environment and hope to remain successful for very long. The changes that have faced business enterprises in recent years include the following:

1. Loss of control over energy sources, and the use of energy as a political and economic weapon.

2. The increasing rate of technological development, such as microprocessor developments, causing rapid diminution of product lifetimes.

3. An increasingly critical focus on the social responsibilities of the business

| | Decision body | Options | Uncontrollable factors | Consequences |
|---|---|---|---|---|
| **Operational structured and independent decisions** | Possible to have a single-person decision body with complete autonomy, since decision is limited, well understood and unlikely to affect other decisions | Likely to have reasonably apparent options but there could be many of them | Likely to be a few uncontrollable factors because of the bounded nature of the decision — what there are will probably be well documented | Could be several attributes of each consequence but likely to be fairly 'forecastable' |
| **Strategic unstructured and dependent decisions** | Likely to need a multi-person decision body, since decision is important for whole organization, prone to different interpretation and wide reaching in its effects | Alternative options unlikely to be immediately apparent but may not be numerous, because options are either difficult to generate (unstructured) or the result of compromises (dependent) | Likely to be many uncontrollable factors, some of which may not even be known and most of which will be difficult to forecast | Likely to be several attributes of each consequence, all of which could be difficult to forecast |

**Figure 1.6** The effect of the type of decision on its elements

organization in such areas as 'environmental friendliness', safety and the 'quality of life'.

4. Political influence over international trading relationships, such as the advent of the single European market, or the dramatic changes in the political orientations of Eastern European countries which have led, among other things, to a huge new potential for East−West trade.

5. The changing role of government in the affairs and activities of work organizations.

## 'Environment' Defined

One way of defining an organization's environment is to think of it as being the totality of circumstances (of whatever kind) under which the organization operates. Everything outside of the boundary of that organization is part of its environment. Experience shows, however, that organizations do not deal with all parts of their environment at the same time or in the same way. While some environmental factors will have a major role to play in creating and shaping any particular decision, much of the total potential environment can often be regarded as being effectively inactive. For example, changes in fashion which raise or lower the hemline have severe implications for dress fabric manufacturers. Their impact on automobile manufacturing companies falls well within the 'inactive' category. So in order to understand the nature of the organization−environment relationship better, we need to distinguish between:

- The 'specific' environment.
- The 'general' environment.

### The Specific Environment

First of all we can separate from the total environmental picture those elements with which the organization relates directly and on a more or less regular basis. These elements can be called the specific environment. For example, a large supermarket has daily contact with such elements of its environment as its customers, its suppliers and the security company which guards the takings. It has a rather less frequent, but nonetheless direct, contact with such other elements as the police, local government and public hygiene and trading standards authorities. It will also have direct contact with more nebulous elements such as the local labour market. Another major element in the store's specific environment will be the other local stores, supermarkets and hypermarkets which operate as competitors.

Managers are likely to be aware of most of the elements in their organization's specific environment and may feel that it contains all that really matters of what is 'out there'. After all, it is the source of most influence on the day-to-day decisions faced by those who manage boundary positions. Yet pressures from the specific environment arise as a consequence of other environmental changes of a more general and long-term nature. Supermarkets owe their existence and success to changes which occurred in the social environment — the increase in living standards, widespread ownership of automobiles, changes in income and working patterns. In turn, they face competition themselves from even larger hypermarkets for similar reasons.

## *The General Environment*

Any one organization will operate with a particular specific environment and, as a consequence, will face up to a unique set of pressures. Many underlying environmental features, however, must of necessity be common to a large number of organizations at the same time. Economic recession, for example, can paint the backcloth for the activities of whole industries and, for that matter, whole economic systems. These common features form a general environment within which organizations, and therefore managers, have to operate.

Considerable change and movement has occurred at a general level in the business environment and clearly will continue to do so in the future. Unfortunately such changes are sometimes seen by managers as being less relevant and certainly less significant than those short-term problems deriving from the specific environment. There are a number of reasons for this:

1. Short-term problems have to be dealt with in the short term, and may absorb so much energy that little is left for longer-term issues. We naturally tend to link immediacy with importance.

2. Trends in the general environment are difficult to identify and to isolate. They are less 'solid' and tangible than issues in the specific environment.

3. Many organizations, particularly small ones, may not have the resources to channel into monitoring the general environment, even when the need to do so is recognized.

## Complexity, Change and Perceived Uncertainty

Two further aspects of an organization's decision environment which affect the context of a decision are:

- Whether the environment is simple or complex.
- Whether the environment is static or dynamic.

Simple environments are those which have relatively few elements, and where those which do exist are probably similar to each other and well understood. Conversely, a complex environment has a large number of factors all of which may be quite different from one another, and their interrelationship difficult to comprehend. A static environment is one that is stable and unchanging over time, whereas a dynamic environment is subject to a certain amount of change which possibly may be difficult to forecast.

These decisions of the environment can make considerable differences to the perceived uncertainty of any organization. For example, contrast a manufacturer of footwear who has longstanding contracts to supply the Military against a fashion-shoe manufacturer. The former has one or perhaps two large customers, and makes a small number of products which very rarely change and for which there is a steady demand. This company has a simple and static environment. By contrast, the fashion-shoe manufacturer might deal with many different customers who buy from many different suppliers. The people comprising the customer group therefore are likely to change with time. In addition, the product range will be subject to continual change as fashion and styles change. The company therefore operates in a complex and dynamic environment.

Duncan[16] maintains that shifts from simple to complex and from static to dynamic environments both tend to increase the degree of perceived uncertainty. However, the static–dynamic dimension is by far the most important. Figure 1.7 relates the two dimensions to perceived uncertainty.

## The Extent of Information Available

The way in which uncertainty manifests itself in a decision is usually as a lack of information. In some decisions there is an abundance of information. All the

|  | Static environment where the factors within the environment do not change | Dynamic environment where the factors within the environment are continually changing |
|---|---|---|
| **Simple environment** where there are a small number of relevant factors, all of which are similar | Perceived uncertainty low | Perceived uncertainty moderately high |
| **Complex environment** where there are a large number of relevant factors which are mutually dissimilar | Perceived uncertainty moderately low | Perceived uncertainty high |

**Figure 1.7** Perceived uncertainty as a function of the environment. (Based on Duncan, R.B., 'Characteristics of organisational environments and perceived environmental uncertainty', *Administrative Science Quarterly*, vol. 17, no. 3, 1972)

possible options can be fully described, the uncontrollable factors have a history which enables the decision maker to predict their probability of occurrence with reasonable confidence, and the various attributes of all the possible consequences can be documented. On the other hand, some decisions may take place in circumstances where very little is known about the options, possible states of nature or resultant consequences. Thus the extent of information available can be regarded as an important aspect of a decision's context. Information plays a central role in many aspects of decision making, and its impact and its management is discussed on a number of occasions in later chapters.

The extent of information may depend on the time available to collect it. Time, effort and money can sometimes change a situation of little information into one where the information is regarded as adequate. This then can be regarded as a cost related directly to the circumstances or context of the decision. Of course, a manager could go on for ever collecting every single piece of information about a decision. One of the skills of decision making is deciding which areas of the decision need further information and when further information is not worth collecting.

## The Time Available

The time available to collect information will itself be determined by the context of a decision. Here the time available is determined by the gap between when it actually becomes *clear* that a decision must be made, and the time at which the decision itself needs to be made. Sometimes the deadline for the decision is clear. For example, if a sealed tender to contract is required by a particular date, then, if management do not make a decision by that date, their opportunity to choose effectively disappears, and the decision is made by default. At other times, the due date of the decision is less clear. For example, suppose a retail chain store is buying a new outlet. There might be several possible sites currently available. As time passes without a decision being made, some of these sites could be sold to other buyers and become unavailable. At the same time, other sites could become available which were not options at the beginning of the decision process. The time available for this decision, therefore, is not a fixed quantity. But the time taken to make it could affect the options available and therefore the decision itself.

In some decisions the timing of the decision, and therefore the time available, can be a decision in itself. For example, a manager purchasing raw materials on the commodity market is concerned to keep his company supplied with the raw materials, and also to buy as cheaply as possible. The fluctuation in the commodity market means that, if he buys consistently when prices are low, he will be supplying the company for less cash outlay than if he were less skilled at the timing decision. In this case the purchasing manager is fortunate in receiving a direct, clear financial feedback from the decision.

Many decisions have a timing element to them. A manager wishing to introduce a new payment scheme, for example, has to decide not only which payment scheme to introduce, but also when to introduce it. A company wishing to expand its production capacity has to decide both who is promoted and when it is an expedient time to make the announcement. Thus, in many decisions, the time available to make the decision and the decision itself are interrelated.

## The Decision Stimulus

The time available also determines what is perceived to be the stimulus to the decision. In decisions where little time is available, pressure on the decision maker will gradually build until the point where a decision has to be taken. Decisions with no time pressures can be taken according to the will of the decision maker. Here, although there are no pressures forcing a decision, the decision maker decides that it is expedient to do so. These two ends of the spectrum, of forced decisions and decisions at will, are called *crisis* and *opportunity decisions* by Mintzberg *et al.*[17] Decisions in between the two ends of the spectrum they term *problem decisions*. Figure 1.8 illustrates this idea. Of course, one type of decision can turn into another, as Mintzberg *et al.* point out:

> a given decision process can shift along the continuum because of a delay or a managerial action: an ignored opportunity can later emerge as a problem or even a crisis, and a manager may convert a crisis into a problem by seeking a temporary solution, or he may use a crisis or problem situation as an opportunity to innovate.[18]

## Managerial Discretion

Before moving on to detailed consideration of the underlying theories and the practical skills of decision making in Parts II, III and IV, we should point out that the character of a decision is shaped not only by the decision itself, but also by the approach the decision maker chooses to take. The decision which a manager sees, and the decision which is formalized as something to be solved, are not necessarily the same thing. Managers have discretion as to how a decision is set up as the 'decision for solution'. The purpose of using this discretion may be to widen the scope of the decision and so make the solution more useful, or to simplify

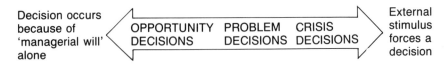

**Figure 1.8** The decision stimulus. (Adapted from Mintzberg, H., Raisinghani, D. and Theoret, A., 'The structure of unstructured decision processes', McGill University Working Paper, 1973)

it so that analysis is easier. The way in which discretion is used is either by changing the boundary of the decision or by changing the way in which elements within the decision are treated. *Boundary discretion* concerns what, or how many, decision elements to include in the analysis, whereas *treatment discretion* concerns the way the decision elements are treated. Some of these areas of discretion are listed below.

## Boundary Discretion

Is it assumed that a single decision maker will make the choice, or will the views of several decision makers have to be taken into account?

Will it be assumed that the decision makers have objectives which are simple and can be represented by a single measure, or that each has several objectives needing different measures?

Will the range of decision options be limited to those which are immediately discernible, or shall the range of options be widened following a comprehensive search for new options?

Shall we include every uncontrollable factor which we think has any influence on the outcome of the decision, or shall we confine our consideration to the single most important uncontrollable factor?

Shall we assume that the consequences of the decision can be described adequately by a single attribute, or shall we include all attributes?

## Treatment Discretion

Shall we describe the uncontrollable factors by taking their most likely values as 'single point' estimates, or shall we use a probability distribution to describe the range of values which the factor could take?

Do we treat factors as uncontrollable which are partly within our control? For example, the demand for a new product may, for convenience, be treated as a random uncontrollable factor. But it is not totally outside the control of most companies. Marketing departments can, and frequently do, spend much of their effort attempting to influence demand.

Do we assume that each possible consequence within a decision situation is known with certainty, or that each combination of decision option and state of nature could produce a range of possible consequences?

The important point is that managers should not regard a decision as immutable. No matter how the decision is originally presented, they have the discretion, and should have the ability, to change their view of the decision, perhaps temporarily, so as either to increase the usefulness of any solution, or to aid the decision-making process itself. This issue of a decision maker's discretion is closely linked with perception, which is discussed in Chapter 2, and decision modelling, discussed in Chapters 5 and 6.

## Summary

In our model, decision making can be viewed as a series of steps following a rational procedure. The process is one of contraction and expansion as follows:

1. *Expansion phase:* moving from an initial awareness that there is a problem of some kind, through the development of objectives, the process of coming to understand the problem in its complexity, and on into the generation of alternatives or optional routes forward.

2. *Contraction phase:* the evaluation of options, the process of choice and then the implementation of chosen solutions.

In most situations, the decision making/problem solving cycle then starts again, moving into a further expansion phase when monitoring results is likely to reveal consequential problems.

In practice, decision making is improved greatly when the opportunity is taken to 'recycle' back to earlier stages in order to improve comprehension or to correct wrong steps.

The elements which are present in any decision are as follows:

● The decision body, characterized by how many individuals it contains, their relationship to each other, and the mechanisms by which they make the decision.

● The decision options from which a choice is made, characterized by how many of them there are and by how obvious they are.

● The uncontrollable factors which cannot be affected directly by the decision body but nonetheless have a significant influence on the decision.

● The consequences or outcomes of the decision, characterized by how many attributes each has and how easy each attribute is to forecast.

Management roles and activities will vary with the level that managers occupy in the organizational hierarchy, with function, with organizational size and with the amount of discretion allowed. Mintzberg has established ten roles which are held to be common to all management jobs. These are grouped into:

● Interpersonal roles

● Informational roles

● Decisional roles

Decision making plays a central part in all types of managerial job. Decisions may be classified as being:

- Strategic or operational

- Structured or unstructured

- Dependent or independent

There is a growing body of thought that managers lower down in the organizational hierarchy than ever before are becoming involved in strategic decision making, where strategic decisions both relate the organization to its environment and have consequences for a large part of the organization.

The environment of a decision is particularly important when the decision concerns a task on the boundary of the organization. The state of the decision environment determines the perceived uncertainty surrounding the decision and the amount or type of information available to the decision body. It can also determine the amount of time available in which to make the decision.

Finally, the decision approach refers to the way in which the decision maker uses his or her discretion as to how the decision should be presented as an issue to be solved. This discretion covers how the boundary of the decision is viewed, and how the elements within the decision are actually treated and identified in practice.

---

## Case Exercise

---

### Rochem Limited

Dr Rhodes was losing his temper. 'It should be a simple enough decision. There are only two alternatives. I just can't understand why it's all blown up into such a big issue. You are only being asked to choose a machine.' The management committee looked abashed.

The problem had been brewing for several weeks now, and although John Rhodes had seen it coming, his anger was real enough. For the last thirteen years, since he had founded the company as a young research chemist, the company seemed to have avoided major arguments over policy. That it should happen over such a trivial issue puzzled and upset him, especially now that the company was so well established.

Rochem Ltd were one of the largest independent companies supplying the food-processing industry. Their initial success had come in the late 1960s with a food preservative, used mainly for meat-based products and marketed under the name of Lerentyl. Other products were subsequently developed in the food-colouring and food-container-coating fields, so that now Lerentyl accounted for only 25 per cent of total company sales.

## The Decision

The problem over which there was such controversy related to the replacement of one of the process units used to manufacture Lerentyl. Only two such units were used, both of the same make, Chemex, a local company. It was the older of the two Chemex units which was giving trouble. High breakdown figures, with erratic quality levels, meant that output-level requirements were only just being reached. The problem was, should the company replace the ageing Chemex with a new Chemex, or should it buy the only other plant on the market which was capable of the required process, the German AFU unit? The chief chemist's staff had drawn up a comparison of the two units, shown in Figure 1.9.

The body considering the problem was the newly formed management committee. John Rhodes had recently decided that the company was now of a size where the rather autocratic (albeit friendly) decision process he had hitherto adopted should be formalized. The committee consisted of the four senior managers in the firm: the chief chemist and the marketing manager, who had been with the firm since the beginning, together with the production manager and the accountant, both of whom had joined the company only six months ago. This was only the second meeting of the committee, and Rhodes was already starting to regret its formation.

What follows is a condensed version of the information presented by each manager to the committee, together with their attitudes to the decision.

## The Marketing Manager

This year the market for this type of preservative had reached a size of some £20 million, of which Rochem Ltd supplied approximately 48 per cent. There had, of late, been significant changes in the market — in particular many of the users of

|  | Chemex | AFU |
|---|---|---|
| **Capital cost** | £590 000 | £880 000 |
| **Unit costs of processing at capacity** | £185 | £183 |
| **Design capacity** | 2200 kg/month | 2800 kg/month |
| **Quality** | 98% ±0.7% purity; manual testing | 99.5% ±0.2% purity; automatic testing |
| **Maintenance** | Adequate but needs regular servicing | Not known — probably good |
| **After-sales service** | Very good | Not known — unlikely to be good |
| **Delivery** | 3 months | Immediate |

**Figure 1.9** Rochem Ltd: a comparison of the Chemex and the AFU machines

preservatives were now able to buy products similar to Lerentyl. The result had been the evolution of a much more price-sensitive market.

Future market projections were somewhat uncertain. It was clear that the total market would not shrink (in volume terms), and best estimates suggested a market of perhaps £24 million in four years' time (at current prices). However, there were some people in the industry who believed that the present market only represented the tip of the iceberg as far as the real potential in food preservation was concerned, especially in the export market which was hardly exploited at all.

Lerentyl was sold in solid, powder or liquid form, depending on the particular needs of the customer. However, despite this complication, prices tended to be related to the weight of chemical used. Thus, for example, this year the average market price was approximately £200 per kg. There were, of course, wide variations depending on order size, etc.

At the moment I am mainly interested in getting the right quantity and quality of Lerentyl each month, and although production have never let me down yet, I'm worried that unless we get a reliable new unit quickly, they soon will. The German machine can be on line in a few weeks, giving better quality, too. Furthermore, if demand does increase, but I'm not saying it will, the AFU will give us the extra capacity. I will admit that we are not trying to increase our share of the preservative market as yet. We see our priority as establishing our other products first. When that's achieved, we will go back to concentrating on the preservative side of things.

## The Chief Chemist

The chief chemist was an old friend of John Rhodes, and together they had been largely responsible for every product innovation. At the moment, the major part of his budget was devoted to modifying basic Lerentyl so that it could be used for more acidic food products such as fruit. This was not proving easy, and as yet nothing had come of the research, although the chief chemist remained optimistic.

If we succeed in modifying Lerentyl, the market opportunities will be doubled overnight, and we will need the extra capacity. I know we would be taking a risk by going for the German machine, but our company has grown by gambling on our research findings, and we must continue to show faith.

## The Production Manager

The Lerentyl department is virtually self-contained as a production unit. In fact, it is physically separate, being in a building a few yards detached from the rest of the plant. The department has its own raw material store and its own packing section, although finished goods are stored in the main store in the main building. Production requirements for Lerentyl were currently at a steady rate of 4150 kg per month. The four technicians who staff the machines are the only technicians in Rochem who do all their own minor repairs and full quality control. The reason for this is largely historical, since when the firm started the product was experimental and qualified technicians were needed to operate the plant. The four had been with the firm almost from the beginning.

It's all right for the marketing manager and chief chemist to talk about a big expansion of Lerentyl sales, they don't have to cope with all the problems if it doesn't happen. The catalyst (*fixed*) costs of the German unit are nearly three times those of the Chemex. Just think what that will do to my budget at low volumes of output. As I understand it, there is absolutely no evidence to show a large upswing in Lerentyl. No, the whole idea of the AFU plant is just too risky.

Not only is there the risk. I don't think it is generally understood what the consequences of the AFU would mean. We would need twice the variety of spares for a start. But what really worries me is the staff's reaction. As fully qualified technicians they regard themselves as the elite of the firm. If we get the AFU plant, all their most interesting work, like the testing and the maintenance, will disappear or be greatly reduced. They will finish up as highly paid process workers.

## The Accountant

The company had financed nearly all its recent capital investment from its own retained profits, but would be taking out short-term loans this year for the first time for several years.

At the moment, I don't think it wise to invest extra capital we can't afford, in an attempt to give us extra capacity we don't need at the moment. This year will be an expensive one for the company. We are already committed to considerably increased expenditure on promotion of our other products and capital investment in other parts of the firm, and Dr Rhodes is not in favour of excessive funding from outside the firm. I accept that there might eventually be an upsurge in Lerentyl demand but, if it does come, it probably won't be this year and it will be far bigger than the AFU can cope with anyway, so we might as well have three Chemex plants at that time.

John Rhodes intervened in the discussion:

Look. I know that to some extent we are arguing in the dark. But this isn't a perfect world and we never will have all the information we want. Furthermore, I think that at this stage any decision is better than just letting things drift.

## Questions

1. What form do (a) the decision body, (b) the decision options, (c) the uncontrollable factors, and (d) the consequences of the decision options, take in this particular case?

2. Classify the decision and the context of the decision, using the frameworks developed in this chapter.

3. Which machine should the company buy, and why?

---

# Bibliography

Ackoff, R.L., *The Art of Problem Solving*, Wiley/Interscience, 1978. We retain our enthusiasm for this marvellously anecdotal and readable book.

Eden, C. and Radford, J., *Tackling Strategic Problems*, Sage, 1990.
Heller, R., *The Decision Makers*, Hodder and Stoughton, 1989. A very readable though perhaps somewhat evangelistic book, focusing on top entrepreneurs and managers.
Thurley, K. and Wirdenius, H., *Towards European Management*, Pitman, 1989. An interesting attempt at defining a distinctively European perspective on management and management issues.

# References

1. Lang, J.R., Dittrich, J.E. and White, S.E., 'Management problem solving models: a review and a proposal', *Academy of Management Review*, October 1978, pp. 854–65.
2. Lyles, M.A., 'Formulating strategic problems: empirical analysis and model development', *Strategic Management Journal*, vol. 2, 1981, pp. 61–75.
3. Mintzberg, H., Raisinghani, D. and Theoret, A., 'The structure of unstructured decision processes', *Administrative Science Quarterly*, vol. 21, no. 2, 1976, pp. 246–75.
4. *Ibid.*
5. Mack, R., *Planning on Uncertainty*, Wiley, 1971.
6. Connor, P.E. (ed.), *Dimensions in Modern Management*, Houghton Mifflin, 1978.
7. Mintzberg, H., *The Nature of Managerial Work*, Harper and Row, 1973, p. 166.
8. *Ibid.*, pp. 54–99.
9. *Ibid.*, pp. 101–2.
10. Stewart, R., *Choices for the Manager: A guide to managerial work and behaviour*, McGraw-Hill, 1982.
11. Harrison, E.F., *The Managerial Decision Making Process*, Houghton Mifflin, 1981.
12. Drucker, P., *The Effective Executive*, Heinemann, 1967, p. 95. His notion of an 'executive' would appear to fit closely with our idea of a 'manager'.
13. Skinner, W., *Manufacturing in the Corporate Strategy*, Wiley, 1978.
14. Aguilar, F.J., *General Managers in Action*, Oxford University Press, 1988, part 1.
15. Simon, H.A., *The Science of Management Decision*, Harper and Row, 1960, originally called these classifications 'programmable' and 'non-programmable'.
16. Duncan, R.B., 'Characteristics of organizational environments and perceived environmental uncertainty', *Administrative Science Quarterly*, vol. 17, no. 3, 1972.
17. Mintzberg, Raisinghani and Theoret, *op cit.*
18. *Ibid.*

# PART II

## The Decision Makers

When contemplating some crucial decision that has been made, it is often tempting to imagine that it is the product of some clinical and dispassionate entity, occupying a position so protected from the everyday world as to be immune from the doubts, fears, uncertainties and ambiguities that most of us as managers feel all the time. Yet decision making is a specifically human activity, and all decisions are made (or at least caused to be made) by human beings working with other human beings. It is the characteristics of the decision makers themselves which add probably the most intriguing dimension to the decision process. Part II examines some of the factors which affect the uniqueness of an individual manager's view of decisions and decision making, and looks at the involvement of other people in the decision situation.

CHAPTER 2 — INDIVIDUAL DECISION BEHAVIOUR — develops the notion of satisficing behaviour to describe the decision behaviour of individual managers. It focuses on the selective nature of the perceptual process and the centrality of human values in the determination of behaviour. Issues involved in the subjective judgement of probabilities and in risk taking are discussed.

CHAPTER 3 — THE SOCIAL CONTEXT — first examines the influence of social pressures felt by the decision maker acting in the presence of others. We then look at work groups, where decisions may be made by individuals or by the group as a whole. Small groups provide an immediate and powerful climate of influences upon the decision maker, and these, together with their consequences, are discussed. The second part of the chapter looks at issues involved in the successful development and use of teams for decision-making purposes.

CHAPTER 4 — DECISIONS WITHIN THE ORGANIZATION — deals with wider social issues, and how they affect decisions, within the organization. In particular, the organization's internal climate and its impact on decision capability is discussed. The chapter then examines the ways in which decision making is affected by the structuring and linking of roles, and focuses on problems of conflict which are caused by the growth and increasing complexity of organizational structures. We look particularly at ways of creating effective human information systems and structures, and also at the choice of management style, particularly in terms of how we should involve people outside the formal decision body.

# 2 Individual decision behaviour

## Introduction

### Rational and Non-Rational Behaviour

Traditionally, the study of decision behaviour in work organizations has tended to be *normative*: that is, it has concentrated on the development of ideas about what decision makers *ought* to do in the best interests either of themselves or of the organization they work for. Underlying such approaches are certain basic assumptions about the general nature of human behaviour and, in particular, about such behaviour when faced with a decision. These assumptions are shared by many approaches to the study of organizations and are based in classical economic theory. They are as follows:

- In a decision situation in a business context or at work, human beings behave in an entirely *rational* and logical manner.

- Other things being equal, the aim of the decision maker is to *maximize satisfaction* by choosing the alternative with the greatest value.

If we turn away for a moment from what ought to be and take a descriptive view, focusing our attention on what people actually do in practice when they make decisions, then experience tells us that these rather simplistic assumptions cannot often be relied on. It may be, of course, that seemingly irrational and sub-optimal decisions are merely the result of a lack of training or, perhaps, of the low quality of the decision makers themselves. On the other hand, there might be something about the nature of the decision or the decision makers that makes our basic assumptions inappropriate. Let us examine the conditions under which it might actually be possible for managers to operate in a rational and maximizing way in their decision making.

Firstly, for any given decision, it would be necessary both for all the alternative choices that are available, and for all of the outcomes or consequences of those choices, to be known by the decision maker (a situation which is sometimes known as the condition of *perfect knowledge*).

Secondly, and in order to maximize, the decision maker must have available some mechanism which will allow the ranking of the desirability or value of the possible outcomes to reflect accurately the decision maker's preferences. We would have to be able to guarantee to judge the relative merits of *all* of the alternatives open in a particular decision in order to be able to choose that one which will bring the maximum satisfaction. This process would also require (at least for the duration of the decision process) the operation of a consistent system of values against which the consequences of alternative courses of action might be judged (a situation which is sometimes known as the condition of *perfect judgement*).

A number of writers have questioned the extent to which the behaviour of decision makers can be regarded realistically as rational activity, and therefore the extent to which our expectations about organizational performance should be based on a model which does not reflect reality. In particular, Simon[1] has distinguished between 'perfect' and 'limited' rationality. Knowledge of every possible outcome is a prerequisite for rationality, but people usually have only limited knowledge and, indeed, limited capability with which to tackle most decisions. Also the *consequences* of particular choices of action may be unknown or unforeseen, and, even in cases where outcomes are predictable, they may often have to be stated in terms of probability rather than certainty. So, in practice, the limited knowledge of decision makers makes perfect rationality an unlikely process.

The other condition necessary for rational decision making, that of the capacity for perfect judgement, is equally hard to defend. Personal and organizational objectives are rarely held as single, isolated and well-defined goals. Rather they exist as complex systems or sets of objectives, within which particular goals may compete with each other for satisfaction. Organizational objectives, against which the utility of alternatives could be judged, are often derived from the goals of a coalition of *stakeholders*[2] in the organization (managers, employees, shareholders, customers, etc.). Goals held by different members of the coalition may not be capable of being pursued equally, or may even be incompatible with each other in particular circumstances or at a particular moment in time. The idea therefore that the desirability of outcomes has, in practice, to be seen in terms of their utility for a range of personal or organizational interests suggests that, in reality, the decision process is one where *minimum acceptable* requirements are met, rather than one which produces the maximum pay-off. Simon describes this acceptance of 'good enough' solutions, based on limited information, as *satisficing* behaviour.

By accepting a view of the reality of decision-making behaviour as one which includes the concept of limited rationality and of satisficing rather than maximizing, we are, of course, abandoning the conditions of perfect knowledge and perfect judgement required by classical decision theory. Unfortunately, we are not able to be as precise about what we can put in their place. While the satisficing approach is clearly more valid as a description of decision behaviour in practice, it is equally certain that, for many managers, it will not be the preferred mode of behaviour. It is likely that, given the choice, they would prefer to achieve solutions which maximize rather than satisfice. Certainly, studies have shown that managers have a particularly high regard for such values as *logic* and *rationality*. Decision making in companies is often at least intendedly rational, and perfect knowledge and perfect judgement are seen as highly desirable goals. While those goals may remain only as idealistic notions, they nonetheless constitute an important target to be aimed for.

Faced with decisions, says Simon, human beings use as a base for judgement their 'personal, limited, approximate, simplified model'[3] of the real situation. This model is built up via a set of perceptual filters operated by decision makers as they select that part of the total situation which is meaningful and significant to them at that particular point in time. The social environment of the decision maker, background and experiences, patterns of aspirations, values and motives, will all go into the construction of the model through which the individual seeks to represent the 'real' world in which the decision is located.

The problem of distinguishing between 'what is' and 'what ought to be' lies at the heart of the matter for the decision maker. The desire to improve the quality of decision making requires us now to focus on those psychological and sociological factors which cause us to adopt a 'limited, approximate, simplified' model of the real situation. In the rest of this chapter we will consider some of the factors that limit the ability of the individual decision maker to behave in a rational, maximizing manner. Chapters 3 and 4 then continue the process to examine decision behaviour in a social and group context and at the level of the organization.

## Perception and the Decision Process

Perception is the process by which the individual receives, organizes and processes data inputs to his or her senses. We are continuously being bombarded by such sensory stimuli, some of them important and necessary to our immediate situation, but many quite irrelevant. (Indeed, some may be disruptive or even positively harmful if they distract us from what we are engaged in.)

The car journey example in Box 2.1 raises a number of important issues for the decision maker. For example, how do we choose to register a stimulus as being particularly important? (Failing to notice traffic lights can be both costly and dangerous!) How do we actually interpret or add meaning to the stimuli we receive, and to what extent is the information-processing system operated at a conscious level?

## Selective Perception

Our own experience tells us that we do not take in and process all the information that is available to us in a given situation. The difficulty that the authorities often

---

*Box 2.1*

Consider this everyday example of selective perception. Try to recall a typical car journey, perhaps from the office to your home.

How many red or green lights do you see during the journey? How many of these are actually traffic lights?

Imagine the anxiety over the sudden perception of the smell of burning rubber, and then the relief when the problem turns out to belong to some other driver! Or the change in engine noise which sounds normal to everyone else in the car but which, to you, clearly heralds the onset of major expensive mechanical breakdown.

Finally, when you reach home, how much of the detail of the actual journey can you then consciously remember?

---

have in getting consistent evidence from witnesses to crimes or to traffic accidents, for example, demonstrates how one person may perceive a particular situation in a very different way to another. This phenomenon can be explained to some extent by differences in physiological capacity, such as eyesight and hearing, and by differences in the relationship the witness has to the incident, such as the extent to which he or she was actually involved or merely a peripheral onlooker. There is considerable evidence, however, to suggest that the way in which individuals see the world about them is coloured by their own particular *needs, background and experiences.*[4]

The phenomenon of interpreting situations through the eyes of our own particular circumstances, our current occupational specialism or our interest group is a very real one.[5] On a post-graduate management programme with which the authors were involved, the different interpretations given to corporate and strategic problems by managers from different specialisms such as finance, operations and personnel were at times marked, and, indeed, became somewhat of a hallmark of the programme.

*Organization of Perception*

Although, by virtue of the process of selective perception, the information we derive from any particular situation is likely to be incomplete, it nonetheless forms a significant basis for our future actions. One way of overcoming the problem of incomplete information is to *organize* the limited stimuli that are received in such a way as to provide a seemingly complete picture of an event and a sensible and satisfactory explanation of what has occurred. This process of 'closure' takes place when information is limited, by our adding in extra elements to the stimuli that actually are received. The search for closure may well be rooted in the very basic human needs for safety, security and certainty that are described by writers such as Maslow. After all, ambiguous situations are often unpredictable ones, where unexpected and perhaps unimaginable and dangerous things can happen. It is very understandable, therefore, that there are strong psychological pressures to fill in or to close gaps in our perception in such a way as to make situations meaningful and controllable.

## Closure Mechanisms

### Categorizing

One of the ways closure can be achieved is to categorize a decision situation by relating it to other problems that have been experienced in the past. By looking for similarities, we can fill in or organize our perception of the present problem by adding to it assumptions which are based on our past experiences of comparable situations. Past experience, of course, plays a valuable role in problem solving and decision making, precisely because it enables us to designate some decisions as being routine or programmable, and thus provides organizations (and individuals) with a degree of certainty and control over their actions. Unfortunately, the process has potential dangers since assumptions of familiarity are often misguided and incorrect. The consequence of treating the novel problem situation as a familiar one can lead to loss of opportunity and of competitive edge, or to the failure to anticipate what might turn out to be a disastrous consequence because of a lack of investigative effort early enough in the situation.

### Stereotyping

A common form of closure mechanism which we use to help make sense of our perceptions of others is the process of stereotyping. We often evaluate an individual on the basis of one particular characteristic, such as sex, race or occupation, and then proceed to base our actions on our beliefs (substantiated or otherwise) about all individuals who have that characteristic. 'Scotsmen are mean', 'All men are chauvinists' and 'Accountants are boring' are all examples of commonly held stereotypes, and individuals often lose a great deal of their uniqueness and contribution when they are pigeon-holed according to the stereotypic image others maintain.

### Perceptual Defence

One rather subtle way to achieve closure is to screen out the stimuli that do not fit our preferred view, or which make the establishment of a coherent picture more difficult. Stimuli which disturb or threaten the congruence of our perceptual model of the situation are left out.[6]

### Set or Expectancy

In many situations we see what we expect to see. When tackling problems or analysing data, we are often preconditioned to organize our perceptions into expected patterns or configurations, perhaps through forewarning or through familiarity with the kind of situation with which we are confronted. Sometimes such a state of *expectancy* (or *set* as it is sometimes known) is brought about by our own needs and our enthusiasm for a particular outcome. The mechanism is clearly a powerful one in the process of selective perception and in the organization of limited data to give them meaning and significance for the perceiver.

Expectancy is just one example of the way in which the context of a decision can play a part in deciding just what information is actually used by the decision maker. The physical, economic and emotional circumstances in which the decision is made will also affect which stimuli are selected as being important. One psychological factor which is regarded as having a profound effect on the perception and evaluation of data is the *value system* of the individual making the decision.

## Values and Value Systems

Values occupy a central position in the determination of human behaviour. One of the most powerful ways in which we form impressions of other people is by our feeling for the values which are important to them. In turn, we attach meaning to this impression through the operation of our own system of values.

The relationship between our own values and those of others connected with the decision can be a complex one. Individuals, groups and, indeed, organizations all seem to construct and maintain systems of values and to use them to evaluate alternative courses of action. However, within an organization such value systems may not always be compatible. A sales representative, for example, whose company adopts high-pressure selling techniques may find herself having to balance her desire to be seen as a success by the company with her feelings about the proper way to relate to customers. A father who desires orderly behaviour from his children may find this at odds with his commitment to treating them as independent and autonomous human beings.

### The Construction of Value Systems

As a result of organizing and giving meaning to the sensory inputs they receive, individuals learn to adopt particular postures or stances in relation to the objects, events and situations they experience. At the simplest level, these stances constitute *beliefs* about specific objects (we each carry about with us vast numbers of beliefs, as basic building material in the construction and organization of our perceptions). Many of these beliefs are *descriptive* (e.g. the sun sets in the west, or 2 + 2 = 4). No judgement or preference is implied. On the other hand, many beliefs are *evaluative*, implying judgement (e.g. this ice-cream is good), and some go even further and become *prescriptive* (e.g. children ought to obey their parents).

Evaluative and prescriptive beliefs clearly involve an assessment of the worth of the object under consideration and, as such, are likely to have a considerable effect on the decision behaviour of the individual who holds them.

## Attitudes and Values

An individual's perception of his or her environment is organized into many thousands of different beliefs, and it is very unlikely that these will stay separate and unconnected with each other for very long. The process which gives rise to their generation in the first place continues when beliefs are grouped together. Where a number of compatible beliefs are organized around a particular object or circumstance, and where this pattern of belief is relatively stable and enduring, then we talk of an *attitude* existing. Attitudes tend to predispose us to behave in a particular way. If we have a good idea about a person's attitude towards someone or something (such as 'the local council', 'blacks' or 'going to work'), then we are able to predict his or her behaviour on future occasions.

At a more basic level, and underlying the range of attitudes held by an individual, we can often identify broader, more general preferences (values) which seem to have a profound effect on behaviour. The 'object or circumstance' around which beliefs are organized at this level tends to be a preferred state of existence or mode of conduct, rather than some more specific focus such as an individual or physical object. 'Honesty is the best policy' and 'Variety is the spice of life' are popular expressions of values. The distinction between attitudes and values is often a subtle one. Values are seen in terms of positive orientations towards desirable end states, whereas attitudes can be either positive or negative. The real distinction, however, lies in their relative status within the individual's belief system. Values form the most basic and generalized level of such a system. Once value systems are established, therefore, their focusing effect will serve as a powerful selective force in the way in which events are perceived and judged. Such selective perception will, in turn, reinforce values already held, thus increasing the likelihood that they will be maintained to provide a relatively permanent framework for influencing behaviour. 'A value may be viewed as a stated or implied conception of what an individual, group or organisation finds desirable.'[7]

Values, along with beliefs and attitudes, also have the characteristics of being learned, of being transmitted from one person to another and, therefore, of being shared and held in common. As a consequence, they are open to influence as a deliberate strategy. Indeed, current management literature tends to place considerable emphasis on the need to influence organizational values in order to create the circumstances for effective organizational performance:

> it is clear that organisations have, in fact, gained great strength from shared values [Box 2.2] — with emphasis on the 'shared'. If employees know what their company stands for, if they know what standards they are to uphold, then they are much more likely to make decisions that will support those standards.[8]

---

*Box 2.2*

Deal and Kennedy[9] claim three specific benefits accruing to the establishment of shared values in an organization:

- Managers pay *extra attention* to whatever issues are stressed in the corporate value system.

- They tend to make *better decisions*, on average, because of the guidance they receive through their understanding of the company's shared values.

- They *work a little harder!*

They also point to a number of potential risks when values are firmly established:

- The risk of *obsolescence* when the business environment changes and values lag behind.

- The risk of creating *resistance* to change.

- The risk of *contradiction* between professed company values and those actually demonstrated by top management.

---

## Managerial Values

In the context of this book, it is worthwhile to look at the extent to which values held by managers might be regarded as differing from those held by other groups. Obviously, if those occupying managerial positions themselves tend to come from the same social or educational background, then we might expect them to have broadly similar value systems. The growth of industry over the years and, in particular, the rise in the number of white-collar, scientific and technical occupations which now play a part in decision-making activities could well give rise to a breakdown of homogeneity in managerial values. At the very least, we might expect more difficulty in maintaining the traditional stereotype of the manager! This expectation is certainly increased by developments in the educational system which now allow and encourage access to managerial positions for people from a much wider range of social backgrounds than has previously been the case.

One of the key studies of managerial values was carried out by England[10] on over a thousand American managers. England distinguished between 'operating values', i.e. those felt to affect behaviour in a significant way, and 'intended values', i.e. those that were owned or claimed by the managers studied, but that were felt not to be very influential in determining actual behaviour. The study demonstrated the significance of the organization in influencing the operating values of managers. As can be seen in Figure 2.1, a considerable number of operating values identified by managers were directly related to the goals of the business organization, while many of the operating values in England's other categories were also company or organization orientated.

| Goals of business organizations | Personal goals of individuals | Groups of people | Ideas about people | Ideas about general topics |
|---|---|---|---|---|
| Organizational efficiency | Achievement Success | My company Customers | Ability Ambition | Change Competition |
| High productivity | Creativity Job | Managers My boss | Skill Co-operation | |
| Profit maximization | satisfaction | My subordinates | | |
| Organizational growth | | My employees Me | | |
| Industrial leadership | | Co-workers Craftsmen | | |
| Organizational stability | | Owners Stockholders White-collar employees | | |

**Figure 2.1** Ranking of operational values by category. (Adapted from Harrison, E.F., *The Managerial Decision Making Process*, Houghton Mifflin, 1981)

For England, the major conclusion to be drawn is that organizational activities are influenced by personal values at all levels, from the corporate to the day-to-day operational decision. At the same time, the organizational environment within which managers operate would seem to be important in moulding and shaping personal value systems. Managers generally take on the values of the organization they work for, and indeed many organizations deliberately seek to recruit employees who already subscribe to their values. A hospital service recruiting nurses, for example, might well look for recruits who show evidence of caring attitudes towards patients. Nonetheless there are occasions when conflicts between personal and organizational values arise, and occasions when these conflicts affect the way decisions are made.

How will the manager resolve such conflicts? The most likely explanations would seem to lie within the mechanism of satisficing behaviour. Non-resolution is only likely to occur if the individual manager requires an optimal decision in terms of his or her own personal goals and values. If, as suggested previously, organizational values are internalized, then the likelihood is that a satisficing stance will be adopted. The individual manager may attempt to achieve personal aspirations within the scope offered by his or her perception of organizational goals. According to Harrison:

> the bulk of the evidence suggests that the values of managers have a strong organisational orientation. Therefore it seems rather doubtful that, in the event of a conflict of values, the personal values of the manager would take precedence over organisational values. It is more likely that the manager will accommodate his personal values to the purposes of the organisation in such a way as to further his own aspirations.[11]

There are other sources of value conflict for the manager in the decision-making process. With the increasing growth of professional groupings within management, more managers are finding that they are influenced by reference groups from outside their organization. Professional bodies, such as the Institute of Personnel Management, the accountancy bodies and the engineering institutions, and, more recently, movements such as the Management Charter Initiative, act as focal points for the development of standards of behaviour and professional conduct to which their members and supporters are expected to adhere. The individual may well find that the standards or values propagated by his or her professional body are at odds with his or her individual aspirations, or with behaviour which is considered acceptable or even desirable by others inside the organization. It is possible, therefore, that judgements made on behalf of a business organization may be influenced by an outside body which has no recognized status in the decision-making processes of that organization.

## Values and the Decision Process

Values and the characteristics of their operation play a considerable part in determining decision behaviour. We can make the following general points in respect of the relationships between values and decision making.

*1.  Values can operate at both an unconscious and a non-conscious level.*

Most of us are not aware in any real sense of the values we exhibit in our behaviour, and we are often unaware that we are making value judgements when we interpret decision situations. Even the manager who insists on looking at the 'cold, hard facts' of the situation is, of course, evaluating data on the basis of a particular value orientation. Data which is felt to be 'subjective' or 'emotional' will be deemed unworthy of consideration. So the operation of the professed values of logic and rationality will cause some items of information to be left out of the decision process.

Information rejection can therefore occur at an *unconscious* level, where the decision maker is genuinely unaware of any process of selection taking place. We are simply not aware of particular stimuli and pieces of information because our value system operates to screen them out below the level of consciousness. Alternatively, even where information is consciously seen or perceived it may not be identified as being relevant to the problem under consideration. Any ideas which occur to us are rejected at a level which, while marginally above that of consciousness, certainly does not involve any active consideration. We might use the term *non-conscious* to describe the operation of value judgements at this level.

Examples of this process of 'instant rejection' can often be observed in exercises such as 'brainstorming'.[12] This technique is used to aid the creative generation of alternative solutions to problems. Participants are encouraged to put forward any ideas which occur to them without any attempt at evaluation. In spite of such encouragement, managers taking part in brainstorming exercises often describe the pressures they feel themselves under to put forward only 'reasonable' solutions. The value of 'not appearing to be a fool' seems to operate strongly at this non-conscious level.

Thus the value systems of individual decision makers, whether operating at the unconscious or non-conscious level, must tend to limit the amount and kind of information which is actively considered, further eroding the 'perfect knowledge' prerequisite of the rational decision maker.

### 2. *Values affect the conscious process of choice among alternatives.*

Judgement between alternatives is made in terms of their perceived utility or worth in the eyes of the decision maker. Worth, even when decisions are clearly made on behalf of the company, is evaluated to some degree in terms of the decision maker's personal values which may not always operate to the maximum benefit of the organization, even if that could be determined. For example, a salesman, deciding which customer to call on, may choose the one who is nearest, rather than the one with the biggest potential sales when he has to balance personal inconvenience against benefits to the company.

### 3. *Our personal values are 'normal'.*

By its very nature, the concept of value is very difficult to think about and to articulate. In everyday life, we develop ideas about other people's values by observing their behaviour, rather than through detailed discussion and careful consideration. Unfortunately, such observations may well be biased towards the support or confirmation of the values that we ourselves already hold. We tend to pick out behaviour in others which supports our personal value system and, in line with the mechanism of perceptual defence, to disregard that which does not fit. This supportive but 'selective' perception reinforces the assumption that it is our values that are normal or correct and that, therefore, there is no real need to challenge them. When such challenges do occur, such as when our decisions are questioned, then they are often felt as personal threats. A likely defence mechanism in such circumstances is to attack the challenger's values and to reassert the correctness of one's own. The resultant unwillingness to re-evaluate may well place limitations on the quality of the final outcome.

### 4. *Value systems are not always consistent.*

Individuals are rarely totally consistent in the way in which they may bring their values to bear when judging the worth of alternatives (Box 2.3). Different values can be triggered by particular stimuli, such that one alternative is judged according to one sub-set of the decision maker's value system, while another is evaluated against a different sub-set which may or may not overlap the first. A commonly

---

*Box 2.3*

A further problem of inconsistency is to be found in the way that the relative weighting of values can vary over even a short period of time, or with a change in circumstances. Consider the problem of buying a pair of shoes. We might set out on a shopping trip, having decided on the style we want and being determined to purchase them at the cheapest possible price. At the first shop we come to, we find the price is £48. Moving on to another shop, we find the same shoes at £42. Encouraged by this, we continue our search but do not find any shoes at a price lower than £42. Finally, we come to a shop where the price is £45. At this point, we might tend to reassess the situation! The cheapest shop is now some distance away, we are late for lunch or for another appointment and we are rather weary of the shopping experience! Different values start to impinge on the decision process with more immediacy and with greater weight than our original criterion of cheapness. The £45 shoes now become the best bargain!

---

experienced situation where this is likely to occur is that of the employee selection interview. The nature and circumstances of the typical interview process allows the candidate to influence the decision situation by appealing (knowingly or otherwise) to different criteria of judgement on the part of the interviewer. The selection decision may be influenced by the dress and appearance of the applicant, by his or her professed knowledge of the employing company, intellectual capacity, emotional make-up, charm and sophistication, and by many other factors which may have less to do with the job under consideration than with personal values held by the interviewer which are brought into play at that moment. The selection interview is often criticized as a technique because of this kind of difficulty.

Values are brought to bear at different times and with different weightings, and this inconsistency prevents the operation of perfect judgement in the evaluation of alternative courses of action.

## Decision Behaviour Under Uncertainty

So far in considering decision behaviour, we have tended to concentrate on situations where the consequence of choosing each of the options under consideration is known to the decision maker. We have assumed that we can assess the worth of a possible outcome and then opt for it or some other outcome in the certain knowledge of what will happen. In real life, however, such certainty cannot usually be assumed. The choice process generally requires the assessment of the worth of a particular outcome and also some judgement about the likelihood of that outcome *actually* happening. For example, an athlete, in deciding whether or not to give up a job and train for the Olympic games, must not only consider how important or desirable it is to him or her personally to take part in the Olympics, but must also make some assessment of the chance of actually being picked. In the same way, our decision to join one of the motoring breakdown services may be affected by the cost and by the range of services offered, but will also be influenced by our view of the likelihood of breaking down. So a decision maker's ability to judge probability and worth accurately or otherwise is an important factor in the maximizing/satisficing debate.

## Assessment of Probability

Probability is the likelihood that something will happen. There are several ways in which a decision maker could assess this, and these will be treated in detail when we discuss the modelling of uncertainty in Chapter 6. For our purposes here we need only distinguish between objective and subjective probability.[13]

*Objective probability* requires that some basis should exist for assessing the likelihood of occurrence which should be independent of the individual who is making the assessment. For example, when we toss a coin the probability of heads or tails is dictated by the nature of the coin. Or our view of the probability of a machine breaking down might be determined by the relative frequency with which it has broken down in the past.

Many managers, however, are confronted by decisions where they are required to make a probability judgement without the aid of objective measures or of accurate statistical data. And, unfortunately, there is considerable evidence to suggest that individual decision makers may well have difficulty in assessing probabilities for complex decision situations. The subjective perception of the likelihood of an event occurring and then its allocation of a probability figure is known as *subjective probability* and is an expression of the degree of personal belief that a particular event will occur.

Gambling is an obvious activity where people are required to make subjective judgements about the probability of particular events occurring. Given fair conditions, any number on a roulette wheel has the same chance of being the winning one each time the wheel is spun. Yet, gamblers may often believe that, because a particular number has not come up for a long time, it is bound to win in the near future. It is as if the roulette wheel is supposed to have a memory and, quite possibly, a conscience as well!

For most individuals, a common method of assessing probability is to search through their experience for previous occurrences of the event. Of course, our own particular experiences and our memory of them may not provide a very good guide to reality. Our ability to recall particular experiences is, of course, itself influenced by the process of selective perception. The following concepts appear to be particularly significant in understanding the accuracy (or otherwise) of this process.

Availability

There would seem to be a number of sources of bias that stem from problems in using information from memory and making it available for judgement purposes.

### Vividness

Our personal and recent experience of a fatal road accident would almost certainly affect our judgement of the likelihood of being involved in one in the future, yet it may be totally unrepresentative of the objective probability we would arrive at through analysis of the relevant historical data. Nisbett and Ross[14] put forward the view that people give more weight to vivid concrete information than they do to abstract and uninteresting information. They argue that evidence which is *emotionally interesting*, which is *concrete* and can be visualized, and which is both *close and recent* has high visibility and may then have a disproportionate impact.

### Organization of Memory

Ability to recall is, to some extent, governed by the way in which memory is organized. The question, 'What is the 12th letter of the alphabet?' is normally answered by reciting and counting the letters from A onwards because that is how such information is stored in our memory. The more 'accessible' the event in our memory, the more likely it is to influence our judgement as to its probability.

### Representativeness

A further source of bias stems from the way in which decision makers attempt to assess probability by judging the incident or circumstances as being *representative*[15] of previously established judgements or stereotyped situations and then applying those same rules in order to make judgements.

There are two kinds of danger here: that the representativeness *does not actually exist* and that we are therefore misrepresenting the situation; and that our *original model is itself wrong* (decision makers are often mistaken in their basic understanding of the statistical rules governing probability!) and that we are therefore likely to be making incorrect assessments.

### The Use of Benchmarks or Anchor Points

We tend to look for evidence of the appropriateness of our judgements under conditions of uncertainty. How often do we wait for others to venture an opinion before we state our own? How much safer do we feel when we know how much a client is willing to spend before we put together our sales proposal? Judgements about relative worth are often made by establishing a benchmark. In selection interviews, for example, candidates may be judged as being better or worse than one particular candidate in an attempt to narrow the field.

*Overconfidence*

Taylor[16] points out that we tend to be more confident of our ability to assess probabilities than is warranted by our actual performance. Factors such as rationalization and readjustment through hindsight, and the ability to suppress embarrassing or discomforting mistakes, help us to believe that we can make probability judgements accurately.

Lindsay and Norman[17] make the following generalizations about the process of estimating probabilities:

1. People tend to overestimate the occurrence of events with low probability and underestimate the occurrence of events with high probability.

2. People tend to exhibit the *gambler's fallacy*, predicting that an event that has not occurred for a while is more likely to occur in the near future.

3. People tend to overestimate the true probability of events that are favourable to them and underestimate those that are unfavourable.

The latter point is particularly important in understanding decision behaviour since it raises the issue of the link between the value placed on a particular outcome by an individual and his or her assumptions about the probability of its occurring. It seems to be the case that, the more we want something, the more likely we are to assume that it *will* happen in the way that we want. Once gain the operation of personal value systems limits the perfect judgement mechanism required for rational decision making.

## Acceptance of Risk

This link between the perceived worth of an outcome and the probability of its occurring is a central factor in decision behaviour. Because of this, we shall now look further at these two components so as to gain more understanding of how the decision maker might actually behave in making choices among alternatives.

Consider the following problem. You have won a ticket in a lottery. The ticket will pay an immediate prize of £10. Alternatively, the ticket can be entered in the second phase of the lottery, where one ticket in ten will win a prize of £100. The losers in the second phase get nothing. What will you do? Should you take the £10, or opt for the chance of £100 and risk getting nothing? Furthermore, would your decision be the same if the prizes were increased to £1000 immediately, or a one in ten chance of winning £10 000? It is likely that many people would give up the chance of an immediate £10 and accept the gamble for £100. When the certain prize is £1000, however, more people might choose not to gamble at all! In fact, the method of using hypothetical lotteries to estimate individuals' utility for different outcomes is well known and is fully described in Chapter 7.

Yet why should our attitudes to these different lotteries change? The probabilities in each case are the same. There is exactly the same chance of winning in the case of the £100 prize as there is in the case of the £10 000 prize. The answer would seem to lie in the worth or *utility* of the amount of money at stake in each particular case. Relative to the normal range of earnings, £10 is a small amount and has little utility. The risk of losing it is therefore correspondingly small. For most people, £1000 has considerable utility, and, although the probabilities in the gamble remain the same, the potential loss has been increased. Of course, although £1000 is a sufficiently large sum to have considerable utility for most people, its magnitude will vary from individual to individual, depending largely on his or her circumstances. To a millionaire, the prospect of losing £1000 may be of little consequence. In some circumstances, though, even a millionaire might prefer the certainty of £10 to the chance of winning more.

The utility of an outcome therefore changes with the particular circumstances of each individual at any point in time, and these changes can take place over the short as well as the long term. Thus our perception of the *riskiness* of a gamble is likely to change, for example, as a winning streak progresses. A gambler who has built up a small stake into a large one by accepting a series of bets involving small amounts of money may decide to take higher risks by betting larger sums. In one sense the risk has increased because the gambler stands to lose larger sums, but in terms of utility these larger sums may have a lower perceived worth than the original stakes because they form a lower proportion of his or her total wealth. In this case the gambler may feel that the risk is now lower than it was previously.

The first stage, therefore, in understanding decision behaviour is to distinguish between an objective view of worth (for example, the assessment of expected profit in pounds) and the notion of *utility*, which relates worth specifically to the particular circumstances, needs and aspirations of the decision maker. The second stage is to build into our concept of utility the notion of subjective probability. The decision maker could combine his or her assessment of the utility of each outcome with a notion of the likelihood of its occurring. This combination has been called *subjective expected utility*,[18] and it forms the basis of decision behaviour under conditions of uncertainty. Of course, it is unlikely that many individuals undertake mathematical computations each time they take a decision under uncertainty. They are more likely to approximate the calculation by taking a more qualitative approach. It is likely that people paint imaginary pictures of possibilities and make choices that fit their most attractive view of the uncertain situation.

## Propensity for Risk

So far, the notion of utility has only been used to describe a decision outcome. It is equally possible to apply the notion of utility to risk itself. In the lottery example, some participants presumably take part because of the attractiveness of taking risks, or gambling, rather than simply because of the utility of the prize money involved. The notion of subjective expected utility therefore might be refined to include an expression of the *utility of risk taking itself*, as well as the utility of the outcome, so that:

Attractiveness of = f (Utility of risk taking, subjective probability
  decision outcome       of outcome, utility of outcome)

This model allows for the possibility of low risk outcomes being regarded as less attractive than those involving high risk. Decision makers who place a high utility on risk itself will behave in very different ways (Box 2.4) from those for whom risk taking is something to be minimized.

An individual manager's predisposition to take risks, or for that matter to avoid them, is a major influence on his or her approach to decision making. A greater understanding of the level of risk acceptance or risk aversion among managers might encourage the search for conditions under which the risk strategies of individual managers might be developed so as to be more consistent with the company's overall strategy.

---

*Box 2.4*

Bazerman[19] puts forward the following generalizations concerning risk neutrality, risk aversion and risk-seeking behaviour:

- Individuals typically are *risk neutral* for 'small' gambles. In such circumstances, value is what seems to matter.

- Individuals are typically *risk averse* where large gambles might lead to gains: i.e. where losing would mean giving up something which is valued, even where the potential gain is large.

- People tend to be *risk seeking* concerning large gambles associated with losses: e.g. the 'double or quits' phenomenon.

- People may be *risk seeking* where they perceive that 'winning' will allow them to breach some important threshold of reward, lifestyle, etc.

- People find the risk of catastrophic loss to be unacceptable, and will pay a premium to avoid any risk.

- In general, *risk aversion is the dominant attitude* towards risk.

---

## Practical Prescriptions

It would be unwise to assume that decision makers in organizations attempt to maximize their decisions in the interests of the organization, or that they are likely to follow an 'objectively' rational model. Individuals (and groups) 'satisfice' in their decision processes, identifying problems and opportunities within a limited perceptual framework, usually leading to the acceptance of 'good enough' solutions which meet minimum-acceptance criteria. This situation is partly a function of organization limitations, such as the lack of clarity of goals and the scarcity or untimeliness of information. It is partly a function of individual factors such as:

1. The selective nature of the perceptual process which imposes limitations on the relationship between the decision maker and the decision situation.

2. The central position of values and value systems in the determination of human behaviour and their effect on the decision-making process.

When making decisions:

1. Be aware of and acknowledge the impact of your own 'bounded rationality' in viewing decision situations. Do not assume that others see the problem in the same way!

2. Resist the temptation to seize on and argue for a favourite solution too early. Adopt an *expansionary* approach during the early phases of understanding the problem and of generating possible solutions, so as to move away from minimally acceptable solutions.

3. Open acknowledgement of personal values (at least to yourself) will allow a critical evaluation of your approach to any particular decision.

4. Clarify decision objectives and make them public as early as possible, so that this particular source of confusion is removed.

5. Establish a common data base, so that all members of the decision body are working from the same sources of information. (This is not the same as giving everyone access to all information!)

In real life, many decisions are made in circumstances where outcomes are uncertain and where the manager must make a judgement in respect of probability without the aid of objective measures or of statistical data.

1. Understand the likely impact that the perceived 'utility' of an outcome will have on the decision maker's assessment of its likely occurrence.

2. Consider also the possibility that risk taking itself may have different utility or worth for different decision makers.

## Case Exercise

Reflect back on a recent important decision you made or were heavily involved in. Make notes describing the situation as it appeared to you.

1. Can you identify any ways in which you 'selectively perceived' the problem? How might these have affected the decision that was reached?

2. Were any of your personal values brought into question while making the decision? How did they influence the final decision?

3. How did you make judgements (if necessary) about uncertain outcomes? In hindsight, how accurate were your judgements?

---

## Bibliography

Bazerman, M.H., *Judgement in Managerial Decision Making*, Wiley, 1986. An excellent text, covering many of the points raised in this chapter (and elsewhere) in considerable detail.

March, J.G., *Decisions and Organisations*, Blackwell, 1988. A collection of readings around the nature and process of decision making in organizations.

Schneider, D.J., Hastorf, A.H. and Ellsworth, P.C., *Person Perception*, Addison Wesley, 1979. A useful book, focusing on our perception of other people and taking our discussion of other people considerably further.

## References

1. Simon, H.A., *Administrative Behaviour* (3rd edn), Free Press, 1976. There is an excellent summary of Simon's work in Pugh, D.S. and Hickson, D.J., *Writers on Organisations* (4th edn), Penguin, 1989, pp. 119–22.

2. See the discussion on stakeholders and coalitions in Johnson, G. and Scholes, K., *Exploring Corporate Strategy* (2nd edn), Prentice Hall, 1988, chapter 5, section 5.3.

3. March, J.G. and Simon, H.A., *Organisations*, Wiley, 1958, p. 139.

4. For an overview of some of the more interesting facets of selective perception, see Buchanan, D.A. and Huczynski, A.A., *Organisational Behaviour*, Prentice Hall International, 1985, chapter 3.

5. See, for example, the classic study by Dearborn, D.C. and Simon, H.A., 'Selective perception: the identifications of executives', *Sociometry*, 1958, vol. 21, pp. 140–4.

6. Mullins, L.J., *Management and Organisational Behaviour* (2nd edn), Pitman, 1989, p. 14.

7. Harrison, E.F., *The Managerial Decision Making Process* (2nd edn), Houghton Mifflin, 1981, p. 152.

8. Deal, T. and Kennedy, A., *Corporate Cultures: The rites and rituals of corporate life*, Penguin, 1988, p. 22.

9. *Ibid.*, pp. 33–6.

10. England, G.W., 'Personal value systems of American managers', *Academy of Management Journal*, March 1967. England's categories serve to show the difficulty in obtaining an operational definition of the notion of value. His category 'groups of people' would not appear to fit in with the definition of values used previously, being too specifically orientated, although operational values in the other categories would be acceptable.

11. Harrison, *op. cit.*, p. 178.

12.  For a description of brainstorming and associated techniques, see Chapter 10.
13.  Taylor, R.N., *Behavioral Decision Making*, Scott Foresman, 1984, pp. 124–9.
14.  Nisbett, R.E. and Ross, L., *Human Inference*, Prentice Hall, 1980.
15.  For an outline of the heuristics of availability and representativeness, see Bazerman, M.H., *Judgement in Managerial Decision Making*, Wiley, 1986, p. 7.
16.  Taylor, *op. cit.*, p. 141.
17.  Lindsay, P.H. and Norman, D.A., *Human Information Processing*, Academic Press, 1972, p. 545.
18.  See Taylor, *op. cit.*, pp. 146–50.
19.  Bazerman, *op. cit.*, pp. 48–9.

# 3 The social context

## Introduction

In considering decision behaviour so far, we have tended to regard the decision maker almost as though he or she were on a desert island: that is to say, we have been assuming that decision makers are not influenced in any way by the presence of or interaction with other people. Since organizations exist especially for the purpose of co-ordinating the activities of numbers of people towards particular goals or objectives, decision making in isolation is likely to be a fairly rare occurrence. We should therefore consider the effects of adding other human beings into the environment of the decision maker, and the likely effect of the *social context* on that individual's decision behaviour.

### Social Needs as Motivators

There is little doubt that human beings are greatly influenced in their behaviour by their relationships with others. The needs both to give and to receive love and affection, and to receive recognition, esteem and respect from others, are held to be important determinants of behaviour for most people. The strength of social pressures in influencing individual decisions has been verified in a number of experimental studies.

Deutsch and Gerrard[1] have put forward the notion of two different forms of social influence on the individual decision maker: normative and informational:

- *Normative social influence* is where the pressure is to conform to the expectations of others in a social situation, even when there is enough information for the individual to make the decision.

- *Informational social influence* is the felt pressure to accept information from others as evidence in the decision situation when the decision maker feels uncertain.

For the practising manager, both forms of social influence are likely to be encountered when making decisions. Pressure, real or imagined, from peers, superiors and subordinates to conform to acceptable behaviour will form a substantial part of the decision environment. So too will the pressure to reduce uncertainty by seeking information on the actions and positions taken by other managers and organization members.

The process of taking up cues, or deriving information from the actions of others, is well illustrated by the work on *bystander apathy*.[2] In one series of experiments, subjects were invited to fill in a questionnaire. Whilst they were doing this, the room would begin to fill with smoke. When the subjects were working alone, a large majority responded by investigating and attempting to report the problem. However, when subjects worked in the presence of two other people who had been briefed not to respond to the smoke, but to carry on as if nothing was happening, most failed to take any action, attempting to persevere with their task even when the smoke levels became extreme. Such experimental results indicate the importance of informational social influence in reducing the complexity of the situation for the individual and thus smoothing the decision process.

## Significant Others

Within a work organization, it is clear that managers, in their role as decision maker, will relate to people in the organization in a variety of ways. Some of these 'others' will be colleagues, from whom the manager may need support and approval in a personal as opposed to an organizational sense. Some may occupy positions of authority, where the relationship owes as much to the role as to the person occupying it (Box 3.1).

Findings such as those on obedience to authority, when translated into the work situation, would appear to confirm what common sense tells us about the very considerable influence of other people in the environment of the decision maker. Managers, in attempting to make the best possible decision, find themselves relying on information that is supplied by or inferred from the behaviour of others, and under pressure to compromise their decision behaviour in a way that will be approved of by the *significant others* in the organization.

## Working Within Groups

The idea of organization — bringing together the activities of people in order to achieve certain shared goals or interests — means that we spend a considerable part of our working lives operating with other people. What is more, we tend to work with a restricted number of people and on a fairly regular basis. Even managers whose decision-making responsibilities and activities affect most of the people in their organization tend to have regular contact with only a small sub-set of other

---

*Box 3.1*

The influence of authority as a factor in determining individual behaviour is particularly strong. Experiments in the early 1960s,[3] where volunteers were asked to administer increasing voltages of electricity to subjects in an experiment on the 'effect of punishment on learning', indicated that people may place a very high value on the authority of occupational roles such as that of the scientific experimenter, even to the extent of apparently inflicting severe pain on others in response to that authority. Over half of the subjects continued to increase the voltage when directed to do so by the experimenter, up to the maximum of 450 volts, well beyond the danger level and in the face of expressions of severe discomfort, pain and the final collapse of the victim (who did not, in fact, suffer at all, but was a collaborator of the experimenter, acting his part behind a screen).

In further experiments,[4] Stanford University students were asked to play the roles of wardens and prisoners in a two-week prison simulation. After a very short time, the researchers observed that the students seemed to adopt behaviours they associated with those roles, the guards taking great pleasure in harassing and humiliating the prisoners who, in turn, became passive and submissive in their responses. The researchers were so concerned that they cut short the simulation after only six days.

---

organizational members. Teamwork and small-group activity is well established in most organizations. When changes in membership or relationships between members do occur (in reality, fairly infrequently), these are often seen as disruptive events to be avoided wherever possible. For this reason, the *settled team* is often held up as a desirable management objective.

## Work Groups and Decision Making

The importance of work groups for management decision making lies in the influence they have over the day-to-day behaviour of their members. Such groups, after all, provide the most immediate and the most tangible environment for the individual at work. They are the most likely source of, for example, standard setting, value setting, support, approval, criticism and censure. Group membership commonly provides the setting in which the decision maker translates what *ought* to be done into what *actually* gets done.

Of course, while some of the social environment of decision makers is provided by groupings that develop informally, work groups and teams are normally set up deliberately in order to achieve some particular purpose or objective. A particular production process, for example, may require that operatives work together to ensure effective monitoring and control of the processes involved. Or it may be thought that a group of executives working on a problem are more likely to come up with good ideas by working together than they would as individuals. Our focus here is on those factors that affect decision behaviour within groups that are deliberately set up with a specific task or remit within the formal structure of the organization.

When we look at what goes on in a formal work group or team, it is possible to pick out a great deal of behaviour that is entirely predictable. After all, the group members are there in order to carry out a particular task or range of tasks, and a great deal of effort is often put in, through recruitment, training and specification, to deciding just what each member of the group is responsible for and should do. But even in situations where much of its behaviour is externally prescribed a group will develop unique and characteristic patterns of behaviour that are 'extra' to external prescriptions. Just as individuals become 'real' to us through developing characteristic ways of behaving, so we can identify work teams through the characteristic behaviours they develop:

> there are consistent codes of dress, style and interaction. If we ask people why they behave the way they do, they say 'That's the way things are done round here', or 'All of us expect to leave a little early.'[5]

Two road gangs, for example, may be employed by the same local council to make and repair roads and footpaths. Each gang has the same number of members, is paid on the same incentive scheme, is given the same tools and equipment, and is trained in the same ways of working. The manner in which each of the groups actually operates, though, tends to emerge in different ways. Each group, for instance, may develop its own pace and manner of working, its own ideas of what is 'a fair day's work' (not always tallying with what the council wants!). An informal pecking order of social status within the group will develop which affects who gets on with whom and, consequently, leads to changes in the way jobs actually get shared out within the group. This *emergent behaviour* develops out of and reacts back upon the externally required behaviour, producing the particular mixture that characterizes the group to its members and to outsiders.

> It is always important to remember ... [however] that, barring outside constraints, what is required is only the beginning. Members of almost any group seem to have a strong need to complicate their life together by developing interactions, activities and sentiments which are not required; and this development can lead to behaviour which is not only different from but in actual conflict with the original ... [external] requirements.[6]

In the developing life of groups and teams, it is perhaps the expression through action of such sentiments which provides the key for a more complex pattern of emergent behaviour. This will include changes in group activities and interactions which may then start to influence their formally required outputs.

## Group Influences on Individual Behaviour

For many decision makers the group situation provides much of the context for their decision making. That context is both a screen which *filters and modifies* decision information and, at the same time, the *actual source* of much of that information. It may be, for instance, that other members of the work group are responsible for collecting and channelling information to the decision maker. Their behaviour (at least as perceived by the decision maker) will form a crucial part of the decision situation and is a major source of influence. By operating within a particular group situation, individual members are faced with stimuli or cues which act to provide information for them, either allowing them to predict what might be considered to be acceptable behaviour, or giving feedback on how they are already doing. Such stimuli fall into two categories: ambient and discretionary.[7]

## Ambient Stimuli

*Ambient stimuli* are those to which all group members will be subjected merely by being members of the group and by occupying a particular physical and social context. They are, in a sense, inherent in the situation and available to everybody. Ambient stimuli can be derived from many of the characteristics of the group and of its circumstances. These can include the physical location, the status accorded to that group within the work organization, the kind of people who work in the group, and the kind of work and tasks that are seen to be done by the group (see Box 3.2). Such stimuli can 'paint a picture' of the group for potential entrants and form a reference point against which individual stances are taken.

---

### Box 3.2

Consider the ambient stimuli emanating from this memorandum!

Memo from: Managing director
To: Members of Senior Policy Review Group

The next meeting of the Senior Management Policy Review Group will be held over a working lunch on Thursday next in the Executive Dining Room. My PA will let you have prior sight of the menu. Please liaise with her as to your choice of main course and drinks requirements.

Or this:

From: Fred Harris
To: SPRG

Can we meet please on Wednesday next in my office to discuss the architect's proposals for phase 3. If we can start at 8.30 prompt, we can all get back to some real work in time for the first melt at 10 a.m. Please let Jim know if you can't make it.

---

For those seeking entry to a particular group, the importance of different ambient stimuli will vary. For example, a recruit from outside the organization to a management team is likely to be influenced to join (or not) by ambient stimuli which relate mainly to the nature of the job, status (maybe as indicated by level), position in the organizational hierarchy, and so forth. On the other hand, someone already working in the organization could be attracted by a rather different set of stimuli, such as the perceived qualities required by (or at least attributed to) members of the group. If status measures are important, then these are more likely to be locally directed and may not mean much to someone from outside (the famous 'key to the executive washroom' for example).

The role and importance of ambient stimuli for individual decision makers within a group should not be underestimated. The notion of ambience provides us with a strong clue in establishing the link between *required* behaviour and *emergent* behaviour, especially in the way guidelines are provided for how an individual should behave within the group. Ambient stimuli provide a picture of *what is available* for new members: whether, for instance, the group is likely to provide social and emotional satisfaction for the individual, whether indeed there will be any real opportunity for intellectual challenge and achievement. Other ambient stimuli, especially the behaviour of other group members, provide the clues as to how one must behave so as to achieve those satisfactions. We learn by observing what personal rewards might be available to us within the group, and what we have to do to go about achieving them. In this way, our individual behaviour is influenced and modified without any deliberate pressure being exerted. The process is one of checking out standards by the individual and the passive demonstration of those standards by the group members. The extent to which ambient stimuli do in fact influence the behaviour of that individual will be determined by how much he or she values, so to speak, what is on offer.

## Discretionary Stimuli

While the ambient stimuli present in the group situation may provide the initial value and attraction for membership, emergent behaviour is influenced over the longer term by a further type of stimulus which is discretionary and selective in nature. By discretionary stimuli we mean those which are in some sense controlled by the group members and which are experienced by individuals as a direct response to the behaviours they actually exhibit in the group. For example, agreement and support, expressed by a colleague when a manager makes a particular decision, is a discretionary stimulus. It is a deliberate and specific action, in response to a particular event or action on the part of one individual. While such discretionary stimuli are potentially available to all members, they can be granted or withheld and are contingent upon particular behaviour. Used in this way, discretionary stimuli can serve a number of purposes.

1. They allow the socialization of group members. While this process occurs

in all groups, it is particularly apparent in cases where the primary purpose of the group is to affect the beliefs, attitudes and values of its members, such as in political education, physical fitness, religious education and so on. In such circumstances, discretionary stimuli may be employed selectively to reinforce acceptable behaviour from group members and to punish what is not acceptable. Obviously the level of reinforcement or of punishment will vary according to the progress made by each member towards some desired end state.

2. They can be used to induce uniformity and reliability. One of the most powerful notions to emerge during the development of a group is that of *the right way of doing things*. Groups very quickly adopt particular patterns of behaviour, stances towards people or situations, and notions of 'what is' or 'what ought to be'. A high degree of uniformity among group members in such matters is often felt to be particularly important, and the use of discretionary stimuli is one of the major ways in which this is achieved.

Group members may well be called upon to act in ways that will have some effect on other members or produce consequences for the group as a whole. In these circumstances, group members will place a high value on 'credibility' and 'reliability' in the behaviour of individuals. This need for predictability is well served by the development of high levels of uniformity. Groups may move towards uniformity of behaviour in order to enhance and reinforce the cohesiveness of the group as a social unit, regardless of the required task needs. Tolerance of highly individual styles and patterns of behaviour would seem to be inversely related to group cohesiveness. The more strongly members value the group, the more likely they are to put pressures on those individuals whose behaviour is seen as non-conformist. In the same way, agreed patterns of decision making (such as always consulting all the members) serve to reinforce the feeling among members that the group really is a group. Unfortunately, from the viewpoint of decision effectiveness, strong pressures to uniformity, while serving to enhance cohesiveness, may well inhibit behaviour which would improve the decision-making ability of the group. New ideas may be played down, for instance, or conflict over different ways of tackling a problem avoided because of the possible disruptive consequences for the group.

3. They may be used to reinforce emergent differences. In direct contrast to the notion of uniformity is the emergence of differentiated activity, particularly in terms of the roles that group members develop. In groups where task activities are already pretty well determined (by virtue of the external system's requirements), this role differentiation may be focused on those behaviours for maintaining the group as a social unit. Roles such as group clown, friend, lawyer and energy bank can be developed within a very short time and rapidly become difficult to break down or to change. Once established, group members often find it impossible to change their roles within the group, however much they may wish to. Equally, new members find it hard to break into roles already occupied by group members of long standing.

The development of a role structure, over and above that required by the external system, seems to be a feature of the move to the position where a group can really be said to be established. The structure provides a focus for members of the group. It is a characteristic which provides a source of identification and point of reference for those outside. Structure reduces ambiguity by providing established patterns for relations between members, setting the scene within which members relate to each other. So, in a curious way, uniformity and differentiation become merged in the need to maintain and protect established patterns of behaviour, of differentiated roles and of relationships.

## The Importance of Ambient and Discretionary Stimuli

The individual joining a group gets a picture of the group situation through the ambient stimuli inherent in that situation. His or her response will then be directly and individually reinforced by discretionary rewards and punishments given by the other group members. The emphasis so far has been placed on the use of such discretionary stimuli, particularly those applied to potential or actual transgressors. It may be, however, that ambient stimuli are equally if not more important in governing individual behaviour in groups. The manager who, after promotion, fits well and easily into a new group is, after all, the one who is sensitive to, and responds positively to, ambient stimuli picked up in the early stages after entry to the group. Indeed, potential members may start to shape or adjust their behaviour *in anticipation* of joining a new work group: for example, a higher echelon of management. Such behaviour, known as *anticipatory socialization* serves two purposes. The process of becoming established in the group is obviously helped if some of the 'fitting in' has been done already. It also acts as a recruitment aid, in that someone who already seems to display behaviour that is approved of is more likely to be seen as a candidate for membership than someone whose behaviour is markedly 'non-group'. (Some attempts at anticipatory socialization go wrong, of course, and do their perpetrators more harm than good!)

## The Dysfunctional Consequences of Group Pressure

Group influences on individual behaviour have dysfunctional consequences, as well as the positive ones we have outlined. Certainly, pressure to conform poses a barrier to the introduction of new ideas and new behaviour into decision groups.

Individuals are often under extreme pressure to conform to existing patterns within the group, whereas there might be considerable benefits to be gained from the new insights and ideas of new members. Of course, new members may be brought into work teams for this very reason. Changes in membership bring about certain accommodations within the group and variations in the patterns of emergent behaviour. In many cases, however, there would appear to be extremely strong

*Box 3.3*

Irving Jannis[8] coined the notion of *groupthink* in identifying what he claimed were the most powerful symptoms of over-conformity. These are:

- The illusion of invulnerability.
- Collective rationalization of failure and of shortcomings in plans and decisions.
- A sense of self-righteousness and inherent morality.
- Stereotyped views of other competing or outsider groups.
- The pressurizing of dissenters.
- Pressure for self-censorship by members.
- Maintaining the illusion of unanimity.

social pressures towards conformity and a resistance to change, rather than towards flexibility and receptiveness.

## The Creation of Norms of Behaviour

We have been concerned so far with the processes of influence towards conformity within the group setting. The question then arises, what is it that group members conform to? Within all groups, expectations exist as to the behaviour required from members. When that behaviour is of particular importance to the group and to its functioning, expectations quickly become clarified and visible to group members. Such expectations about behaviour are known as *norms*. Porter, Lawler and Hackman[9] identified three characteristics of norms:

1. They apply only to behaviour, not to private thoughts and feelings. (Public expressions of feelings or beliefs count as behaviour!)

2. Norms generally develop for what behaviour is seen as most important by group members.

3. Most group norms still allow a range of acceptable behaviours by individuals.

Norms of expressed sentiment (shared values and beliefs) are often reflected in the development of emergent activities and interactions, sometimes in a way that is of benefit to the task being undertaken, sometimes less so. Suppose, for example, that a work group develops a strong norm for consensus and agreement. This norm may manifest itself in a number of ways. It may, for instance, result in an atmosphere where disagreement and the expression of differing views are to be avoided at all costs. Decisions will be reached quickly and by consensus but, because of a lack of discussion and evaluation, low-quality solutions may result. A further consequence of the consensus norm might be that the group adopts the process of complete consultation and agreement seeking among members before any decisions or actions are taken. There are clearly circumstances where this would greatly improve the quality of decisions taken by the group. Equally there are many circumstances — for instance, where speed of decision is more important than quality — when this approach would be quite inappropriate.

Some norms delimit behaviour very precisely, while others allow very wide variations. For example, norms about the way decisions are made within a group may be a very central issue, allowing little or no variance. Yet the same group may have norms about language, dress or even work output, which allow a considerable variation on the part of each member of the group.

## Group Processes and Decision Making

Ideas about the functioning of work groups, and, in particular, the notion of emergent behaviour, are especially significant when we examine many of the decision-making processes that go on in organizations. They enable us to understand more clearly the way such decisions are made and how organizational problems are tackled.

### Group decision-making outcomes

A useful starting point is to consider the potential outcomes of a group's decision-making activities. These outcomes might be thought of in terms of:

1. Productivity.
2. Satisfaction.
3. Individual development.

#### *Productivity*

Of the three outcome areas, productivity is almost certainly the one that will most interest those who set up the group. After all, management teams are put together primarily with a view to 'what' they are going to achieve or to produce, rather than 'how' they are going to do it. We usually recruit engineers or accountants, for example, for their output capabilities, rather than for their skills in working together in teams. The basic objective of teamwork in work organizations is measured in terms of productivity. We assemble decision-making groups to make those decisions in particular areas or circumstances, and they are judged by whether or not they achieve that purpose.

Productivity is affected by emergent behaviour in several ways. It is often observed, for example, that work groups determine their own level of output through the development of norms that are concerned with such notions as 'reasonableness', 'effort', and 'a fair day's work'. While this kind of result is usually reported in studies of groups which are concerned with routine production output, it is likely that all work groups have the potential to develop such productivity norms and that the same group control over output will be found in those groups whose primary concern is in decision making and problem solving. Such control might be reflected in the time taken to make a decision, the energy expended, the number of decisions taken at any one time and so on.

The organization's notions of required productivity might also be affected in that decision-making groups often seem to attempt to re-negotiate or re-define the ground on which they operate. The nature of organizational problem solving is such that it tends to be a broadening process, laying stress on the interaction of various potential solutions, and the 'knock-on' effect of decisions that are taken. Under these circumstances, group members will often seek to broaden or, in some cases, to make more specific, the areas to which they relate their efforts. A special project team, for example, may be set up to decide on the viability of launching a new product. In doing this they may find it necessary to consider and make recommendations about modifications in the current product range in order to take best advantage of the new product. The idea of such modifications may well not have been in the minds of senior management when they set up the special project team. When the external system emphasizes ends rather than means — objectives rather than processes — changes may be detected only after the decision has been reached. Even then, the changes may not be challenged. They may not be made explicit by the group, but remain part of their shared understanding of the problem to be worked on. The changes may occur over a long period of time, gradually filtering through and influencing the external system's perception of what is to be produced. In all events, those others within the work organization who have set up and who depend upon the outputs of the work group may well be faced with products they were not expecting, with decisions that encompass areas not previously considered, or perhaps that are based on too narrow a view of the problem to be useful.

## Satisfaction

Membership of a working group and the involvement with others in decision making can often be a source of great satisfaction to individuals. Such satisfaction, however, is not automatically linked to productivity — and certainly not to those measures of productivity that are determined by the external company or organizational system. Emergent patterns of behaviour, such as shared values or, in particular, patterns of interaction, provide many of the rewards that are available for group members, and it may be that conflicts will occur between those activities which are 'in the interests of the company' and those which generate other reward and satisfaction for group members. In this event, it is likely that the behaviour of the group will evolve towards a compromise situation which, while maintaining output or productivity at a level which the external system will accept, tends to enhance and increase the satisfaction available for group members. A decision-making group may evolve methods of working and systems and procedures that work best for its membership, rather than being orientated towards the best possible solutions. Some groups in this position, whose task is largely concerned with decision making (for example, planning groups or management committees), are at a position high enough in the organization so that there is relatively little prescription from the external system and, therefore, a great deal of freedom about the choice of behaviour during the decision process. It is often this freedom which allows the growth of rewarding emergent behaviour.

> A point worth stressing: although satisfaction does not necessarily lead to productivity, productivity can often lead to satisfaction. The pride and sense of achievement that comes from being a member of an effective group can lead to satisfaction if the individual values the group and the work it is doing. This has been called a sense of competence, and the 'competence motivation'.[10]

### Individual Development

Decision groups vary considerably in the extent to which they allow members the freedom to grow and develop. The norms which develop within the group will, to a large extent, set the boundaries within which individual members will be able to meet their personal need for psychological growth and self-actualization. Situations that provide individuals with high levels of satisfaction through relationships with others in the group do not necessarily provide the kind of environment in which those same individuals can find the opportunity for personal development and learning.

Decision-making groups, however, may provide an opportunity for potentially high levels of both satisfaction and development (for example, in situations where there is the requirement for a considerable individual contribution to the decision process). Groups that place a high value on individual opportunity for growth and development are likely to evolve decision-making strategies that focus on the provision of such opportunities, rather than directly on the needs of the task as seen by the external system.

## The Move to Group-Acceptable Decisions

Pressures on the individual decision maker operating in a small-group situation are considerable. For many decision makers, their contact with other members of the organization realistically means regular and direct contact with only a small number of people in the work group and very much less frequent and more impersonal contact with others. For them, the reality of organizational life *is* the work group. This situation has several implications:

1. Individual behaviour is most immediately judged by other group members. Such behaviour is therefore likely to be calculated so as to produce favourable judgements from colleagues, the need for esteem from others being such a powerful motivator for most people.

2. Support and sanction for decision behaviour is most likely to come from those who have been most directly involved — again the other members of the work group. This support is likely to be particularly powerful in that it is available on an immediate and ongoing basis. Provided that the actions of the group member are contained within the range allowed for by the norms of that particular group, then the support will also be consistent.

3. The individual is likely to be providing such support for other group members. Supportive behaviour is reciprocated within the group, and so individuals develop obligations towards each other, strengthening the value of the group and its value to members.

Under these circumstances and faced with such pressures, there is likely to be a move towards decision-making processes (and towards decisions themselves) that are aimed primarily at acceptance by the group, rather than at maximizing the interests of the organization. Simon's concept of *satisficing*[11] behaviour might well be applied in a group context here. The driving force in the group's decision making or in the activities of its individual members may be the desire to make the decision in such a way that maintains established procedures and that enhances the value of the group in the eyes of its members. It may become more important, under these circumstances, to make a decision than to make *the* decision. In some cases, the best solution for the group is to put off making any decision at all, if the group is likely to suffer in the making of it. The criterion of group acceptability becomes the dominant one in producing the 'good enough' solution.

## Decisions Made by Groups

In looking at groups, we have so far considered decisions made by individuals within a group. There are, of course, some circumstances when, for various reasons, the decision is taken by the group as a whole. These reasons include the following:

1. *Tradition:* it may be customary for certain kinds of decision within an organization to be taken collectively (for example, the selection of senior staff or the purchase of items costing over a certain amount).

2. *Structure:* the organization may be designed so as to bring together managers with certain responsibilities for decision making (for example, departmental

heads who are given joint responsibility through a management board for areas such as strategic planning).

3. *Communication:* this may be helped if the people concerned are there and take part in making the decisions (for example, joint consultative meetings).

## Group Process and Decision Success

The creation of a group to make decisions does not, of course, in itself mean that those decisions will be successful. Once the group is established, actual decision processes can take many forms. The group setting might, for example, merely provide the forum for a powerful individual decision maker to dominate the proceedings, the other group members acquiescing and falling in with the decision. Conversely, the group setting may be one in which all group members participate genuinely in the decision-making process. Studies of the effectiveness of different processes in group decision making have tended to centre around the areas of:

1. The quality of decision output.

2. The speed of the decision and the appropriateness of decision timing.

3. The extent of commitment to the decision produced.

### The Quality of Group Decisions

In some circumstances and with the right internal processes, groups can produce very high-quality solutions to problems. Sometimes, solutions can be better than those capable of being produced by members of the same group acting as individual decision makers. Suggestions for *right* processes have included the following factors:

1. A high level of participation by all group members.

2. Equal status in the treatment of ideas, whatever the source.

3. A consensus approach to the taking of the decision, where genuine attempts are made to secure the agreement of all group members to the decision that is finally arrived at.

### Speed of Decision Making

It is clear that, in the 'choice' phase of decision making, there are very few situations in which a decision taken by a group is going to be more speedy than that taken by an individual. If, however, the scenario is broadened to include all the phases of decision making outlined in Chapter 1, or even the full problem-solving cycle, then, as indicated in Figure 3.1, the issue becomes much less clear cut.

The speed of the decision process is certainly an issue in choice of method, but

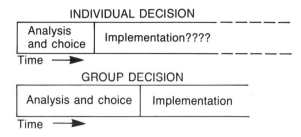

**Figure 3.1** Speed of individual and group decision making

one which may well be over-emphasized when compared with the need for quality or for commitment. Vroom and Yetton,[12] when considering the importance of speed as a decision attribute, suggest that it should become a criteria only after other more important issues such as quality and commitment to implementation have been taken into account.

*Commitment*

Work on participation in decision making suggests that one of the major benefits to be gained is that of increased commitment to the decisions that are reached and to their successful implementation.[13] The general conclusion would seem to be, 'if you make it, you make it work'. Taking part in the decision-making process builds a sense of ownership in the decisions taken, and a consequent determination to put them into effect. Decisions imposed on people from outside do not create this ownership, with a consequent lack of energy and commitment to their success.

## Group Decisions and Risk Taking

An additional factor we might wish to consider in choosing to use groups for decision making is the extent to which groups and individuals might differ in their approach to risky decisions. A traditional expectation of groups is that, if anything, they will be conservative in their approach to risk taking. In other words, they will tend to choose less risky options than individuals who are faced with the same decisions. There is, however, a growing body of evidence to suggest that something approaching the reverse is often true. Some individuals are more likely to choose options with higher risks attached when that decision is arrived at as part of a group than when they make the decision on their own.

Experiments on the *risky shift phenomenon*, as it has become known, usually involve giving individual subjects a problem where they have to choose between outcomes with different probabilities of success (for example, a range of chances of survival for a major surgical operation). Each subject is asked to state the minimum level of success probability he or she would accept. The same problem is then discussed in a group, and a new consensus view formed. The groups characteristically recommend a risk level which is higher than the average of the individual recommendations of those taking part. A shift towards accepting a more risky solution must therefore have taken place on the part of some of the members of the group (Box 3.4).

While the precise reasons behind risky shift are not clearly understood, the potential consequences for organizational decision making may be considerable. Imagine, for instance, a situation in which the chief executive of an organization decides to move towards a more participative approach in relationships with senior management. Decisions that were made autonomously and then presented for implementation are now discussed and agreed collectively. Policy and strategy are now formulated by group decision. Obviously, such areas will involve the

---

## Box 3.4

Various explanations[14] have been put forward for risky shift:

- *Diffusion of responsibility.* This notion relies on the assumption that some individuals are heavily influenced by considerations of what might happen if things go wrong. The sharing of responsibility for blame then becomes a liberating factor which allows individuals to accept higher-risk strategies than they would normally.

- *Leadership of the group by high risk takers.* There is some evidence to indicate that group members who are able to cope with and to accept risk tend to gravitate towards leadership roles within the group and to have considerable influence on group discussion and decision making.

- *Exposure to a wider range of views.* Group discussion leads to new ideas being put forward and basic concepts being more fully examined and explored. This process enables individuals then to re-evaluate their view of the problem and their assessment of the risks involved. While this does not appear to be a very complete explanation in itself, several writers have put forward the view that it is the *process* of discussion that is important in producing the shift, rather than the requirement to make a group decision. Certainly, classroom exercises carried out by the authors, where groups of senior managers have used a range of decision methods (including consensus, voting, 'taking the feel' of the group and, on a number of occasions, where no overt decision has been reached), have generally tended to produce the shift.

- *Expressions of high risk are more socially acceptable than those of low risk.* It may be that individuals are under pressure in the group situation to profess acceptance of high risk because this is seen as being socially valued. The phenomenon of 'egging on' under pressure is one which seems to be prevalent in other social group situations (within street gangs, for example, or during prison riots). There would seem to be no reason why social pressure to take high risks should not be present in management groups.

consideration of risk and uncertainty and, if the experimental findings on risky shift occur in practice, then that organization's strategic decisions might well become more risky as a result of a move towards participation, rather than through any deliberate choice.

Experience tells us that there are many situations where the idea of group decisions being more risky than individual ones is not sensible. We may have to distinguish between the idea of a 'group' decision, which involves at least a basic level of participation in either information sharing or in making the decision, and a 'collective' decision, where such levels of participation are not reached in practice but the decision is then owned by members of the group as far as the outside world is concerned. Clearly, much more work needs to be done before it is known precisely what kinds of group make risky decisions, and under what circumstances. Even so, the addition of the measure of risk taking to those of quality, speed and commitment may well be worthwhile in making the choice to use groups in decision making and in evaluating their performance.

## Developing Effective Groups and Teams

High personal skill levels in the manager are of considerable importance in organizational decision making, but they are a necessary rather than a sufficient condition for effective decision making. Vroom and Yetton[15] emphasized the importance of others in the decision process, for the provision of information and in the successful implementation of decisions. Four of their five decision styles, for example, require the manager to depend in varying degrees on others for successful outcomes. The activities of subordinates, singly and collectively, largely determine the success or otherwise of attempts at problem solving. Managers who work with a skilled, effective work team are likely to be able to produce more high-quality results than those whose work teams are ineffective. Organizations can further increase their capacity for high-quality decision making by bringing together and developing effective teams of managers (Box 3.5).

Managers who work with a skilled, effective work team are likely to be able to produce more high-quality results than those whose work teams are ineffective. Unfortunately, effective work teams do not just happen, they require the investment of considerable energy and resources. For any work group to be effective, several distinctive sets of needs have to be met. Broadly speaking, these needs can be divided into two major categories:

- *Content needs.* These are essentially concerned with 'what' it is that the group or team is doing. The need may be for particular specialist skills or abilities, for knowledge or information. Clearly, groups who do not possess the necessary 'content' capability are at a considerable disadvantage. In fact, members are usually recruited into work groups on the basis of their ability to provide content.

*Box 3.5*

## The Advantages of Group Decision Making

When considering the potential advantages to the organization of using groups to make decisions, it is important to distinguish between two groups of features. First, there are those features which, in a sense, characterize group decisions *only* because they are group decisions; second, there are those features which might be achieved if the group works particularly well. Just as an individual decision maker can be more or less effective, dependent upon expertise, practice, skills and so on, a group can also vary in its performance effectiveness. In the same way that individual decision skills can be improved by training, so groups can be made more effective through experience and through practice in decision making.

### The Built-in Advantages

Decision making by groups would appear to have the following built-in advantages:

- *It reduces the need for communication.* The more that those who are involved or affected actually take part in making the decision, the easier will be the task of communication after the decision has been taken.

- *It improves co-ordination.* Group decision making is in itself a co-ordinating mechanism. Action on implementation can be agreed at the time the decision is taken.

- *It increases commitment.* Members of the group making a decision want to see it put into effect. Obviously the level of such commitment will depend on the way the decision is made within the group, but the mere fact of involvement seems to be an important factor in increasing commitment to implementation.

### The Potential Advantages

Advocates of group decision making point to a further range of possible benefits from group decision making which can be obtained under the right circumstances. For maximum effectiveness, groups need:

- *Competent people* as group members.
- *Training* in group decision methods.
- Opportunity to *practise*.
- *Appropriate leadership* by the manager.
- *Encouragement* and positive feedback.
- *Support* from the external system.

Given these conditions, groups can make high-quality decisions by producing:

- *Wider ranges of alternative solutions.* Groups tend to generate and to consider a wider range of alternatives than an individual decision maker does.

- *More information.* In situations where the problem is unstructured — that is, where there is uncertainty over what information might be needed and what form it might take — then groups tend to bring more information to bear on the problem.

- *Increased creativity and risk taking.* Group situations provide a good vehicle for the generation of creative ideas. Individual ideas can be built on and modified; members may adopt more risky and 'way-out' solutions if they get support within the group.

- *Process needs.*[16] These are essentially concerned with 'how' the team actually operates. Group members need skills in working together and in 'living' together as a group. Although group members are very rarely recruited primarily for their skills in this area, process issues can often make or break the effective operation of the work group.

Process needs can be further subdivided. Some process needs are concerned directly with problem solving or *task* accomplishment. Other *maintenance* needs are concerned with the long-term cohesiveness and well-being of the group. Satisfaction of these process needs makes the group attractive to its members, generating energy and enthusiasm. The two sorts of process need are related in that both are essential for long-term effectiveness (Box 3.6).

## The Flexible Role Structure

The particular balance between the need for content understanding and expertise and that for task and maintenance process skills is likely, of course, to vary from one situation to another. Not only that, but the balance will change at various points during work on a particular problem. In order to be consistently effective, therefore, work group members need to be sensitive to the needs of the situation and to vary their behaviour accordingly. Groups which operate with a rigid structure of roles, prescribing the behaviour of members, do not allow this variability. Effective problem-solving teams need to adopt a flexible role structure, allowing changes in behaviour so as to meet content or process needs as they occur.

## Organizing for an Effective Team

In the same way that managers cannot be expected to be effective leaders without the necessary skills and experience, work team members cannot be expected to work together effectively without possessing an adequate level of skills and understanding of what is required. Managers may have to be prepared to invest considerable energy and effort in putting together a problem-solving group, and in creating the right conditions in which they can operate. Steps need to be taken in each of the three areas of content, task process and maintenance process.

---

*Box 3.6*


Examples of activities which meet task and maintenance needs in the group situation are as follows.

## Task Process Activities

- *Initiating:* putting new ideas forward or starting up new activities.
- *Asking:* getting information or views, actively searching out facts and ideas.
- *Giving:* volunteering information and ideas, making suggestions.
- *Clarifying:* helping in understanding, restating, defining terms, asking for explanations.
- *Summarizing:* bringing ideas together.
- *Testing for agreement:* checking if the group is ready to make a decision.

## Maintenance Process Activities

- *Harmonizing:* bringing others together, exploring and reconciling disagreements.
- *Gatekeeping:* bringing others into the discussion, allowing everyone to participate.
- *Encouraging:* agreeing, responding positively to others, building and supporting.
- *Listening:* showing that ideas are heard, showing understanding.
- *Standard setting:* stating feelings and beliefs, bringing things out into open discussion.

---

*Development of Content Capability*

In stable or routine situations, it is relatively easy to determine what content knowledge and skills are required within the group. In non-routine situations, the existing *content capability* of team members places limits on the way in which new and novel problem situations are perceived and interpreted. It will also affect significantly the way in which the problem is then worked on, and the direction or area from which solutions are sought. In order to enhance the content capability of the work team, the manager can:

- *Recruit* within the overall boundaries set by the general field of orientation, bringing in as wide a range of content skills and expertise as possible. In this way, problems get looked at from a variety of angles and viewpoints.

- *Encourage* team members to keep their knowledge and expertise up to date. Members recruited for their particular content ability must be allowed to use it in practice. In addition, opportunity should be provided for updating of knowledge and skill through reading, courses, workshops, internal seminars and so on. The particular method of updating has to vary according to circumstance, but the key point here is that team members should be *expected* to keep adding to their content expertise and be *encouraged and helped* to do so.

## *Task Process Skills*

Skills in this area are gained both through training and through experience. The manager can help group members to gain skills by using regular group tasks as learning vehicles. Valuable insights can be gained by *debriefing* and by *reflecting* on what was done well and what was not so successful in the way tasks were tackled. Behaviour by members which helps the group in task accomplishment can be picked out and acknowledged and perhaps rewarded. It will help if group members are given training in systematic problem solving, so that increased awareness of the importance of the stages in the process can be developed.

Process skills require to be developed, in the main, within the team situation. Basic concepts and ideas can be learned individually, but the translation of these into effective action really has to be learned *in situ*. Team members need to learn by experience what behaviour is appropriate and will produce the desired results, given the particular membership of the team and the way in which relationships have developed. In order to increase task process skills, then, the manager can:

● Ensure that team members are trained in problem-solving strategies.

● Ensure that the team looks regularly at its own performance and effectiveness in problem solving and task completion. Constructive behaviour should be identified and built upon; mistakes and ineffective behaviour can be corrected and improved.

## *Maintenance Process Skills*

There is no doubt that, however strong it is in content capability and task process skills, a group's performance can be severely affected by poor maintenance process. Groups with low cohesion, and whose members find little reward in the group situation, are unlikely to maintain an effective performance over any length of time. Preparation and organization in this area would seem to be particularly difficult. One method that has been developed to help individuals to understand more about their own behaviour, and how others perceive it, is the sensitivity training group, or *T-group* as it is commonly called. T-group training is experiential in nature, the learning material being the growth and development of structures and relationships within a participant group (Box 3.7). By focusing on such developments with the help of a 'trainer' or facilitator, members learn about group processes at first hand. At the same time, they can begin to understand more about their own behaviour and its impact on others, through giving and receiving feedback and by experimenting with new behaviour.

Personal and interpersonal processes are, of course, not always of importance in the accomplishment of group tasks. There may well be situations where a

*Box 3.7*

## Sensitivity Training

The area of sensitivity training is a controversial one, and there are widespread criticisms[17] as well as claims for its success.[18] It is clearly an area in which great care must be taken. Dessler[19] suggests the following guidelines to be used in conducting T-group training:

- T-groups should only be used where an open, flexible style is appropriate for organizational needs.
- Attendance on a T-group should be voluntary.
- Participants should be carefully screened before going on a T-group.
- The trainer should be an experienced professional.
- Mechanisms must be built in for transferring learning back into the work organization.
- Trainees should know beforehand what kind of experience they are getting into.

concentration on such issues actually gets in the way! Too much honesty about likes and dislikes may prove to be destructive rather than constructive. The point to be made is that increased sensitivity to maintenance process allows the relevant issues to be sorted out and worked on, and the irrelevant to be left alone.

## The Characteristics of an Effective Team

The next stage, after organizing and preparing the ground for effective teamwork, is to check out how successful these efforts have been. What does an effective team actually look like? What kind of characteristic behaviour might we expect? McGregor[20] has listed the following characteristics, based on his observations, of particularly effective teams:

1. The task or objective of the group is well understood and accepted by the members.

2. There is a lot of discussion in which virtually everyone participates, but it remains pertinent to the task of the group.

3. The members listen to each other. Every idea is given a hearing.

4. There is disagreement. The group is comfortable with this and shows no signs of having to avoid conflict or to keep everything on a plane of sweetness and light.

5. Most decisions are reached by a kind of consensus in which it is clear that everybody is in general agreement and willing to go along.

6. The chairperson of the group does not dominate it, nor, on the contrary, does the group refer unduly to the chair.

7. The group is conscious about its own operations. Frequently it will stop to examine how well it is doing, or what may be interfering with its operation.

8. When action is taken, clear assignments are made and accepted.

These descriptions of effective team behaviour fit very well into our requirements for decision-making effectiveness. Not only does such a group come through with high-quality decisions and solutions, but its members enjoy and look forward to the experience of working together. Process issues are recognized and worked on, allowing maximum use to be made of the group's content capability. This leads to a flexible and adaptive approach to problem solving. McGregor's eight characteristics form a very useful checklist for effectiveness.

## Recruiting for the Decision-Making Group

For most managers, the main strategy for improving team effectiveness is, as described previously, one of training and development of existing team members. Nonetheless, there are occasions when new members have to be brought in. Even in situations of high stability, team members leave for other employment, are promoted and so on. In other circumstances an entirely new team might be brought together. Such cases present an opportunity to strengthen the team in terms of its professional skills as well as its content capability. Belbin[21] has identified a number of *team types* which together form the basis of an effective team in terms of process (see Box 3.8). These types or roles are considered essential to successful operation, and therefore can be used in the construction or building up of a balanced team.

### Personality Characteristics as Key Variables

Over a period of seven years, Belbin and his colleagues were able to observe and investigate the performance of a considerable number of teams undertaking the same competitive task. Team members were subjected to a number of psychometric tests in an attempt to relate observed team behaviour to specific psychological traits. In this way, individual characteristics could be linked to behaviour within the team, and the balance of this behaviour in turn related to overall team effectiveness. The four traits which appeared to be most significant were:

- Intelligence
- Dominance

*Box 3.8*

## The Team Types

Belbin has identified eight roles as being necessary or useful in team work. The team type best suited to fill each role is characterized by a particular combination of personality traits.

### Chairman

Traits: dominant, extrovert, stable.
Focuses on objectives; establishes work roles and boundaries for others; concerned to use human resources as effectively as possible; clarifies and sets agendas, summarizes and makes decisions when necessary; not necessarily highly intelligent or creative; a good listener and communicator.

### Shaper

Traits: anxious, dominant, extrovert.
High nervous energy; full of enthusiasm and drive; continually looks for opportunities for action from discussion and ideas; heavily involved personally in the team's actions and successes; the task leader of the group.

### Plant

Traits: dominant, high IQ, introvert.
The creative ideas person; tends to bring new insights and imagination to the task; concerned with basics rather than details; tends to criticize; may switch off if ideas are rejected.

### Monitor Evaluator

Traits: high IQ, stable, introvert.
Objective and serious; concerned with analysis of ideas rather than idea creation; skilled in assimilation and interpretation of data; may be the least highly motivated team member, but provides sound judgement.

### Company Worker

Traits: stable, controlled.
The practical organizer; concerned with order and feasibility; methodical, efficient and systematic; does not cope well with novelty and lack of structure; does not value ideas and suggestions that do not seem to be directly related to the task; may be somewhat inflexible, but responds to direction.

### Resource Investigator

Traits: stable, dominant, extrovert.
Friendly and sociable, enthusiastic and positive about ideas and suggestions; tends to be the member who goes outside the team and brings back ideas and information; enthusiasm for tasks may fade quickly; tends to be stimulated by others; keeps the team in touch with outside reality.

## Teamworker

Traits: stable, extrovert, low in dominance.
Highly sensitive and aware of feelings and emotions within the team; a popular and supportive member; uncompetitive and disliking friction; a good listener and communicator, tends to weld the team together.

## Finisher

Traits: anxious, introvert.
Concerned with detail and order; tends to worry over possible mistakes; communicates to others a permanent sense of urgency; may get bogged down in detail, losing sight of the main objective.

For Belbin, the full range of types is essential for a balanced and effective team. The absence of one or more types has a considerable weakening effect. Similarly, the presence of too many of one or more types can reduce effectiveness by upsetting the balance. The problem of groups with fewer than eight members is solved by the finding that individuals tend to have a *secondary role* which they can play in addition to their preferred role if this is required.

- Extroversion/introversion
- Stability/anxiety

The balance of ratings an individual achieves on these measures, together with ratings on a number of secondary scales, determines team type: that is, the role within the team that an individual is best fitted for.

The idea of selecting a problem-solving team by personal type is naturally still somewhat controversial. These research findings, however, have now been applied in a number of industrial companies and organizations, with evidence of some success. It does seem sensible, therefore, that member selection, as well as training and development, can be used in organizing for the effective team.

## Practical Prescriptions

Managers are influenced through the behaviour of others both to fill the gaps in their understanding of decision situations and to look for guidance as to what is acceptable in their decision behaviour. The work group most commonly provides the setting in which the individual decision maker operates and also the arena in which decision situations are interpreted and acted upon.

As a manager, you need to understand and be aware of:

1. The importance of the 'authority figure' in the decision maker's social environment.

2. The fact that individuals become familiar with what behaviour is acceptable

through ambient stimuli which are inherent, and through discretionary stimuli which are direct attempts to influence individual group members.

3. The fact that emergent group 'norms' can determine decision productivity, together with methods of working and processes that work best for the group rather than for the organization as a whole. In some cases there may be a move towards a 'group-acceptable decision'.

Decision making by groups has the built-in advantages of reducing the need for communication, improving co-ordination and increasing commitment. Well-trained effective problem-solving groups can produce a wide range of alternative solutions, more information and increased creativity, leading to high-quality decision making.

Decision-making capability in colleagues and subordinates can be increased by:

1. Recruiting as wide a range of skills as possible and encouraging team members to keep their knowledge and expertise up to date.

2. Improving process skills through training in problem-solving strategies and through regular review of team performance in problem solving.

Research has indicated that it may be possible to recruit members to fill a number of roles which may be necessary or useful in effective teamwork. When team building, consider recruiting team members for their process skills as well as their content strengths.

## Case Exercise

1. Choose one recent decision made by an individual manager in your organization that would, in your view, have been better made by a group.

   (a) What was the decision?
   (b) Who made it?
   (c) Who, in your view, *should* also have been involved in making the decision?
   (d) What benefits would that involvement have brought, if the decision had been a group one?

2. Now try the reverse. Find, if you can, a decision that was made by a group or team which, in your view, ought to have been made by an individual manager.

   (a) Who was involved in making the decision?
   (b) What was the rationale (if any) for their involvement?
   (c) What were the dysfunctional consequences of using group decision making in this instance?

# Bibliography

Hastings, C., Bixby, P. and Chaudhry-Lawton, R., *The Superteam Solution*, Gower, 1986. An exploration of the vision of the high-performance team and how it might be created and sustained.

Payne, R. and Cooper, C.L., *Groups at Work*, Wiley, 1981. A selection of material on group dynamics, based on real-life situations.

Zander, A., *Making Groups Effective*, Jossey Bass, 1983. An interesting and very readable book.

# References

1. Deutsch, M. and Gerrard, H.B., 'A study of normative and informational social influences on individual judgement', *Journal of Abnormal and Social Psychology*, 1955, vol. 51, pp. 629–36.
2. Latane, B. and Darley, J.M., *The Unresponsive Bystander*, Appleton, 1970.
3. Milgram, S., 'A behavioral study of obedience', *Journal of Abnormal Psychology*, 1963, vol. 67, pp. 371–8.
4. For a review of this experiment and of the area as a whole, see Feldman, D.C. and Arnold, H.J., *Managing Individual and Group Behaviour in Organisations*, McGraw-Hill, 1983, Chapter 17.
5. Scott, W.G., Mitchell, T.T. and Birnbaum, P.H., *Organisation Theory: A structural and behavioral analysis* (4th edn), Irwin, 1981, p. 106.
6. Lawrence, P.R. and Seiler, J.A., *Organisational Behaviour and Administration*, Irwin Dorsey, 1965, p. 161.
7. See Hackman, J.R., 'Group influences on individuals', in Dunnette, M.D. (ed.), *Handbook of Industrial and Organisational Psychology*, Rand McNally, 1976, pp. 1455–95.
8. See the article by Jannis in Morgan, G., *Creative Organisation Theory: A resource book*, Sage, 1989, pp. 224–8.
9. Porter, L.W., Lawler, E.E. and Hackman, J.R., *Behaviour in Organisations*, McGraw-Hill, 1975.
10. Handy, C.B., *Understanding Organisations*, Facts on File, 1986, p. 161.
11. See Chapter 2.
12. Vroom, V. and Yetton, P.W., *Leadership and Decision Making*, University of Pittsburgh Press, 1973, pp. 37–8.
13. Feldman, D.C. and Arnold, H.J., *Managing Individual and Group Behaviour in Organisations*, McGraw-Hill, 1983, pp. 500–1.
14. The risky shift phenomenon is reviewed in Clark, R.D., 'Group induced shift towards risk: a critical appraisal', *Psychological Bulletin*, vol. 76, 1971, pp. 251–70. The issue is presented as one of 'polarization' (and therefore includes the notion of 'caution shift') in Fincham, R. and Rhodes, P.S., *The Individual, Work and Organisation*, Weidenfeld and Nicholson, 1988, p. 124.
15. Vroom and Yetton, *op. cit.*
16. Handy, *op. cit.*, pp. 177–80.
17. Dessler, G., *Organisation Theory: Integrating structure and behaviour*, Prentice Hall, 1986, p. 455.

18. Campbell, J.P. and Dunnette, M., 'Effectiveness of T-group experiences in managerial training and development', in Scott, W. and Cummings, L., *Readings in Organisational Behaviour and Human Performance*, Irwin, 1973, pp. 568–95.
19. Dessler, G., *Human Behaviour: Improving performance at work*, Reston Publishing, 1980, p. 430.
20. McGregor's characteristics, together with those of ineffective teams, can be found in Stuart-Kotze, R., *Introduction to Organisation Behaviour*, Reston Publishing, 1980, pp. 165–6.
21. Belbin, R.M., *Management Teams: Why they succeed or fail*, Heinemann, 1981.

# 4 Decisions within the organization

## Introduction

In looking at decision behaviour during the last two chapters, it has become evident that the context that is provided for the decision maker by the work organization itself is of crucial importance. At one level, the role of the organization is both obvious and absolute — without the organization there is no need for the decision. The organization, its aims and objectives, the business it is in, sets up the situation in which decisions are needed, and both provides and limits the resources with which decisions are made. But, at the same time as generating the 'need' for the decision, the organization produces a *climate* within which managers must operate and which may either facilitate or impair decision-making effectiveness. Such a climate is one of the major components of the specific environment for the decision maker.

## The Concept of Climate

In everyday usage, the notion of climate is usually felt to be the concern of geographers, meteorologists and holidaymakers! When we think of different regions or countries throughout the world, one significant way in which we form a judgement of them, and perhaps distinguish between them, is our impression of their climate, their rainfall, humidity levels, temperature, sunshine and so on. Some climates are attractive, some are not. In a very similar way, it is possible to form an impression of the internal climate which develops within a company or organization and within which employees have to operate. Just as a geographical climate can be more or less attractive for different individuals, the climate within a company can be supportive, encouraging and motivating, or it can be inhibiting and frustrating to the people who work there and to the tasks that get done.

While two companies may share very similar goals and face the same external operating conditions, the internal climates generated within each can lead to vastly different decision behaviour on the part of managers. Within one company, strong pressures may exist towards involvement, consultation and sharing, while in the other, managers may feel that they are judged heavily on their contribution as individuals, and so come to regard sharing activities as a sign of managerial weakness. Creativity, innovation and risk taking may be encouraged in one company, while in the other, the emphasis is on 'doing things by the book'.

Climate is therefore, in a sense, an *intervening variable* between the goals and structures of an organization on the one hand and the activities of its decision makers on the other. If the climate within a company is not a supportive and encouraging one, then the decision-making activities that are essential to its well-being and even survival may just not happen. It is notoriously difficult, for example, for managers in organizations under the threat of cutback, redundancy or even closure to work together in the kinds of collaborative decision-making ways that might be necessary to get them out of a crisis. The idea of climate as an intervening variable is a useful one in that it helps us to think of the internal climate as part of an organization's reserves or assets, which can be built up or run down and which allow or prevent that organization from achieving its objectives. A company's 'climate account' may be healthy, or it may be in overdraft! A difficulty is that, while we may think of internal climate as affecting decision behaviour (and, of course, all employee behaviour), the reverse is also true. While climate is affected by factors that are, broadly speaking, organizational or structural, such as policies and rules, systems and procedures, it is also affected by the consequences of the decisions and other behaviour of individuals both in their formal and informal activities. A shift in climate prompts or encourages decision makers within an organization to behave in a particular way. That new behaviour in turn reinforces the change in climate.

## The Dimensions of Climate

> Organisational climate is characterised therefore, by the nature of the people—organisation relationship and the superior—subordinate relationship. These relationships are determined by interactions amongst goals and objectives, formal structure, styles of leadership, the process of management, and the behaviour of people.[1]

Writers and researchers[2] have identified many different components or contributing elements in their views on the nature of climate. Campbell *et al.*[3] have grouped measures of climate around four major dimensions which would seem to be fruitful both in terms of their general utility and in their specific relevance to decision-making behaviour. These dimensions are:

1. Individual autonomy.
2. The degree of structure imposed.
3. The orientation of rewards.
4. The degree of consideration and support.

*Autonomy*

Autonomy is essentially concerned with freedom and independence. When autonomous work groups[4] are set up, for instance, they are given wide discretion in the ways they operate in order to achieve their goals. For the individual decision maker, autonomy means the freedom and the responsibility of choosing how to set up the decision and how to go about tackling it. For many managers, such freedom and independence is highly motivating, and a very considerable source of satisfaction at work. The independence brought by autonomy is essentially that of *independence of choice*, allowing the manager freedom to consider the whole spectrum of possibilities in choosing how to approach and work on a problem. It follows, therefore, that autonomous climates are at their most effective when the manager actually has the skills and ability to choose the most appropriate approach from that whole spectrum.

Circumstances often exist where, in order to be effective, organizations require such independence of choice and action from their managers. The extent to which managers actually behave autonomously is often determined more by the subtleties of climate than by obvious need or by any prescription of style.

Obviously, formal requirements, such as regular or frequent reporting to superiors, or progress checks, can have a sizeable impact on felt autonomy — managers are unlikely to feel that they are trusted to act independently if they are constantly called upon to justify their actions or to account for their time. A good deal of the impact of management action is determined not by any formal requirement for autonomy, but by a 'feel' for what behaviour is acceptable and by the way superiors and subordinates operate together in practice and on a day-to-day basis.

*Degree of Imposed Structure*

The degree of structure imposed on a decision maker has to do with the extent to which the 'rules' for decision-making behaviour are established and spelled out by others. One problem of decision making in an organizational climate even where there is a high degree of autonomy can be uncertainty among top management about the degree of competence and awareness among the (autonomous) decision makers. Indeed, a number of writers[5] have argued that, since any increase in the size of an organization tends to lead to some increase in autonomy on the part of subordinates through the need for delegation, such uncertainty and a corresponding desire to retain control is likely to occur even in organizations where the climate might not be particularly encouraging of autonomy. One common reaction to such concern is to impose some degree of structure on the decision maker, thus providing a framework (or imposing limitations) within which that manager can then be 'autonomous'. Such limitations on managerial activity, through the imposition of structured approaches to decision making, play a major role in creating a climate which restricts effective decision making.

The difficulty is compounded once ideas about what is an acceptable structure or approach become part of the pervading climate. The issue then of whether such limitations are *myth or reality* becomes rather blurred. In any event, once part of climate, myth and reality have much the same impact on actual decision behaviours. Changes in the degree of structure imposed which are intended to change decision behaviours are masked by the intervening variable of climate. Managers may, for example, persist in referring all expenditure decisions upwards, even when senior managers no longer require it. The extent to which decision activities are felt or perceived to be structured, restricted and prescribed forms a very powerful element in organizational climate, and it is that climate which has first to be altered before one can seriously expect to alter the actual behaviour of the decision maker over the long term.

### Orientation of Rewards

Organization life offers rewards and satisfaction to members; otherwise they would not be there. The contribution of rewards to our understanding of climate comes through an awareness of *what exactly it is that rewards are aimed at*. Obviously, there are circumstances in which some employees find rewards and some do not, but we can generalize about organizational rewards in such a way as to add to our understanding of the climate existing within an organization and its effect on the way in which managers might approach decisions (Box 4.1).

---

## Box 4.1

Here are some questions managers might ask themselves in their early days in a new company:

- How do I get on in this company?

- What is it they are paying me to do around here?

- Do I get rewarded for getting results, or for not making mistakes?

- Should I take this good idea to my boss, or to my colleagues who might be able to improve on it?

And here are some of the things they might tell the next manager who joins the organization:

- 'Keep your ideas to yourself, that's how you get ahead around here!'

- 'Keep your head down and do your own job, that's what you are paid for.'

- 'Sure you can take risks. If they work, you're the blue-eyed boy; if they don't, you're in big trouble!'

These comments all represent particular perceptions of the way in which managers might get rewards in our mythical company. They may, in fact, be realistic perceptions; they may be distorted. Either way, they are likely to have a profound effect on the way in which the managers concerned behave.

---

The primary objective in the establishment of reward systems in organizations is to influence the behaviour of people who work in them. Both the intended and the unintended messages of such systems provide evidence which all employees use in building up their 'feel' for the organizational climate. Elements of the *formal reward system* which contribute to climate include:

- *The type of system used:* e.g. piece work, measured day work, salary.

- *Fringe benefits and special privileges:* e.g. company car, stock issues, expense accounts, methods of promotion and regrading.

It is very difficult, for example, to achieve genuinely collaborative working under a payment system which is heavily geared to individual performance, particularly on a comparative basis, or where some members of the team get special privileges and others do not.

Other elements of the reward dimension are rather less tangible or explicit than the formal system. These will include ideas about which kind of behaviour is likely to be approved of and seen as acquiring merit in the eyes of superiors. Additionally, there are likely to be more general views about what broad areas of activity within the organization are likely to be held in high esteem. It may be that work in particular departments, or on particular projects, acquires a high status, and, consequently, decision making and problem solving in those areas are seen to be more 'worthy' or important than in other areas. In recent years in the United Kingdom, production and engineering management has suffered from a particularly poor image and a lack of status even within manufacturing companies, and, consequently, within the wider society. It is only recently that its importance has been recognized and that attempts have been made to create stronger links between rewards and activity in this area. At various times, other areas such as marketing and personnel management have suffered in a similar manner.

Reward orientations are likely to influence decision makers in a variety of ways. It is likely, for example, that managers will form an impression as to whether or not taking decisions is, in itself, a rewarding activity. If the organizational climate is such that *fear of failure outweighs the rewards* that are felt to be linked with success, then there might well be a tendency to put off difficult decisions or to pass the buck on to someone else. On the other hand, climates which encourage decision taking are likely to emphasize a task orientation and to support a view of the manager as a problem solver. Such a climate needs to be backed up by a system that is oriented towards rewarding managers who actually do behave in this way.

## Degree of Consideration and Support for the Individual

One vital element in the establishment of organizational climates (closely linked perhaps to autonomy) is the extent to which managers feel they will be given adequate consideration and support in their actions. Managers who believe and see that they are supported and encouraged by their superiors are likely to be creative and flexible in their approach to decision making. *Innovation and good ideas need something to grow on!* This dimension of climate, consideration and support is one which is probably least open to prescription or to formal structuring, and one which is most affected by individual behaviour and by the building of relationships. In that respect, it may be the dimension which is least under the control of the organization itself. Managers have a choice of emphasis in their relationships with other managers and subordinates. Such relationships can be essentially 'controlling' in nature, or they can be 'supportive'. The choice is largely influenced by perceptions of the prevailing climate. Supportive climates are built up by reciprocal activity, the manager, as decision maker, contributing through his or her behaviour towards others in the work group. The more support one gives, the more supported one is likely to be!

## The Interaction of Dimensions

While organizational climate can be measured or judged separately along each of our four dimensions, it is most likely that they are related quite strongly to each other. Climates which, for instance, provide a high degree of autonomy for managers are most likely to be perceived as having relatively low structure, to be high in support and consideration, and to contain reward orientations which are geared to results rather than methods. In other words, we can expect some measure of consistency, at least in stable situations, between the dimensions of climate. Changes along one particular dimension, once they become extreme, tend to induce an element of 'drag' such that the total climate changes so as to accommodate the new situation. The difficulty might be in introducing and establishing a change along one or more dimensions that is sufficiently severe as to have an effect on existing climate, rather than being moderated and accommodated by that climate.

It might be that certain dimensions, particularly those which provide bridges outside the localized situation of the organization, are likely to be key ones in stimulating changes in climate. Changes along the dimension of reward orientation, for example, such as a change from individual and local towards national and industry-wide pay settlements, or a reduction in promotion opportunities (both common occurrences in the United Kingdom during the depressed economic conditions of the late 1970s and 1980s) are likely to have a major knock-on effect on the other three dimensions of climate, reducing managerial autonomy by increasing the rules and guidelines under which pay decisions are made and adversely affecting supportive relationships.

## Managing Organizational Climate

The importance of actually managing, or at least attempting to manage, the climate of organizations has come to be recognized in recent years. Long-term strategies to create organizations that are effective in their relationships with their outside 'environments', which adapt well and take maximum advantage of changing conditions, have begun to include efforts to alter the 'internal' climate. These strategies, attempting to create the favourable climate required so as to allow managers and other decision makers to operate in the way that the organization needs, have become known as *organization development*:

> Organisation Development techniques are aimed at changing the attitudes, values and behaviour of participants, with the specific objective of getting the people themselves to develop more open, supportive, organic types of organisations, in which innovation can then prevail.[6]

It seems clear that the proponents of organization development have in mind a particular climate they feel is necessary for improved organizational performance. A fairly representative statement might be the following:

> By fundamental change, as opposed to fixing a problem or improving a procedure, I mean that some significant aspect of an organisation's culture [climate] will never be the same. In the case example, it was the reward system. In another case, it might be a change in the organisation's management approach or style, requiring new forms of exercising authority, which in turn, would lead to different conformity patterns since new norms would be established, especially in the area of decision making.[7]

## Organization Structure and Decision Making

So far in this chapter, we have been concerned with the somewhat intangible notion of climate and its impact on the decision maker and on decisions made. A rather more directly observable feature of organizational life which materially affects the way decisions get made (or even whether they get made at all) is the manner in which decision-making roles within the organization are structured and linked together. As an example, Figure 4.1 shows the structure of authority relationships and responsibilities within the sales department of a company.

Suppose the sales manager is required to estimate future orders for a product and, based on those estimates, to make recommendations for production and stocking

**Figure 4.1** The structure of a sales department

levels. The regional sales supervisors who have the basic information are geographically dispersed. The manager could either bring them together and involve them in the decision each time one has to be made (not very convenient, but potentially perhaps the most accurate way of obtaining the estimates), or evolve a system whereby the regional sales managers provide information on a regular basis which the sales manager can then use to make the decision, providing the estimate centrally. Alternatively, investment in some form of technology-based conferencing facility might be developed, albeit at great expense. Whichever method is chosen, in practice, will dominate the others. The manager has to invest in a particular decision-making procedure in order to cope with the way the sales department is structured. This structure has a considerably restricting effect on what decision processes dominate in practice, and the flexibility and scope the manager might have for changing them if required.

## Information Flow and Structure

The key problem for the sales manager in our illustration was the fact that the 'information' and judgement capability needed to make a high-quality decision was separated (in this case geographically) from the point at which the decision was required. The increasingly important role of information in decision making, its quality, location and flow patterns, is a growing area of concern in management theory and practice. The way in which organization structures are designed can very often create problems for decision makers in that it restricts or corrupts the information available to them. An interesting point here is that, while we now have available the information technology to deal with complex information needs in decision making, it is often used to compensate for structural problems and difficulties, rather than as the cornerstone of organizational design. Figure 4.2 illustrates a more detailed organization chart, again of our mythical company, which has been specifically constructed so as to highlight some of the problems that can arise. Such problems might include the following.

1. *Location.* Those members of the company required to take part in decision making may be based in different locations. These might be within the same plant or in different parts of the country. Indeed, with the growth of multinational corporations, it is not uncommon for management teams to be spread across several continents! Physical separation of those involved in decisions, and the inconveniences this causes, not unnaturally often leads to decisions being taken centrally, not because the requirements of a high-quality decision indicate that approach, but because it is the only one that is deemed to be practicable.

2. *Direction of communications.* Communication channels in large organizations have traditionally tended to emphasize the vertical, rather than the horizontal. The points at which information is gathered are usually at or near the bottom of the chain for most routine decisions. These are often separated, as in our organization,

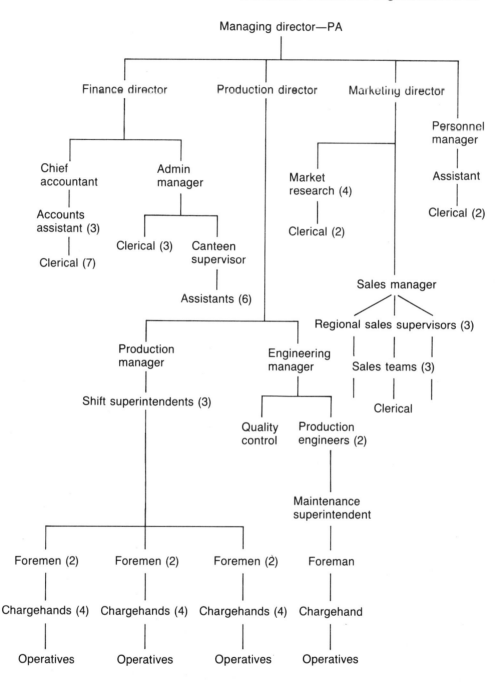

**Figure 4.2** Organization chart (greatly simplified)

by several stages from the decision-making levels, allowing considerable scope for delay and for reinterpretation on the way up. Even in non-routine decision situations it may be that, while information sources and the decision makers are closer together, the communication channels to those who are expected to implement decisions can often be very extended. For decision-making purposes, structures which reduce the distance between those who have the needed information, those who actually make the decision, and those who implement it, create a considerable advantage.

## Changing Patterns of Work Attendance

As work organizations grow and become more complex in structure, patterns of work attendance often become more varied. It may be that the technological processes or the economics of large-scale production require shift working, a different team of managers being responsible for each shift. Handling continuity and the co-ordination of 'non-problematic' activities in this kind of operation can be severe. Getting decision makers together to solve problems that cut across shifts is often more difficult than pulling together teams that are geographically dispersed! More recent changes, such as those brought about by the introduction of flexitime systems, where there is more freedom for the individual in deciding on attendance hours, might well have some considerable impact on organizational decision making. One can speculate further on technological advances in production and in communication that will no longer require people to congregate together as they do now, and the effect this might have on the way decisions get made.

## Status Differences

The status of particular roles within the organizational hierarchy can facilitate or impede the decision-making process. Making decisions is itself sometimes the prerogative of high-status managers. Status differentials and the expectations and assumptions that often accompany them can create obstacles in decisions which require that contributors be drawn from different parts of the organization. More weight may be given, for instance, to the view of senior managers, just because they are senior managers. Conversely, ideas put forward by junior managers may be discredited or discounted because of their low status within the organization.

## Communication Networks

A number of experimental studies have been undertaken which have examined the effect of limiting and prescribing the channels through which people involved in decision making can communicate with each other. Some of the earliest, and perhaps the best known, in this field was that done by Alex Bavelas,[8] and his findings have generally been supported and enlarged upon by other researchers.[9] Such studies have usually examined a range of different communication structures or networks as represented by those in Figure 4.3.

Although the networks are constructed for experimental purposes, they do, of course, approximate very closely to the communication networks that are found as sub-systems in many work organizations. Indeed, we can overlay, for instance, the star and the chain at several points on the organization chart of our mythical company (see Figure 4.2). Experimental findings from the study of communication networks have thrown up a number of issues that are of particular interest and value to the organizational decision maker.

## Differences Between Networks

One way of categorizing communication networks is by the degree of centrality they display. The star, for instance, is highly centralized, all information channels flowing through one point, and the other points being peripheral. The circle on the other hand, is highly decentralized, all points in the network having the same

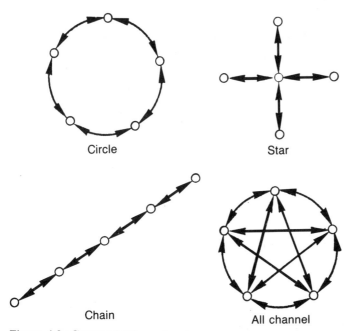

**Figure 4.3** Communication networks

number of channels. Research has tended to indicate considerable differences between centralized and decentralized networks in three main areas:

1. Getting started.
2. Solving problems.
3. Involvement and commitment.

### Getting Started

Networks with high degrees of centrality, such as the star, are generally more efficient in getting started than are the more decentralized networks. It is clearly possible for the person at the centre of the star to initiate action and get some form of decision-making effort going quickly. In work organizations this may be an important factor. 'Getting to grips' and 'being seen to be doing something' can provide high *face validity* for a centralized network.

The speed of start-up can vary in networks like the chain, depending on the point within the chain at which initiating action is taken, but, in network terms, they are fundamentally inefficient in this respect. This problem is often faced in work organizations, where long communication chains stretch down through the organizational hierarchy. The responsibility for getting things started is often held by the senior manager at the top of the chain, and unfortunately that may not be the best position for recognizing that a problem exists in the first place, especially if key information is being received further down the chain.

### Solving Problems

Networks vary in their effectiveness in solving different types of problem. For routine or 'simple' problems, the more centralized networks have the advantage in both *speed* and *accuracy*. In such cases, procedures for solution have already been or can easily be established, and are handled at the centre. Peripheral members of the network are merely required to provide information and to pass it to the central position where it is then processed. Many organizational problems fall into this category. Other kinds of problem, however, require different action on the part of network members. They may be required to generate and to develop information, or to search for data that might be pertinent to the situation. They might be required to put forward ideas or to suggest ways in which the problem might be tackled. In these more 'complex' problem situations, it is the decentralized networks with the highest number of communication channels between members that would seem to be the most effective.

### Involvement and Commitment

Satisfaction and enthusiasm for the problem-solving process is most uniformly shared among members of *decentralized* networks. In centralized networks, not unnaturally, those at the centre tend to derive most satisfaction, provided that they are able to cope with the high workload. Morale among network members seems to be directly related to the extent to which they are involved in and participate in the decision-making process. It also seems to correlate very highly with the level of communication that goes on: that is, with the number of messages sent. It may be, therefore, that organizational health, at least in terms of morale and satisfaction, depends not just on the genuine *possibility* of involvement by members, but also on a base level of actual communication between them.

## Other Findings Related to Decision Making

### Saturation and Inefficiency

For some problem situations, the sheer volume of work to be carried out can easily saturate central positions in networks, and lead to the inefficient use of those occupying the more peripheral positions. Of course, the worse the level of saturation, the worse the network becomes at working on the problem, and the more disenchanted and de-motivated team members become. Such a situation is very difficult to get out of as it is the central initiating position which is overburdened, and the other positions where people have more time to think do not find it easy to take on the initiating role. The job of the manager here is to decide on the most appropriate allocation of resources to central and peripheral positions, thus reducing the likelihood of saturation and increasing the workload of those at more peripheral positions in the decision-making network.

### Centrality Produces Leaders

When a leader has not been previously designated, the centrality of the network in giving and receiving messages seems to contribute to producing leaders. Here is a case where the formal structure, within which a decision-making group may be expected to work, in itself requires leadership behaviour from whoever occupies central positions in the network. Other group members may then come to look for leadership from that person in other fields.

### Flexibility

Flexibility seems to be much higher in the more decentralized networks, in terms of:

- Willingness among members of the network to change jobs and to adapt their behaviour. Centralized networks tend to produce rigidity and a reluctance to try new approaches to problem solving.

- The network members' ability to adapt to new tasks and to take on new or novel types of problem.

The Development of Open-Channel Networks

The adoption of an appropriate communication network for dealing with the kind of problem confronting us is obviously a key step in establishing the decision situation. Unfortunately, managers are often faced with severe restrictions on what they can achieve in this area in practice. At best, we may have to settle for the kind of network that suits the majority, or, perhaps, the most crucial of our decision situations. At worst, the communication structure may be forced upon us, leaving no choice at all.

As work organizations face increasingly complex decision situations and have to tackle more and more non-routine problems, then it should follow that organization structures will develop to include more open-channel networks to deal with them. Deciding 'how to decide' and which kind of communication network to use might well become one of the key areas of a manager's problem-solving responsibility.

## Organizational Growth and Specialization of Function

As work organizations grow in size, one seemingly inevitable feature is the shift from a relatively homogeneous structure to one that is much more differentiated. In order to capitalize on the use of resources, most organizations divide up their activities into specialist functions. Departments or sub-units may be formed, for instance, based around a particular product or, more commonly, a particular stage in the production or commercial process. So, in even a medium-sized company, we may find sales and production departments, quality control, packing and dispatch, maintenance, personnel, finance and many other specialist activities.

The economic benefits of such specialization are easy to understand. It allows the development of skills and expertise, leading to the efficient use of resources and corresponding economies of scale. The co-ordination of such specialized activities so as to capitalize on such benefits is, of course, a major management activity. Co-operation between specialist departments and, indeed, between all sub-groupings within the total organization is a fundamental requirement for its effective functioning. Yet, almost without exception, managers regularly experience situations where conflict, rather than co-operation, is the order of the day, and where groups seem almost to go out of their way to compete with each other.

Inter-Group Conflict

Examples of conflict between departments and between groups within the organization are widespread. Production and sales departments, which are so clearly interdependent, often spend considerable effort in conflict situations. Similarly, employees involved in work study and those in production often see themselves as being in opposing teams, each out to beat the other. In a telecommunications company where one of the authors worked, relationships between the design department and the assembly department were so bad that, at one stage, the assembly manager issued explicit instructions that assemblers were to follow design blueprints to the letter, *even when they knew there were mistakes!* The costs to the company were, of course, substantial, and the manager's action did nothing at all to improve relationships between the two departments.

Many factors can contribute to inter-group conflict, and the cause is often seen as lying with the personalities involved. The assembly manager, for example, is being juvenile and pig-headed. The difficulty is that, *whatever* the cause, conflict is bound to express itself through the behaviour of the people involved. Some writers[10] would actually suggest that conflict between groups is essentially a structural phenomenon, being born out of the process of specialization. The potential for conflict is set up through the very act of subdividing the total organization structure in order to improve efficiency. Schein sees the problem as one of groups focusing in on their own goals and objectives, and coming to regard these as their *raison d'être*:

> This problem exists because, as groups become more committed to their own goals and norms, they are likely to become competitive with one another and seek to undermine their rivals' activities, thereby becoming a liability to the organisation as a whole.[11]

## The Consequences of Inter-group Conflict

Inter-group competition within work organizations may not always actually outweigh the positive gains of specialization, but it can often reduce organizational effectiveness to a level which is far below that which is potentially attainable. For the decision maker, inter-group conflict can lead, for example, to a lack of provision of vital information, or to problems in getting solutions implemented. In short, it can lead to difficulties in any area where effective problem solving means crossing the boundaries between sub-units of the organization.

Conflict between departments or groups is often seen as the inevitable and unavoidable consequence of working in a large organization, and reduced levels of decision effectiveness come to be regarded as the best that can be achieved. It is certainly true that the pressures towards specialization inevitably bring with them the *potential* for conflict between groups, but that conflict can be managed at different levels. Perhaps the traditional way is to use an 'after the event' style, overcoming obstacles when these are recognized and coping with the difficulties that arise. This approach is, of course, also a 'high-energy' strategy, as are all reactive strategies, requiring extra effort and resources to overcome unexpected difficulties and unnecessary hurdles.

Many managers will find the suggestion of avoiding win–lose situations (see Box 4.2) particularly difficult to accept. This is because of the traditionally held

---

*Box 4.2*

Schein has identified a number of 'pro-active' steps[12] that can be taken by management in order to reduce the level of inter-group conflict by taking away many of the conditions which foster its occurrence:

- *Increase the emphasis on total organizational effectiveness.* Departments and teams should be encouraged to focus on the total effectiveness of the company or organization. Furthermore, they should be rewarded on the basis of their contribution to that effectiveness and in proportion to it. This strategy focuses attention on to superordinate goals and away from the 'us and them' situation.

- *Stimulate high interaction and frequent communication between groups.* It is very difficult to maintain negative stereotypes of people you see and work with frequently! In work organizations, therefore, interaction between the members of *inter-dependent* groups should be encouraged, and the communication channels between them should be opened up as much as possible. Group members should then be actively encouraged to use these channels, on the basis that it is the actual frequency of communication, rather than its mere feasibility, which reduces conflict.

- *Swap members between groups.* Members of interdependent groups and departments should be rotated among those groups so as to 'stimulate a high degree of understanding and empathy for one another's problems'.

- *Keep away from win–lose situations.* Managers should avoid creating situations where groups or departments find themselves in the position of competing for some scarce or limited organizational reward. In such situations, one group is bound to win, and the other to lose. Such situations obviously cannot be removed entirely, but they are often set up and entered into unnecessarily. Instead, attention should be focused on win–win situations, where groups can compete against external standards and targets, rather than against each other.

---

belief that competition improves and stimulates performance. Such beliefs usually centre around expectations about the performance of the winners rather than the losers, and even less around total overall performance.

> If managers wish to prevent such [negative] consequences, they must face the possibility that they may have to abandon competitive relationships altogether and seek to substitute intergroup collaboration towards organisational goals. The more 'interdependent' the various units are, the more important it is to stimulate collaborative problem solving.[13]

Very few management decision activities are now so independent that they do not require collaboration and co-operation from other units within the same organization. The level of inter-group conflict that exists can be a significant factor in the decision situation, perhaps determining absolutely which alternative course of action is selected. Management of such conflict, through a pro-active strategy based on Schein's four stages (see Box 4.2) can prepare the ground for higher-quality and more effective decisions.

# Organizing for Decision

The consequences of most decisions are relatively minor in their impact on medium- and long-term organizational goals. The many alternative routes that are available, and the effect of subsequent decisions in correcting or confounding earlier ones, will make that inevitable. The real impact of poor decision making is created by the cumulative effect of large numbers of poor-quality decisions, which combine together to reduce organizational effectiveness.

In order to avoid this, it is necessary to set up processes and mechanisms within the organization which will enhance the potential for 'high-quality' decision making to go on, on a regular and frequent basis. Such processes have to take into account two separate but linked needs:

- That when problems arise, decisions do actually get taken.

- That when decisions are made, they are good decisions.

## Deciding to Decide

In many cases, problems are endured rather than solved. For example, we first become aware that something might be wrong through experiencing some minor irritation or difficulty. We get round that difficulty, since the effort of getting to the root causes seems disproportionate to the irritation suffered. If the size and impact of the problem gradually increases, we may continue to cope and to put off the effort of solving the problem once and for all, though the total energy expended in dealing with the irritating symptoms may now exceed that needed to deal with the root causes in the first place. The problem never comes to a head, and so a decision never gets made.

In many circumstances, employees who are in a position to locate and experience problems, particularly in their early stages, may not be in a position to make decisions. They may be precluded from doing so, decision-making authority being restricted to more senior personnel. They may have no effective communication channels to those who can make decisions, or they may not realize that what they are experiencing actually constitutes a problem that ought to be solved.

There are many reasons why decisions do not get taken at the point where they would be most effective, or, sometimes, why they never get taken at all. Of course, *to do nothing* might well be the most effective solution in some cases. There is a world of difference, however, in arriving at a 'do nothing' strategy through a definite decision process and in doing nothing by putting off making a decision at all, or being unable to make a decision because the problem is not recognized by the right people. *Deciding to decide*, establishing that a decision must be made, may actually be more important in some circumstances than the eventual quality of whatever decision is made.

## The Processes

Organizational processes which will meet the needs for high-quality decision making and for ensuring that decisions really do get taken have several components. They will clearly require the development of new systems and procedures which provide for the possibility of identifying problems and for the implementation of solutions. They also require the generation of new skills in those who have to make the required decisions. The major areas where the development of such skills and procedures can bring rewards are:

- The collection and use of information.
- The development of effective management styles in decision making.

## The Collection and Use of Information

Perfect knowledge, and therefore perfect information, has previously been identified as a necessary operating condition for rational decision making. Even if we accept that this condition is not likely to be achieved, it is clear that information will play a vital part in the quality of solution achieved. In addition, information plays two other roles in the organizational context:

- Managers need to gather and to collate information in order to decide whether or not a problem exists.

- Information is needed after the implementation of the chosen solution in order to determine its effectiveness.

The first task, therefore, in establishing an information process for decision making is to identify and establish the nature of the information required and the sources from which it is likely to come. These will vary according to the nature of the task and problems being worked on. Ullrich and Weiland[14] identify three basic factors which will affect the complexity of the information process required:

1. *Task uncertainty.* The greater the degree of novelty and uncertainty in the task or problem to be faced, the greater the amount of information that has to be processed and shared among those involved in the decision making. Companies and departments that work extensively on non-routine problems or one-offs therefore need to develop communication structures which allow such sharing of information. In network terms this would require the use of decentralized structures. On the other hand, where the problems being worked on are relatively routine, much of the information needed will be known and information channels can then be set up. This allows the use of a centralized network with advantages of speed and initiation of action.

2. *The number of elements involved.* The decision situation is complicated by the size of the organization, the range of different activities involved in decision

making, and the number of tasks or products undertaken at any one time. Each of these factors is likely to require an increase in the number and intensity of information flows.

3. *The interdependence of decisions.* In situations where there are likely to be knock-on effects when decisions are made, there is a need for extensive communication of information between departments, project teams and decision makers. A change in body styling for a motor car, for instance, may lead to an increase in weight. This may then cause problems for the suspension, which has to be redesigned. This, in turn, may affect cost, or it may allow further possibilities for the designers which were not possible with the old suspension.

The complexity and nature of the system for sharing and using information seems, then, to depend on the nature of the task. Managers working in organizations where tasks are relatively stable and routine, where there is little interdependence, need relatively simple systems for processing information. Those who have to cope with relatively high degrees of novelty and uncertainty in the problems they face need as much information as they can get, together with highly developed channels of communication, so as to make the best possible use of that information. In both situations, managers are faced with the problem of 'what kind' of information is needed and 'where' it might come from. Again this is likely to be related to the nature of the predominant or key tasks they face.

## Establishing Sources of Information

Gathering information in order to make a decision, once the problem has been identified, is almost of necessity a unique process. While one can obviously learn from experience gained in similar situations, much of the information needed is likely to be specific to that particular decision and so needs to be identified and obtained at that point in time. Yet the process of gathering and collating information which allows us to recognize the emergence of a potential problem is one that must be carried out on a continuous basis. The focus of this 'monitoring' process will vary according to the business that organizations are engaged in and the nature of the problems they face. In general, regular information is needed:

1. To monitor any changes in input conditions from the environment (technological, political, economic, etc.) which may have a bearing on the decision situation.

2. To check on how well the chosen solution has been put into effect within the organization or department responsible, using measures of efficiency such as costs, scrap rates, capacity and usage.

3. To evaluate the performance of the chosen course of action in meeting the set objectives (sales figures, profit levels, market share, etc.)

## Information Needs in Stable Conditions

Managers who operate in relatively stable product/market environments find most of their information needs concentrated in 2 and 3. The basic nature of the product or service is likely to be well established, and will vary only in limited and predictable ways. The problems that arise tend to be concerned with internal issues, such as snags in production or processing or in the implementation of the decision, and with monitoring effectiveness. Changes in input conditions do not have a great impact, and therefore the amount of effort which is put into obtaining input information can be reduced. This situation is represented in Figure 4.4.

The danger here, of course, is that companies whose operations and markets have been stable for some considerable time may neglect to monitor such outside conditions altogether. Then, when changes do occur, any response has to be reactive rather than pro-active, with the corresponding loss of initiative and advantage. Even in stable situations, therefore, it will be necessary to gather information about one's environment in order to detect any movement away from that stability. The number of organizations, and for that matter the number of managers who operate in an environment that can genuinely be said to be stable, must clearly be declining rapidly. The ever-increasing rate of technological, economic and political change affects more and more organizations in industrial, commercial and service fields. Information sources and systems must be adapted to meet situations of instability and uncertainty.

## Information Needs in Conditions of Uncertainty

The more decision makers are faced with variety and variability in the problems they face, the more they require to invest in gathering information on input conditions. These information needs are represented in Figure 4.5.

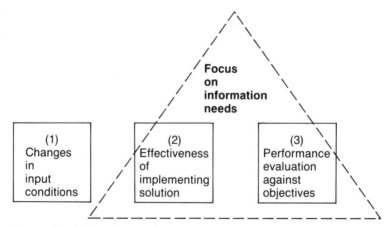

**Figure 4.4** Information needs under stable conditions

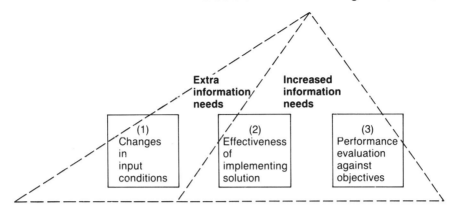

**Figure 4.5** Information needs under uncertainty

As well as this relocation of focus, uncertainty often means that 'extra' resources have to be allocated to information gathering and evaluation. Firstly, this is because the lack of routine means that any information system has to be flexible enough to be able to draw information from many outside information sources so as to meet the needs of a range of one-off decisions. Secondly, the task of monitoring implementation effectiveness and the achievement of objectives for a series of one-off decisions is made more difficult in such circumstances. Thirdly, the sheer amount of information that is available to be monitored, and in some cases the highly technical nature and format of that information, can mean that the decision maker is highly dependent on other people in the organization for its supply and for its interpretation. The more complex organizations have become, the more they have developed specialist functions, recruiting employees with widely different skills and expertise. For instance, a company may employ scientists, engineers and designers to keep abreast of developments in knowledge and applications, relying on their competence and judgement in assessing which of them might be of potential value and use to the company. The same company may rely heavily on its sales force in monitoring customer interests and market trends. As products and services become more sophisticated, the number of separate skills to be managed increases, and consequently the volume of information necessary for their successful integration goes up. The argument here is not that increases in the volume of information are the 'unfortunate consequences' of change and of uncertainty. The establishment of adequate information channels is a *necessary precondition* for effective decision making in these conditions. The danger, of course, is that the cost of gathering information outweighs the benefits that are gained from it.

## Establishing the Decision Point

Just as different organizational circumstances generate different information needs, so it is possible to envisage variations in the point at which the actual decision gets made. The right to make decisions has perhaps traditionally been reserved for senior positions in the organizational hierarchy. There is a strong argument, however, for varying the point of decision according to the nature of the problem or task. The level at which decisions are made will depend on the following.

### Routineness of Task

The more routine the task or the problems faced, the more it is possible to centralize certain aspects of the decision-making process. Pre-planning at the centre can cope with most, if not all, contingencies. Rules and procedures can be established which lay down the actions managers should take under any particular set of circumstances. The manager then uses these centrally produced 'decision rules' to work through the decision and arrive at the correct course of action.

Non-routine problems and wide variations in task, on the other hand, would require too many decisions too frequently from a centralized authority and therefore cannot be routinized in the same way. In such circumstances, a possible solution is for central authority to set guidelines in terms of goals and objectives, rather than detailed decision rules, and then to devolve decision rules downwards within those broad frameworks. This strategy would limit the need for information to travel through great distances within the organization, and also reduce the chance of blockages resulting from the overloading of the central decision makers.

### Interdependence of Task

The effect of interdependent tasks on the complexity of the information required for adequate decision making has already been raised. Where a high degree of interrelatedness is found, decision making is likely to be focused at a level which is high enough (see Figure 4.6) that co-ordination can be achieved.

### The Devolvement of Decision-Making Power into Problem-Solving Units

Many if not most organizations now operate under conditions which produce both greater variety of problems and decision situations and much more uncertainty

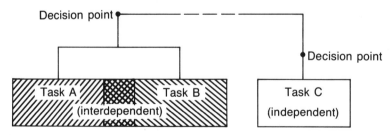

**Figure 4.6**  The effect of task interdependence on decision point location

about the tasks that they have to carry out. Under such circumstances, the retention of centralized decision making is likely to be less than effective. A more appropriate guideline might be: *locate decision-making power at the lowest point where the problem can be solved.* This strategy has the following advantages:

1. It reduces the volume of information moving vertically through the organization, reducing the risks of distortion and overload.

2. It shortens both the distance and the time between information being received and decisions being taken, allowing a quick response.

3. Involvement in decision making is a highly motivating factor for employees, encouraging awareness, creativity and idea generation, and a commitment towards getting solutions implemented.

4. The more employees are directly involved in solving problems as opposed merely to experiencing them, the more problem solving will become part of the organizational culture.

The devolution strategy still allows for considerable variation in the 'end result', since the key factor in determining the location of the decision point is the level or point at which the problem can be identified and then solved. This will vary considerably between organizations. Those which perform very routine operations may face few problems (in the sense of decisions where innovative solutions have to be found) at lower levels in their hierarchy. Conversely, organizations whose activities require a great deal of interaction and co-ordination are likely to find that the only effective decision point is some way up in the hierarchy. Nonetheless, the central point of the strategy is that decision making should take place as close as possible to the relevant sources of information and, for many companies, this will mean devolving decision-making power downwards to employees who previously did not have it.[15]

## The Development of Effective Management Styles

Management positions are distinguished from others in work organizations by the fact that the holder is usually appointed from outside the immediate situation, usually by organizational superiors, to a specific role within the work group to which is delegated both responsibility and authority. The manager is usually given responsibility for some phase of operations or segment of an organization's activities, and is delegated, by virtue of his or her position, the authority deemed necessary to carry out those duties. As this task almost certainly involves influencing other people, the managerial role is clearly a *leadership* role. While, as is often pointed out, the exercising of delegated authority cannot be avoided, the manager usually has discretion as to how he or she will put it into operation: 'Although managerial leaders cannot choose whether or not to exercise authority, they can often choose how they will exercise it — that is to say, they can choose a leadership style.'[16]

## Management Style and Decision Effectiveness

So far, in looking at issues centring on decision making in groups, we have not assumed any particular structure of relationships within the group. When we come to examine the position of many managers in group situations, it is apparent that their relationships and interactions with others in the groups are somewhat special. In terms of decision making, the one distinctive and overriding feature of many decisions is that it is *one manager*, rather than the whole group, who carries responsibility for the decision. When confronting a problem, therefore, the manager has to face an immediate issue in deciding how to go about taking the decision.

The exercise of choice over leadership style is essentially concerned with the *extent* to which and the *basis* on which the manager might involve the 'non-managerial' members of the work team. Three factors would seem to limit the freedom of choice any manager has in this respect:

1. The basis of managerial power.

2. Relationships between the manager and subordinates.

3. The nature of the decision to be taken or of the problem to be solved.

### *The Basis of Managerial Power*

By virtue of being appointed to the position, the manager acquires a particular source of power, that of the *authority* vested in the role. Values in most work organizations reinforce the notion that managers have the 'right' to lead and to be obeyed. Of course, this source of power is at its strongest when the objectives of the workforce coincide with those of the external system, but even challenges or threats to the 'manager's right to manage' usually concern its scope, rather than its absolute basis.

Authority, although central to the managerial position, rarely exists on its own as the sole basis for managerial power and influence. It is often backed up by:

1. The ability to dispense rewards (such as promotion or pay increases) and punishments (such as the withholding of expected rewards and privileges, or more extreme sanctions such as dismissal).

2. A demonstration of skill and expertise, including technical skill and ability, and organizing ability.

3. Respect and affection for the manager as a person.

In the same way that authority and power based on rewards and sanctions tend to be linked together, so is the power and influence derived from skill and expertise linked with that gained from respect and affection. The former are based in the role that the manager occupies, the latter on the personal abilities and attributes of managers themselves. Managers who can draw on the full range of sources of managerial power are more likely to be able to influence others and, consequently, to have a wider range of options in leadership style open to them.

### Relationships Between the Manager and Subordinates

The essential area of concern here is the degree of trust and openness of communication between managers and their subordinates. This relationship can be affected by many factors, including the values and aspirations of the manager and of other members of the group, the degree of confidence each has in the other and, perhaps most importantly, the extent to which the manager recognizes the skill and expertise of group members.

### The Nature of the Task

Different types of decision will require different action on the part of the manager as leader. As we suggested in Chapter 1, decisions can be:

1. Strategic or operational.
2. Structured or unstructured.
3. Dependent or independent.

## The Choice of Management Style

The diagnosis of a decision situation in terms of power, relationships and task type may enable the choice of a style which will aid an effective outcome (see Box 4.3).

---

### Box 4.3

Guidance in the choice of an appropriate style can also be obtained by looking at the work of Tannenbaum and Schmidt[17] in their attempts to illustrate the links between the degree of authority used by the manager and the amount of freedom in decision making enjoyed by subordinates.

In terms of our criteria of quality, commitment and timing, leadership styles which involve consultation and participation should score well in increasing the quality of decisions and commitment to them, but they are not likely to be as effective as the more autocratic styles in terms of the speed with which decisions are actually made. Such increased participation may, of course, be a desired goal in its own right and this will influence a manager's choice of style. In terms of decision effectiveness, however, it may be more appropriate to choose a management style on the basis of the particular decision being faced, and only then to overlay this with longer-term considerations.

Vroom and Yetton[18] have been particularly influential in the advancement of *situational* approaches to choosing a management style. They develop a set of rules which follow the form of a decision tree, thereby guiding the choice of style. A range of styles is presented from being highly autocratic, where managers make decisions on their own, to being highly democratic and participative. Their range of styles has five basic strategies as follows:

Style (a)  The manager takes the decision personally, using the information which is immediately available.

Style (b)  The manager obtains required information from subordinates and then makes the decision. Involvement by others is limited strictly to the provision of information.

Style (c)  The manager discusses the problem with subordinates on an individual basis, while still retaining the decision-taking role.

Style (d)  The manager discusses the problem collectively with subordinates, encouraging collective thoughts and ideas, while still retaining the decision-taking role.

Style (e)  The problem is discussed and tackled collectively. The manager and subordinates attempt to reach a consensus on a solution which is then adopted.

Vroom and Yetton have identified a number of decision dimensions which, when considered together, allow a manager to decide which of these five styles to adopt. Their diagnostic questions are designed to force a consideration of the following.

## The 'Quality' Dimension

To what extent does it, in fact, matter which of the alternative solutions is chosen? In some decisions, any one of a number of solutions would be acceptable and, other things being equal, any of the five styles might be used. In others it is certain that one solution will be better than another. Where this is the case, the manager has to ensure that a *high-quality* solution is put forward.

## The 'Information' Dimension

Who has the information necessary to make a high-quality decision? Does the manager know enough about the problem to solve it alone? If not, is it known just what information is needed and where it can be obtained? If there is uncertainty, either about what information is needed or where to get it, then subordinates may help to produce a high-quality solution by sharing ideas about the problem and by working on it collectively, thereby generating information and understanding. If the problem is 'structured' (so that the manager knows what information is needed and where it is to be found), such collective involvement may not be necessary, and subordinates can be consulted for information individually.

### The 'Commitment' Dimension

Many decisions depend on the actions and interpretations of others for successful implementation. To what extent is acceptance and commitment by others crucial to a successful outcome? The underlying assumption here is that the more people are involved in the decision-making process, the more they will be committed to its successful solution.

### The 'Capability' Dimension

It is only sensible to use group consensus methods if the group is actually capable of producing a high-quality decision. Are group members likely to share the aims and objectives of the organization in their search for solutions? Is there likely to be disagreement over the preferred solutions, even where there are shared goals? Decision strategies which allow group involvement and discussion are useful ways of exposing and resolving such conflicts, but if a quality solution is required, the manager may sometimes have to retain the final decision.

By considering each of these dimensions in turn, managers can derive a rationale for their choice of management style. For example, others may be involved in the decision so as to provide information, to help illuminate the problem or to generate commitment. So the extent of involvement is determined primarily through an examination of the 'capability' dimension.

In practice, the process is essentially one of exclusion rather than of positive choice as such. It is one of discarding inappropriate styles rather than choosing one which is particularly appropriate. For example, a lack of information on the manager's part should prevent the use of a heavily autocratic style if a quality solution is required. This 'discarding' process often means that several acceptable styles will exist for any particular decision. Figure 4.7 illustrates how the dimensions can be used to obtain a set of acceptable decision styles.

### Other Deciding Factors

Where a range of acceptable styles exist, factors other than those in the 'dimensions' need to be included. For example, Vroom and Yetton use *time* as the governing factor. Other things being equal, and provided that there is more than one acceptable style, the one which is likely to get the decision made most quickly should be chosen. Then again there may be other factors more important to the manager than the time spent on the decision. The existence of a range of acceptable styles may be exploited to promote the development of long-term personal or organizational

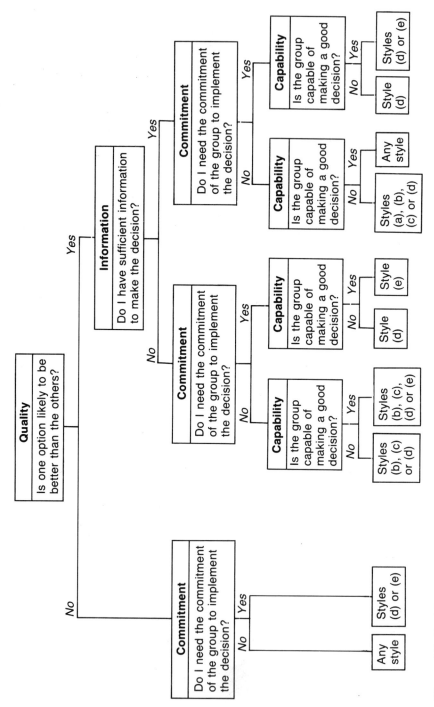

**Figure 4.7** Decision process flow chart

strategies. For example, a manager might have a moral commitment to participative management and will therefore always tend to the more consultative styles. Alternatively, the manager may wish to establish a departmental reputation for staff involvement so as to recruit the best employees and again, given the choice, will tend towards consultative styles.

## The Need to be Flexible

The situational approach to analysing decisions highlights the inherent weakness in the rigid adoption of one particular decision style (Box 4.4). *There is no single decision style that is appropriate for all situations*. The adoption of an autocratic style, for example, where a manager makes decisions without consultation of any kind, is seen by Vroom and Yetton as being appropriate in only a very few cases. It would therefore seem that, rather than let long-term issues of style override the needs of a particular decision, the more effective approach is to:

1. Determine the type of decision being faced by considering the four dimensions of 'quality', 'information', 'commitment' and 'capability'.

2. Isolate the range of acceptable styles by *excluding* those which are unacceptable in the circumstances.

---

*Box 4.4*

## Problems in the Situational Approach

An approach which bases decision style on the demands of the situation poses a number of problems. Most importantly, managers are expected to select from a range of styles according to the situation, and this presupposes a willingness on the part of the manager that may not actually be there. Some managers adopt a fairly limited set of styles, or may even use the same style with only minor accommodations, regardless of circumstances.

Many factors can combine to produce such rigidity, including:

- Past experience of successes and failures.
- Comfort and familiarity with a particular style.
- Encouragement in using a particular style by senior management, or by the prevailing organizational climate.
- Current trends, e.g. towards participation and democracy in decision making.
- A belief that getting help from others is 'weak management'.
- A lack of skill in diagnosing different problems.
- A lack of skill in operating a wide range of different styles.

3. If there is more than one acceptable style, choose the one which fits in with long-term aims, or alternatively choose the style which is likely to get the decision made most quickly.

Situational approaches such as that taken by Vroom and Yetton provide us with a systematic basis for examining and understanding decisions. Because they *are* systematic they can be a very supportive aid to managerial decision making. The choice of style need no longer be entirely a matter of fashion or organizational culture. Indeed, such a model may provide support and justification for managers who go against the prevailing organizational climate in their decision-making style. However, the real test must be in the quality of the final choice, and unfortunately the ability of a manager to diagnose a decision situation and decide on the most appropriate style does not, in itself, guarantee a high-quality solution. It may be that, after consideration, the manager discards a particular style, even though it is an appropriate one, because he or she recognizes that the skills needed to carry it through successfully are lacking. Alternatively, and perhaps more frequently, a particular style is adopted but applied in an unskilful manner. This may lead to poor-quality decision making and, quite possibly, the long-term rejection of that style. The move from a long-established way of doing things towards a more flexible approach does actually involve some personal risk taking by the individual manager concerned.

Managers cannot be expected to be flexible in their decision-making styles if they do not possess the necessary skills to operate across the full range. Providing managers with skills through training in the use of different decision styles is a fundamental part of preparing and organizing for high-quality decision-making capability. Not only does this allow for the possibility of a range of styles to be used successfully, but it also provides the stimulus and encouragement for managers to take a flexible approach. When people possess skills, they do tend to look for opportunities to use them!

## Practical Prescriptions

Decision climate can be grouped around the four dimensions of: autonomy; degree of imposed structure; orientation of rewards; and degree of consideration and support for the decision maker. Monitor the dimensions of climate to determine whether or not:

1. They are in balance.

2. The climate supports the kind of decision behaviour you want to achieve.

Inadequate organization structure can severely impede decision-making activities.

1. Choose the kind of structural network that suits the majority or the most crucial of your decision situations.

2. For routine problems, choose centralized network structures.
3. For novel problems, choose decentralized networks.

As work organizations face increasingly complex decision situations, and have to tackle more non-routine problems, organization structures will include more open-channel networks to deal with them effectively.

As organization structures become more specialized, conflict between departments and groups becomes more widespread. Manage inter-group conflict at an acceptable level by:

1. Increasing emphasis on total organizational effectiveness.
2. Increasing communication and interaction between groups.
3. Avoiding win−lose situations.

Information needs for decision making in an organization depend on the degree of uncertainty in the decision situation, the number of elements involved and the interdependence of decisions within the organization. Create a rapid-response problem-solving culture by:

1. Locating decision-making responsibilities at the lowest point in the organization where the problem can be solved.
2. Investing in information systems which allow adequate monitoring of input conditions from the environment, together with rapid provision of information to the decision maker.

Check to make sure the management style you choose is appropriate for the quality, information, commitment and capability needs of the decision situation.

---

## Case Exercise

---

### Industrial Air Products Limited

Fred Dawson founded IAP in 1979 with the redundancy payments he got when he left his job as chief engineer with a large engineering company. IAP has since grown from seven employees in that first year to over eight hundred in 1989. The company makes pneumatic and (since 1986) hydraulic control systems for a range of industrial tools and machinery. As well as making a range of standard systems, the company also offers a custom design and development service to its larger customers and to those who are willing to pay for it. Sixty per cent of staff are employed at head office, which handles production, design and development, marketing, accounts, personnel and other central services. The remainder are more or less evenly split between seven regional offices, each under a regional manager. The regional staff are split into sales, engineering (installation and maintenance) and administration. The functional heads of each of these three areas are at head office, although all regional staff are on the establishment of the regional manager.

Engineers typically work out on customer premises, either on their own or with a single colleague, being given job sheets by and reporting to an engineering supervisor at the region. The majority of work is fairly routine, and the opportunity for initiative taking is limited.

The company has gone through a period of tremendous growth over the last ten years, and this is likely to continue into the foreseeable future. Fred Dawson is aware that organizational systems and structures, together with managerial expertise, have developed on the back of engineering competence and demand for the product. He is constantly on the lookout for 'high-flyers' within the organization, and promotion possibilities are certainly available to those who demonstrate capability and resourcefulness. The payment system is also fairly *ad hoc*, having evolved into broad grades together with annual merit awards given on the recommendation of the employee's immediate line manager supported, in the case of regional staff, by the regional manager.

In late 1988 Fred gave John Carter the task of heading up a special Customer Support Unit to provide advice and a problem-solving service to users and potential buyers of IAP equipment. The unit consisted of John, based at head office and reporting to the chief engineer, two development engineers also at head office, and a senior engineer at each of the regional offices. These regional engineers were attached to the unit in addition to their normal duties in the region. Each engineer specialized in either pneumatics or hydraulics, and the seven were chosen so as to provide as wide a range of experience as possible on different types of system and installation.

Within a few months of the unit being established, John and his team were busy at work. Requests for advice came to John through the appropriate regional manager (in some cases, customers contacted John direct), and decisions and recommendations for action went back down the line. John, however, was unhappy about the quality of help customers actually received from the unit. His development engineers reported that some of the regional engineers seemed to resent their advice, and the hoped-for teamwork in bringing the wide range of expertise to bear on problems was certainly not happening. At a monthly management meeting, two of the regional managers complained strongly that they were understaffed and that it was unfair to take out their best engineers to deal with customer problems in other regions.

In an attempt to knit the team more closely together, John set up a two-day seminar at head office, arranging 'teach-ins' on the latest equipment and a review of methods for solving technical problems. To his dismay, one regional manager refused to release his regional engineer to attend the seminar on the grounds of pressure of work, two engineers were late arriving on the first morning, and one more said he would have to leave after the first day in order to carry out an installation in his region. Feeling angry and frustrated, John asked for an urgent meeting with Fred Dawson. 'You've got to do something', he said. 'This unit idea just isn't working out ...'

## Questions

1. What might the internal climate be like at IAP? Is it likely to support collaboration in the Customer Support Unit?
2. What structural factors are likely to impact on the likely success of John's unit? What effect might they have?
3. If you were Fred Dawson, what exactly would you do in response to John's request for changes in order to improve the smooth running of the unit? How would you go about it?

---

## Bibliography

Alston, J.P., *The American Samurai*, de Gruyter, 1989. Attempts to contrast and also to blend a number of the prevailing organizational philosophies and practices which face managers today.

Kolb, D.A., Rubin, I.M. and McIntyre, J.M. (eds.), *Organisational Psychology: A book of readings*, Prentice Hall, 1984. Contains many readings which will support material contained in this chapter and throughout the book.

Warner Burke, W., *Organisation Development: A normative view*, Addison Wesley, 1987. An excellent overview of organization development, tracing its evolution over the last three decades.

## References

1. Mullins, L.J., *Management and Organisational Behaviour*, Pitman, 1989, p. 489.
2. See Payne, R.C. and Pugh, D.S., 'Organisational structure and climate', in Dunnette, M. (ed.), *Handbook of Industrial and Organisational Psychology*, Rand McNally, 1976.
3. Campbell, J.P., Dunnette, M.D., Lawler, E.E. and Weick, K.E., *Managerial Behaviour, Performance and Effectiveness*, McGraw-Hill, 1970.
4. For a discussion of autonomous work groups, see Bailey, J., *Job Design and Work Organisation*, Prentice Hall International, 1983, pp. 106–12.
5. A summary of these ideas is provided in Dalton, G.W. and Lawrence, P.R., *Motivation and Control in Organisations*, Irwin Dorsey, 1971, Chapter 1.
6. Dessler, G., *Organisation Theory: Integrating structure and behaviour*, Prentice Hall, 1986, p. 452.
7. Warner Burke, W., *Organisation Development: A normative view*, Addison Wesley, 1987, p. 9.
8. Bavelas, A., 'Communication patterns in task oriented groups', in Cartwright, D. and Zander, A. (eds.), *Group Dynamics*, Row-Peterson, 1953.
9. See, for example, Shaw, M., *Group Dynamics: The psychology of small group behaviour*, McGraw-Hill, 1976; Rogers, E.M. and Rogers, R.A., *Communication in Organisations*, Free Press, 1976.
10. For an excellent article on inter-group conflict, see Brown, L.D., 'Managing conflict

amongst groups', in Kolb, D.A., Rubin, I.M. and McIntyre, J.M. (eds.), *Organisational Psychology: A book of readings*, Prentice Hall, 1984.

11. Schein, E.H., *Organisational Psychology*, Prentice Hall, 1980, chapter 10.
12. *Ibid.*, pp. 179−80.
13. *Ibid.*, p. 180.
14. Ullrich, R.A. and Weiland, G.F., *Organisation Theory and Design*, Irwin, 1980, pp. 122−3.
15. For an interesting and powerful discussion of the decentralization of decision-making power within organizations, see Mintzberg, H., *Structuring in Fives: Designing effective organisations*, Prentice Hall International, 1983, chapter 5.
16. Sadler, P., 'Executive leadership', in Pym, D. (ed.), *Industrial Society*, Penguin, 1968.
17. See, for example, Tannenbaum, R. and Schmidt, W.H., 'How to choose a leadership pattern', *Harvard Business Review*, May/June, 1971.
18. Vroom, V. and Yetton, P.W., *Leadership and Decision Making*, University of Pittsburgh Press, 1973.

# PART III

## Decision modelling

There is an understandable desire by many managers to look for help in their decision making through the use of a 'technique' or decision model, and, indeed, there are many of them. Since the application of mathematical methods to tackle industrial problems started in the first half of this century, numerous methods, techniques or models have been developed. Now, although these decision models cannot take the responsibility of the final decision from the manager, they can provide valuable support. To get the most from decision models, managers must be aware both of the principles which underlie their development and the variety of decision models which are available. Part III deals with these issues.

CHAPTER 5 — MODELLING DECISIONS — examines what we mean by a 'model' of a decision and develops a step-by-step approach to building decision models. Some particular types of model are described, including the more recent types such as simulation, heuristic and 'corporate' models, which help in finding a good or an acceptable solution rather than the 'best' solution to a decision.

CHAPTER 6 — MODELLING UNCERTAINTY WITH DECISION TREES — looks in more detail at models which treat those decisions whose major characteristic is their uncertainty. The ways in which uncertainty may be quantified, and the resulting probabilities manipulated, are examined. Probability theory is then used as a basis for reintroducing the 'decision matrix' as a simple uncertainty model, followed by the more complicated 'decision tree' as a multi-stage model. Finally, 'risk simulation' is used to illustrate a procedural model for incorporating uncertainty into the decision process.

CHAPTER 7 — MODELLING PREFERENCE — deals with the introduction of the concept of utility into decision models. For our purposes this means examining two types of model. First, there are those which reflect how people's ideas of the value of money change depending on how much they have. Second, there are the models which treat decisions where possible consequences cannot be adequately described by one measure alone (such as money) but need several (money, prestige, risk and so on).

# 5 Modelling decisions

## Introduction

A model is an explicit statement of our image of reality. It is a representation of the relevant aspects of the decision with which we are concerned. It represents the decision area by structuring and formalizing the information we possess about the decision and, in doing so, presents reality in a simplified organized form. A model, therefore, provides us with an abstraction of a more complex reality.

When the term 'model' is used in this sense, it is apparent that managers are communicating by means of models all the time and using them in the decision process. Suppose a manager has just observed a meeting: for example, a negotiation with a trade union over the coming year's pay increase. Rather than giving a verbatim account, he is likely to try to convey the gist of what has occurred by giving a thumbnail sketch or painting a 'word picture' of what he considers to be the main events of the meeting. In doing this, he is modelling or abstracting a particular version of the reality he has just witnessed by constructing a *verbal model* of the meeting.

## Verbal Descriptive Models

In presenting his model of the meeting, he will probably be simplifying what occurred in two ways:

1. He will deliberately *exclude* much of what has happened, and so is making a judgement of the relative importance of events. Of course, he might reveal some of his modelling process by stating what it is that he is excluding: for example, 'I won't bore you with the preliminaries . . . ' or ' . . . and then there was a lot of detailed discussion until . . . '.

2. He will *compress* or *aggregate* several comments, reactions and events into one overall result. For example, the statement 'they agreed the agenda' may

mean that they only did so after considerable argument, but the manager judges the statement an adequate summary.

In this way the 'bones' of the events will be conveyed, but some of the information, richness and flavour of what occurred is inevitably lost.

So far, the observer at the meeting has confined himself to constructing a model that relates what was said and what occurred. At this level the model is merely *descriptive*. If nothing else, the model has communicated some of the necessary information on which decisions can be based, and therefore has aided the decision process. This *verbal descriptive model* is equivalent to the 'scale model' which architects and industrial engineers use to convey the appearance of a new housing estate or a rearranged workshop. However, there is more to a 'scale model' than just a change in dimension. Some information is lost. So, for example, of the many attributes which make a real house, some (like the details of its construction) are only implied by the shape of the model, while others (like cost) are not represented at all.

## Analogue Models

The next level of abstraction in the modelling process involves using analogy: representing one set of properties by another. The observer of the wage negotiation might compare the progress of negotiation to something quite different. For example, he might say, 'They made one concession after another until they finally capitulated . . . it was like a stick bending until it finally snapped.' The analogy of the stick breaking conveys the slow change in position accompanied by an increase in stress until that stress brings about a sudden change.

Analogy can be poetic, and goes some way to retain the richness which would otherwise be lost by straight description. It can also be economical and effective — a contour line is an elegant method of describing the altitude of land while not interfering with other information on the map. Thus the contour map is an *analogue model* of the terrain it portrays. Graphs are probably the most frequently used physical, as opposed to verbal, analogue models. They represent the relationship between two variables by a line on a chart, and in doing so convey the gist of the relationship in an efficient and convenient way.

The problem with analogies is that one can take them too far. Not only are there doubts regarding the *validity* of a particular analogy chosen for the specific set of circumstances, there is the important practical problem of how far one can project or extrapolate the analogy outside the set of circumstances for which it was originally appropriate. Analogies rely on implication and association to describe the underlying structure of a problem; they do not necessarily reveal the relationships between the various elements which give the problem its character. What is needed is the next stage in the process of abstracting the 'reality' of the problem — a *relationship model*.

## Relationship Models

In the event, it would be difficult for the observer to avoid giving clues to his opinion of the relationship between the elements of the meeting: the attitudes of the negotiators, the interests they represent, their opening positions, their willingness to compromise and so on. For example, he might say, 'It was only when our personnel manager said that he would be willing to reduce the working week that they started to compromise on the working conditions issue.' The relationship between the two events being described models a small part of the meeting. The manager is attempting to hold his perception of the *cause—effect links* within the meeting. The relationship may even be quantified. For example, 'Every time we increased our offer by 2 per cent, they reduced their claim by 1 per cent.'

The step towards using models which formalize the relationships between the elements in the decision is an important one. Not only is this the most important part of understanding the problem, but the model is now capable of being translated into a more formal language, such as the language of mathematical symbols. Words, although conveying the flavour of a decision, can be ambiguous and may not focus upon the important features within the decision as effectively as a diagrammatic or a mathematical formulation. Furthermore, words are essentially a serial form of modelling — one idea follows another — and are inadequate for complex interrelated non-serial decision problems. When mathematical symbols are used the model is known as a *symbolic model*.

Figure 5.1 compares the verbal models we have discussed with the conventional categories of 'scientific' models: namely, *iconic models*, where there is a change in scale; *analogue models*, where one set of properties is represented by another; and *symbolic models*, which use mathematical symbols to convey relationships.

## The Process of Modelling

As we discussed in Chapter 2, psychological differences in perception are likely to cause the reality of the decision situation to be viewed in different ways by different individuals. Each observer's 'mental model' of the decision is therefore likely to be different. Since people reach decisions by interacting with their models of the problem, it is quite likely that different individuals' decisions will not be the same.

For this reason, it is important to be aware of the process of formal model building. Clearly, we wish to develop as 'good' a model of the decision area as possible. Here, a 'good' model is one which reflects accurately our perceptions of the decision area and can be used to aid the decision process in one of the three ways already described. Essential prerequisites to the development of such a model are:

1. An understanding of the key variables within the decision.

| Level | Verbal model of the negotiations | Conventional 'scientific' modelling categories |
|---|---|---|
| **Descriptive** | *Description* of what the observer perceived — subject to exclusion and aggregation | *Iconic* models, i.e. the scale of reality is changed and usually some properties are ignored (e.g. scale models for layout) |
| **Analogy** | *Comparison* of the observed situation with an analogous situation | *Analogue* models where one set of properties are represented by another (e.g. contour lines in maps or graphical representation of sales) |
| **Relationship** | Influence relationships are implied between elements or events in decision situation — these relationships may be quantified | *Symbolic* models where mathematical symbols, letters and numbers are used to convey the relationship between elements in the decision |

**Figure 5.1** The three basic levels of modelling — descriptive, analogy, relationship — as applied to verbal and 'scientific' models

2. Knowledge of the 'cause—effect' pattern of influence between the variables.

3. An appreciation of how mathematical formulations can be used to formulate powerful models.

## The Variables in a Decision Model

A *variable* within a decision is some element in the decision which takes on different values. The converse of a variable is a *parameter*, which is assumed to have a constant value over the period of time studied or the range of options considered. In practice, many factors in the decision which in reality are variable are treated as constants. This is part of the process of simplification which characterizes the modelling process. For example, when deciding between alternative investment projects the prevailing interest rate on borrowed money might be assumed constant, although in practice it will fluctuate.

Variables can be classified as either *input* or *output*. Input variables (sometimes called exogenous variables) are the independent inputs to the model which may be taken as acting upon the decision. They can be either controllable or uncontrollable. Controllable input variables are the inputs to the decision over which the decision maker has influence. The values which the controllable input variables take are directly determined by the decision options. Uncontrollable input variables are those which affect the decision but are generated by the uncontrollable factors in the decision environment.

Output variables (sometimes called endogenous variables) are generated from the interaction of the model's input factors and the structure of the decision itself. Thus output variables indicate the consequences of the decision. Because consequences do not exist independently of the decision itself, a directly controllable output variable is a contradiction and cannot exist. Figure 5.2 illustrates this classification of decision variables.

For example, suppose a decision needs to be made by a wholesaler about the quantity of a particular item to be kept in stock. The major controllable input variable is the quantity to order from the supplier, since this will control the average stock level. Also, the stock level at which the product is reordered is a factor which can be controlled and will have some influence on the effectiveness of the wholesaler's stocking policy. The output variables reflect how the effectiveness of the decision will be measured. Possible output variables include the amount of money tied up in stock, the organizational effort required to control the stock, the cost of providing storage facilities and the probability of running out of stock. Yet the order quantity and the reorder level do not entirely determine the consequences of the decision, since there are the uncontrollable input variables to consider: for example, the rate of demand for the product, the cost of capital in the future, customer willingness to accept a substitute product and the lead time for delivery from the suppliers. Figure 5.3 lists all these factors for this decision.

It is the uncontrollable input factors which pose an immediate problem to the decision maker. Because they are uncontrollable, we cannot determine the exact value that they will take. Consequently, our belief regarding their form will often best be represented by a probability distribution rather than a single point measure. If this is the case, they are described as *probabilistic* rather than *deterministic* variables.

In practice, the way in which we treat uncontrollable variables is governed largely by the particular output variables we select to measure the effectiveness of the

|  | Controllable | Uncontrollable |
|---|---|---|
| **Input or exogenous variables** | The variables which represent the decision options | The 'environmental' variables which represent the uncontrollable factors |
| **Output or endogenous variables** | Do not exist | The variables which represent the consequences of the decision |

**Figure 5.2** Classification of decision variables

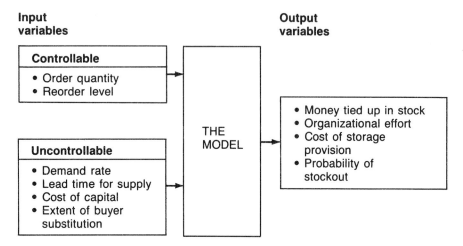

**Figure 5.3** The variables in the stock control decision

decision. For example, in the stock control decision, running out of stock occurs as a result of demand rate being greater than allowed for, or supply lead time being longer than allowed for, or both. If we choose not to use stockout probability (or similar measures, such as service level) as an output variable, then there is less reason for describing demand rate or supply lead time in a probabilistic manner, and a deterministic estimate could be assumed. Similarly, by making assumptions about demand rate, supply lead time, buyer substitution and interest rate, for example, the decision model could be greatly simplified to the form shown in Figure 5.4. One of the arts of decision modelling is judging the 'reasonableness' of such assumptions.

The next level of sophistication in the modelling process is to make the cause−effect structure explicit, thereby linking the input factors with the output factors.

## Cause–Effect Diagrams

The simplest method of indicating that some relationship exists between two factors within a decision is to show the direction of influence by arrows on a cause−effect diagram. If, for example, it is thought that price and promotion expenditure influence the total demand for a product, we could show this as in Figure 5.5.

These diagrams can be drawn by working backwards from the output variables, specifying the influencing factors, until the input variables are reached. Figure 5.6 illustrates this process for one part of the stock control decision. The output variable 'total ordering cost' will be determined by the organizational cost of making an order together with 'order frequency'. The order frequency is in its turn a function of 'demand rate' and 'order quantity', both input variables.

Following this procedure of tracing the reverse influences, a model can gradually

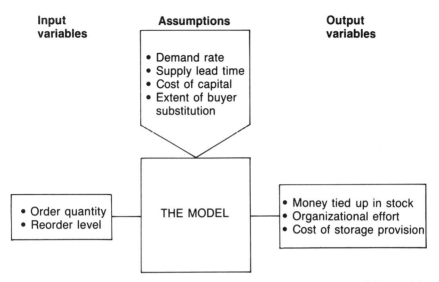

**Figure 5.4** The variables in the stock control decision with the uncontrollable variables estimated and assumed in the model

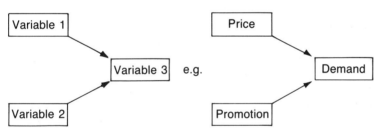

**Figure 5.5** Simple cause–effect relationship

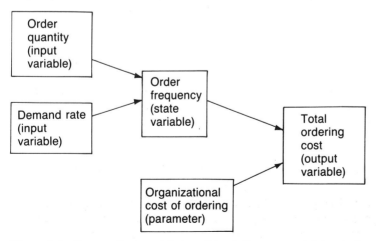

**Figure 5.6** Cause–effect model describing influences on total ordering cost

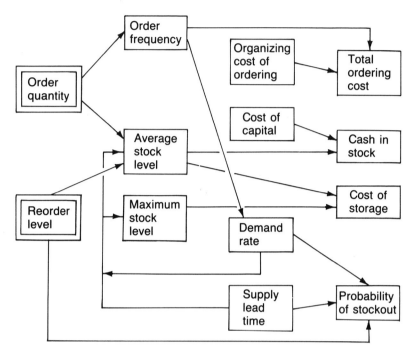

**Figure 5.7** A cause–effect model of the stock control decision

be built up of the interactions between the factors in a decision. Figure 5.7 shows a fuller model of the stock control decision.

As well as input and output variables, there are intermediate variables in this model: namely, 'order frequency', 'average stock level' and 'maximum stock level'. These variables are influenced by the input variables and in turn influence the output variables but are internal to the model. They are sometimes referred to as *state variables*.

Cause–effect models are a useful step in understanding a decision. Their major disadvantage is that they are not capable of describing the *nature* of the relationships between decision factors in any detailed manner. To do this, we need the more formal symbolic notation of mathematics. Cause–effect models, however, are often used as a preliminary step towards the development of more powerful symbolic models.

## Mathematical Models

A symbolic model is one which uses any set of symbols to describe decision variables and the relationship between them. The most convenient set of symbols for such a task are the conventional mathematical ones, since there are well-established rules for their manipulation.

The mathematical model of the relationships implied by the cause−effect model in Figure 5.6, for example, is shown below:

$$T_0 = C_0 \times \frac{R}{Q}$$

where $T_0$ = total ordering costs in time period
$C_0$ = organizational cost of placing an order
$R$ = demand per time period
$Q$ = quantity.

Now we have, for the first time, a description of the *form* of the relationship between the output variable $T_0$ and the controllable input variable $Q$. The form of the relationship between other pairs of variables can be modelled mathematically, and these *sub-models* of the total decision combined in some way to model the whole decision. However, fitting the sub-models together so that the whole model reflects accurately the complex interactions between all the problem's elements is usually a difficult task. Furthermore, it is not always worth the effort. One of the skills of model building is the ability to decide sensibly how all-embracing to make a decision model, and how much of the decision process to leave outside it.

## The Uses of Modelling

There is widespread misapprehension among managers that models need to be sophisticated, mathematical and 'high powered' before they can contribute to decision making. This is far from the truth. Models can be used to aid decisions in many ways and at all stages in the decision process. Models can be of assistance:

1. To enhance the decision maker's understanding of the decision.

2. To stimulate creativity in the search for possible solutions to the problem.

3. To help in the evaluation of alternative courses of action.

### Enhancing Understanding

The simplest way in which a model can enhance our understanding of a decision is by acting as a vehicle for communication. Our understanding of the problem can be communicated to other decision makers for them to share and possibly improve. Any subsequent debate regarding the nature of the problem will then centre around the model. In this way, the model is slowly enriched or enhanced, until it reflects more accurately a consensus view of the decision area. The very act of making our view of the decision explicit can lead to greater understanding. It forces us to be aware of, and perhaps challenge, the assumptions upon which we based our model of the decision. Specifically, it focuses attention on assumptions concerning the structure of the decision itself — that is, what is influenced by what — and also the relative importance we attach to the various factors within the decision.

## Stimulating Creativity

Once we have a statement of our perception of a problem, we have a vehicle that is open to challenge and debate. Debate can aid the generation of new ideas that are either fresh combinations of the factors we are manipulating in the decision, or totally new alternative solutions. Some mathematical models are specifically designed to explore the feasible combination of decision variables and search out fresh solutions.

## Evaluating Alternatives

Models are used for evaluation both directly and indirectly. Direct evaluation requires the model to identify the single best option or, alternatively, to identify an option that will prove satisfactory to the decision maker. In this way, the model is aiding a choice based on either the *optimizing* or the *satisficing* modes of behaviour discussed in Chapter 2. In some decisions the consequence of a particular course of action depends on predicting the behaviour of a system. Here models are used to predict the behaviour of that system under specified circumstances prior to evaluation by the decision maker: that is, the model is being used indirectly to aid evaluation. The use of models for evaluation purposes, whether optimizing, satisficing or predicting, requires a far more powerful model than is needed for either enhancing our understanding of the problem or aiding creativity. It is for evaluative purposes that mathematical models have traditionally been used (Box 5.1).

# Some Common Decision Models

Building quantitative models to aid managers in their decision making is the keystone of *operational research* (also known as operations research and management science). Operational research (OR) originated immediately prior to the Second World War, when teams of scientists from several disciplines turned their scientific procedures to solving the problems of managing the technology that they had helped to develop. Originally applied to the management of newly invented radar systems, the approach was used for other military management applications and then for industrial management. Since that time, OR has developed in two ways: first, as

---

*Box 5.1*

For a long time the early stages of decision modelling were undervalued. An elegant mathematical model was looked on as the only legitimate outcome of the modelling process, even if it turned out to be both mystifyingly complex yet simplistic in terms of the real decision.

No longer. One eminent decision scientist at the London Business School[1] sees the answers which are generated by decision models almost as a by-product of the total modelling process. The major benefits of the process come from actually building the model. In order to build an effective model, managers must clarify their views on how their organization works and on the 'structure' of the decision. This idea is reinforced by managerial practice.[2] Royal Dutch/Shell's chief planning strategist has described the process of decision modelling as 'planning as learning'. In other words, by examining how they arrive at decisions, how they 'model' the problem, they become more effective strategic thinkers.

---

an *approach* to aiding management decisions through modelling; second, by producing powerful *standard models* and methods to fit some well-defined commonly encountered classes of decision.

It is worth describing briefly some of the better-known classes of model in order to understand the scope of the contribution of this aspect of OR to management.[3] The models examined here are:

1. Linear programming models.

2. Queuing models.

3. Competitive models.

4. Heuristic models.

5. Simulation models.

There are many other classes of mathematical model. One is especially useful — the decision tree — and a large part of Chapter 6 is devoted to it.

## Linear Programming Models

Linear programming models treat the class of decision where resources have to be allocated to one or more activities. Generally, there are rules which govern the feasibility of an allocation. These rules either limit the level of the resources which can be committed to the activities, or affect the way in which the resources can be combined. The rules are called *constraints*. The combination of resources is then linked to a formal measure of the objectives called the *objective function* and can be maximized (if it is expressed, for example, in profit terms) or minimized (if expressed in cost terms) by computational procedures. When both the constraints and objective function are linear functions, a linear programming model can be formulated.

For example, suppose a manufacturer is deciding the production volume for each of his two products A and B. The most important resources he has to allocate to each of the two products are the amount of machine department time and the amount of assembly department time. The times taken by each product in the two departments are shown in Figure 5.8.

If we know the total amount of time each department has available in a week, we can model the constraints on the decision:

If the number of product A made per week = $X_A$
    the number of product B made per week = $X_B$
    the total machine department time available = 120 hours/week,

then the total load on the machine department must be not more than 120 hours, i.e:

$$6X_A + 6X_B \leq 120$$

Similarly, if the total assembly shop time available = 120 hours/week, then:

$$8X_A + 4X_B \leq 120$$

Whichever combination of $X_A$ and $X_B$ is chosen must satisfy these two constraint expressions.

The objective function which links the input variables to the output variable will enable the valuation of all combinations of $X_A$ and $X_B$ within the area of feasibility. For example, suppose the gross contribution from the product is £30 for product A and £35 for product B, then:

$$\text{Total gross contribution} = 30X_A + 35X_B$$

So, the problem can be stated as selecting values of $X_A$ and $X_B$, so that:

$$6X_A + 6X_B \leq 120$$

and

$$8X_A + 4X_B \leq 120$$

and

$$30X_A + 35X_B \text{ is maximized}$$

| Department | Time to process one product A | Time to process one product B |
|---|---|---|
| Machining | 6 | 6 |
| Assembly | 8 | 4 |

**Figure 5.8** Processing times for products A and B

Linear programming provides a computational procedure to achieve this, although generally the mathematics are executed by a computer.

## Queuing Models

Queues occur as a result of short-term imbalance between supply and demand. The nature of demand for a service is often predictable only in the sense that we can describe the form of its unpredictability over the long term. Thus, for example, a hospital accident department might know the average demand on its services on Saturday nights, but cannot predict the number of casualties it will treat this coming Saturday. Likewise, the hospital might know the average time that a casualty occupies a medical team, but cannot predict the severity of each accident in advance. Thus, there are two sources of short-term unpredictability: the time between arrivals to the system, and the 'processing' time required by each arrival. Several 'longer than average' gaps between customer arrivals, together with some 'shorter than average' processing times, can mean idle service facilities, while conversely a high rate of arrivals with long processing times will result in a queue building up.

Queuing problems can take many forms depending on the manner in which the basic input—service—output systems are arranged. Some of these queuing systems are shown in Figure 5.9.

Queuing models do not 'solve' queuing problems as such. They are generally used to predict the behaviour of queuing systems, so that behaviour and costs can be combined to evaluate alternative arrangements. Unfortunately, there are some severe limitations on the ability of mathematical queuing models to treat some

**(a) Basic system, e.g. aircraft waiting to land at airport**

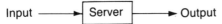

**(b) Parallel arrangement, e.g. supermarket checkout**

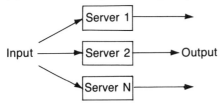

**(c) Series arrangement, e.g. manual assembly line**

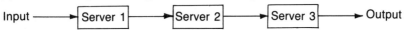

**Figure 5.9** Single, parallel and series arrangements of queuing systems

of the more complex systems encountered in practice. Major practical restrictions concern the nature of the distributions of customer arrival and processing time, the priority rules applying to customers waiting in the queue, and the size of the system (the number of service units), especially in series systems.

## Competitive Models

The distinctive characteristic of competitive problems concerns the nature of the uncontrollable input variables. In the two classes of model so far described, the uncontrollable factors are assumed to be independent of the decision variables themselves. However, in competitive problems not only are the uncontrollable variables related to the controllable variables, but the relationship is rarely benign or even neutral. In other words, there are factors within the decision area which are controlled by competitors who will react against our interests.

The classic example of such a situation is the children's game of scissors—paper—stone. In this game, the two players simultaneously indicate one of the three alternative plays: 'scissors', 'paper' or 'stone'. The winner is the one with a play which dominates the other. However, the rules governing dominance are circular, so scissors cut paper, paper wraps stone, stone blunts scissors, scissors cut paper and so on. Since there are two players, both of whom can adopt three alternative plays, there are only nine possible outcomes, as illustrated in Figure 5.10.

Game theory models have been developed to resolve this type of decision in terms of the optimum mix of plays to adopt in order to optimize the 'value' of the game: that is, minimize expected losses or maximize expected gains, assuming an equally rational opponent.

## Heuristic Models

As we observed in Chapter 2, managers might often desire optimality in their decisions but find it a difficult concept to use in practice. Mathematical models which optimize generally do so for a rigid set of assumptions concerning the

|  |  | Player A plays | | |
|---|---|---|---|---|
|  |  | **Scissors** | **Paper** | **Stone** |
| **Player B plays** | **Scissors** | Draw | B wins | A wins |
|  | **Paper** | A wins | Draw | B wins |
|  | **Stone** | B wins | A wins | Draw |

**Figure 5.10**  A game outcome matrix for a scissors—paper—stone game

| MODEL | ASSUMPTIONS CONCERNING ... | | |
|---|---|---|---|
| | **Objectives** | **Time horizon** | **Nature of decision** |
| **Linear programming** | • Maximize a single measure of utility | • Until parameter values change | • Linear constraints and objective functions |
| **Queuing models** | • Predict utilization characteristics | • Until parameter values change | • Exponentially distributed arrival and service times<br><br>• Steady-state operating conditions |
| **Game theory** | • Maximize single measure of utility | • Until parameter values change | • Well-defined strategies<br>• Simultaneous decisions<br>• Rational opponent |

**Figure 5.11**  The assumptions in three common decision models

objectives of the decision maker, the time horizon under consideration, and the nature of the decision itself. Figure 5.11 describes the assumptions of the three classes of model described previously.

As a consequence of the desire of OR practitioners to reflect the 'bounded rationality' concept of decision behaviour, a class of models known as *heuristic* have emerged. Heuristic models do not attempt to optimize (although they can do so by chance!), but rather to derive *good sub-optimal* solutions. That is, they adopt a satisficing approach. The heuristic approach adopts 'short cuts' in the reasoning process, and uses 'rules of thumb' in the search for a satisfactory solution. It has been described as being analogous to the 'trial and error' procedure which human (as opposed to mathematical) decision makers adopt when evaluating a restricted range of possible solutions. The similarity with human behaviour is even closer when the heuristic is *adaptive*: that is, it 'learns' by adjusting some decision parameters as it progresses.

There is no novelty in the use of heuristics for decision making. Commonly quoted examples from everyday life include:

- Don't use a new golf ball at a hole with a water hazard.
- Take a raincoat if it looks like rain.
- Don't try out a new dish when the boss comes to dinner.

There are two areas where heuristic models (Box 5.2) have proved particularly useful:

1. Where the decision is ill-structured and does not fit the assumptions of a standard mathematical model.

*Box 5.2*

## The CRAFT Heuristic Model

The facilities layout decision is one which every operation has to face: namely, how to arrange the departments relative to each other. The major criterion of the 'value' of a layout will be the cost of the total flow of traffic between, for example, the departments within the factory. The deterrent to finding the optimum arrangement is the combinational complexity of the problem (that is, there are very many alternative arrangements). In fact, there are factorial $N$ (factorial $N = N! = N \times (N - 1) \times (N - 2) \times \ldots \times 1$) ways of arranging $N$ facilities relative to each other. Realistic layout problems therefore involve billions of alternative layouts. One approach, described by Armour and Buffa,[4] is called CRAFT (computerized relative allocation of facilities technique).

Three inputs are required: a matrix of the flow between departments; a matrix of the cost associated with transportation between each of the departments; and a spatial array showing an initial layout. From these:

- The location of the centroids of each department is calculated.

- The flow matrix is weighted by the cost matrix, and this weighted flow matrix is multiplied by the distances between departments to obtain the total transportation costs of the initial layout.

- The model then calculates the cost sequence of exchanging every possible pair of departments.

Where there are

$$\frac{N!}{2!(N - 2)!}$$

possible ways of exchanging two departments in an $N$ department layout (this is far more feasible than calculating $N!$ alternatives), the exchange giving the most improvement is then fixed, and the whole cycle repeated with the updated cost flow matrix. These iterations are repeated until no further improvement is made by exchanging two departments.

Thus the heuristic procedure is as follows:

Step 1. Input details of flow between departments and relevant costs.

Step 2. Input initial layout.

Step 3. Find out which pairs of departments can be changed.

Step 4. Calculate distances between centroids of all departments.

Step 5. Calculate total 'traffic' cost for current version of layout.

Step 6. Calculate 'traffic' costs for all possible layout configurations with two departments changed.

Step 7. Check to see if one of these layout configurations reduces traffic cost.

Step 8. If cost can be reduced, choose lowest cost layout, arrange departments in a logical form, establish this as new layout configuration and return to step 3. If no reduction possible, stop.

2. Where the range of feasible solutions is so large that even modern computing power does not allow complete enumeration.

One major problem in assessing heuristic models in general is in finding something with which to compare them. If the models are satisficing (that is, they are not attempting to achieve the single best decision), how do we establish the extent of one model's superiority over another? It has been suggested that a manager should examine the output of a heuristic model with four questions in mind:[5]

1. Does it produce better results than our existing methods?
2. Are there incremental savings in resources?
3. Are computational effort and expense reduced without sacrificing the quality of work?
4. Is the information produced more timely, and are decisions reached earlier than by present methods?

## Simulation Models

Viewed in one way, *all* modelling is a 'simulation' in as much as it imitates reality. Yet the term 'simulation' in modelling jargon has come to mean something separate from the approaches to modelling which attempt to develop predictive devices purely by mathematical means.

The essence of simulation models is that they rely on a statement of *procedure* which underlies the logical relationships between variables. In fact, what are generally called simulation models should more properly be called *procedural* models, since the model is a procedure expressed in precise symbols. The term 'simulation' actually refers to the method by which the model is used to make predictions. A simulation model usually takes the form of a logical flow chart which describes the interrelationship between variables. The model is then used to execute the procedure described in the flow chart, and thus the behaviour of whatever system is being modelled is simulated.

In some ways simulation is one of the most fundamental approaches to decision making. Children play games and 'pretend' so as to extend their experience of novel situations; likewise, managers can gain insights and explore possibilities through the formalized 'pretending' involved in using simulation models. Simulation explores the consequences of decision making rather than directly advising on the decision itself: it is a *predictive* rather than an *optimizing* technique.

Simulation models are especially useful for predicting the dynamic behaviour of systems, and also for modelling systems where some of the uncontrollable input variables are described in probabilistic terms. For example, let us return to the stock control decision described earlier.

Suppose that, after examining the records of past demand and delivery statistics, it is found that they conform to the distributions shown in Figure 5.12. We can simulate the operation of any particular stocking policy (the combination of *order*

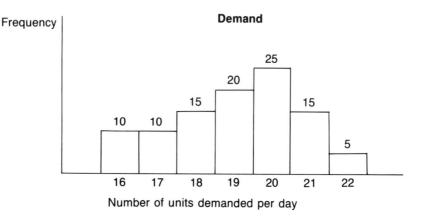

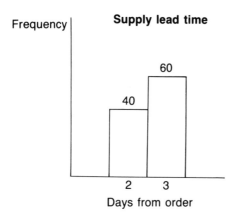

**Figure 5.12**   Histograms of the demand per day and supply lead time from placing an order

*quantity Q* and *reorder level R*) by sampling values of daily demand and delivery lead time in a random manner. In order to generate values which represent daily demand, we can simply place pieces of paper in a box with values written on them in the following proportions:

10 pieces with 16 written on them
10                  17
15                  18
20                  19
25                  20
15                  21
5                   22

After mixing the pieces of paper, one is drawn out at random, read and replaced. Likewise, to simulate delivery time, pieces of paper with 2 days and 3 days are mixed in the proportion 40:60 respectively, and randomly sampled in the same way.

Since we are aware of the basic cause—effect logic which links variables in the stock control, it is now possible to simulate the operation over a period of time. For example, if the effect of a control policy is to be evaluated where the quantity ordered at any time is 100 ($Q = 100$), and orders are placed when the stock level is 60 or lower at the end of the day ($R = 60$), the system can be simulated as shown in Figure 5.13 to determine the effect of the policy on service level (the percentage of orders supplied).

In this way, the system can be manually simulated for as long as the modeller has the energy. Of course, such a procedure would rarely be performed manually as the logic of the operations used in the simulations is simple and repetitive — just the process to be handled by a computer. Before a computer can be programmed, however, the logic of the procedure must be formally stated, and the usual method of doing so is by using flow charts.

A flow chart describes the paths through the logic of a procedure in terms of questions and operations. Figure 5.14 shows the flow chart which describes the procedure used to perform the stock control simulation.

In the early days of simulation, the approach came under severe criticism from the more traditional OR practitioners as a 'lazy analyst's' method of avoiding the more rigorous challenge of mathematical modelling. After all, mathematical models can give proven solutions, whereas simulation models merely *sample* from simulated behaviour. So, in simulation, there are two areas where the modelling process could misrepresent rather than reflect reality:

1. In the structuring of the procedure itself. Is the flow chart a true representation of what is being simulated?

| Day | 1 | 2 | 3 | 4 | 5 | 6 | 7 | 8 | 9 | 10 | 11 | 12 |
|---|---|---|---|---|---|---|---|---|---|---|---|---|
| **Brought forward** | 100 | 81 | 60 | 38 | 20 | — | 84 | 64 | 45 | 27 | 9 | — |
| **Orders delivered** | — | — | — | — | — 100 | — | — | — | — | — | 100 |
| **Starting stock** | 100 | 81 | 60 | 38 | 20 | 100 | 84 | 64 | 45 | 27 | — | 100 |
| **Demand** (sampled from distribution) | 19 | 21 | 22 | 18 | 21 | 16 | 20 | 19 | 18 | 18 | 9 | 20 |
| **Finishing stock** | 81 | 60 | 38 | 20 | — | 84 | 64 | 45 | 27 | 9 | — | 80 |
| **Order quantity** | — 100 | — | — | — | — | — 100 | — | — | — | — |
| **Delivery lead time** (sampled from distribution) | — 3 | — | — | — | — | — 3 | — | — | — | — |
| **Shortage** | 1 | | | | | | | 10 | | | | |

**Figure 5.13** Twelve days' simulated stock behaviour

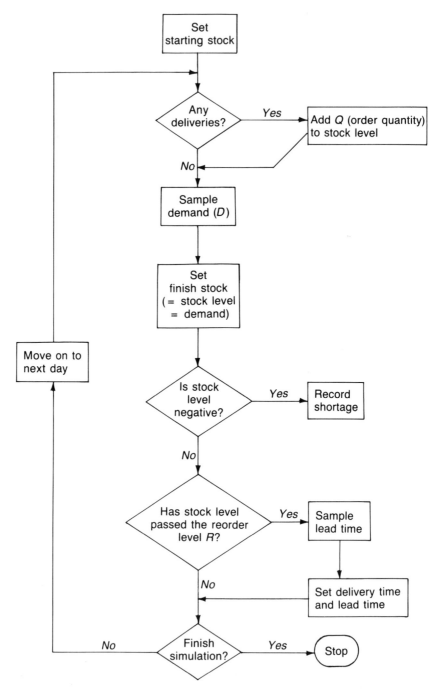

**Figure 5.14** Flow chart which describes the procedural logic involved in simulating stock behaviour

2. In the sampling procedures which are adopted. Are the relevant variables being sampled? Is the sample itself unbiased?

In spite of these dangers, simulation is probably the most widely used approach to modelling within OR. Its power to model decisions outside the scope of most mathematical analytical methods makes it a valuable practical tool for decision making.

### Financial Simulation

In Chapter 1 we discussed the nature of decisions which are conventionally classed as corporate or strategic. Just as other classes of decision have caused the development of specific models, so corporate decisions can be aided by corporate models. Corporate models differ from others not necessarily in their approach to modelling, but rather in the nature of the variables, especially the output variables, they include. In fact, 'corporate modelling', as it is conventionally called, is something of a misnomer. Corporate strategic decisions involve consideration of a very wide range of variables, social, legal and technological as well as financial, and an equally broad collection of objectives. However, the term 'corporate modelling' has come to mean:

- Models which use conventional accounting measures and relationships.
- Deterministic simulations, representing a fairly long time scale (years, rather than months).

Indeed, the process is sometimes called *financial modelling* or financial simulation, rather than corporate modelling.[6]

Nevertheless, since corporate decisions concern the long-term objectives of organizations, models of corporate activity must evaluate decisions in terms of an organization's long-term health, using such measures as profit, net cash flow and net present value.[7] It is this type of factor which constitutes the output variables in corporate models. But the further away the input variables are from the output variables, the more complex the model will be. For example, the cause–effect model which links the output variable 'sales revenue' with the input variables 'production capacity', 'utilization of capacity', 'sales demand' and 'unit price' is shown in Figure 5.15.

Now it is quite possible to develop this cause–effect model further back down the chain of influence, but the relationships become more numerous and less clear. Furthermore, it is common practice in corporate modelling to avoid describing some of the less clear relationships *within the model*. The absence of a link between 'sales demand' and 'unit price' illustrates this. In reality, the demand for a product and the price that is charged for it are related for most products. Yet in this model they are not linked. This is because the objective of corporate modelling is typically not to examine the relationship between price and demand *per se*, but rather to explore the effect of different price–demand (or other factor) combinations on the output variables concerned.

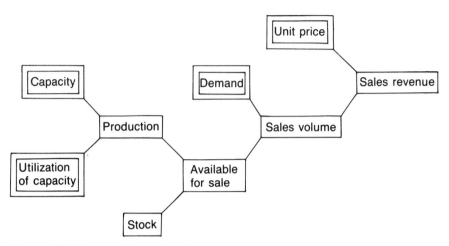

**Figure 5.15**  Cause–effect model of the influences on sales revenue

*An Example of a Financial Simulation*

A pharmaceutical company manufactures a single product, the sales for which are forecast to grow only slightly over the next six years, but whose market price (at today's prices) is likely to fall by about 10 per cent over the same period. The company has developed a new product which it could introduce on to the market within two years. Sales for the new product could then grow very rapidly, outstripping the old product within three years. Figure 5.16 shows sales and price forecast for the two products. The company decided to test the effects of alternative capacity expansion programmes on the profitability of the plants and its cash flow position. Figure 5.17 shows the cause–effect model for the profit and loss account.

The cause–effect relationships indicated were then written in the form of a computer program[8] and used to simulate the activity of the plant over a six-year period. Figure 5.18 shows the print-out from one particular simulation run.

By changing the input variables, the decision makers can assess the effects not

| Year | Old product | | New product | |
| | Price (£s per unit) | Volume (000 units) | Price (£s per unit) | Volume (000 units) |
|---|---|---|---|---|
| 1992 | 1.00 | 25 000 | — | — |
| 1993 | 0.95 | 25 200 | — | — |
| 1994 | 0.94 | 25 600 | 1.15 | 3 000 |
| 1995 | 0.93 | 25 700 | 1.10 | 16 000 |
| 1996 | 0.92 | 25 800 | 1.00 | 25 000 |
| 1997 | 0.90 | 25 800 | 1.00 | 27 000 |

**Figure 5.16**  Sales volume and price forecasts for a pharmaceutical company

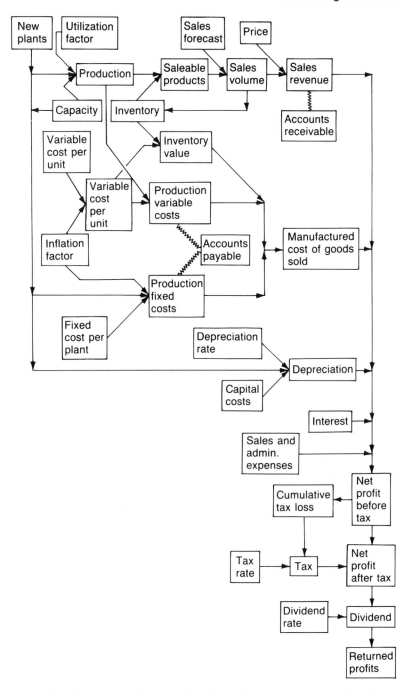

**Figure 5.17** The cause–effect model for the profit and loss account of the pharmaceutical company

| Year | 1992 | 1993 | 1994 | 1995 | 1996 | 1997 |
|---|---|---|---|---|---|---|
| New product capacity (000s of units) | 0 | 0 | 5 000 | 15 000 | 25 000 | 25 000 |
| **(a) Profit and loss account** | | | | | | |
| Sales income | 26 000 | 24 940 | 28 514 | 42 501 | 49 736 | 50 220 |
| Cost of goods sold | 17 914 | 17 892 | 21 819 | 30 918 | 37 106 | 37 786 |
| Depreciation | 725 | 725 | 1 205 | 2 165 | 3 125 | 3 125 |
| Interest payable | − 388 | − 461 | − 324 | 309 | 671 | 768 |
| Sales and admin. | 6 000 | 6 000 | 6 000 | 6 000 | 6 000 | 6 000 |
| Net profit before tax | 1 749 | 784 | − 186 | 3 109 | 2 833 | 2 541 |
| Tax incurred | 1 237 | 754 | 0 | 0 | 0 | 0 |
| Dividend declared | 256 | 15 | 0 | 1 555 | 1 417 | 1 270 |
| Retained profit | 256 | 15 | − 186 | 1 555 | 1 417 | 1 270 |
| **(b) Cash flow** | | | | | | |
| Sources of cash | | | | | | |
| Sales and inc. credit | 25 830 | 24 940 | 29 195 | 43 322 | 50 552 | 50 220 |
| Uses of cash | | | | | | |
| Manufact. cost | 17 750 | 17 750 | 23 424 | 30 268 | 37 068 | 37 068 |
| Sales and admin. | 6 000 | 6 000 | 6 000 | 6 000 | 6 000 | 6 000 |
| Interest, tax, dividend, debit | 1 172 | 905 | 874 | 1 987 | 3 094 | 2 243 |
| Capital payment | 0 | 2 000 | 68 000 | 9 600 | 5 600 | 0 |
| Total cash out | 24 922 | 26 655 | 37 098 | 47 855 | 51 761 | 45 310 |
| Net cash flow | 908 | − 1 715 | − 7 904 | − 4 532 | − 1 209 | 4 910 |
| Cash and trade investments | 5 760 | 4 045 | − 3 858 | − 8 391 | − 9 600 | − 4 691 |

**Figure 5.18** Print-out from a simulation run showing the effect on the profit and loss and cash flow statements of one capacity introduction strategy

only of changes in the controllable variables, such as plant capacity, but also of departures of the uncontrollable variables from their forecast values. Thus, the model is used in an exploratory way by asking 'What if?' questions,[9] such as:

*What if* sales of the new product are 10 per cent lower than forecast?
*What if* we can increase demand by 10 per cent? (How much extra profit would it generate, and therefore how much extra promotion expenditure could we use to get the increased sales?)

In this way, alternative strategies can be evaluated in common terms, the sensitivity of future performance to changes in the input variables can be assessed, and the nature of the problem can be better understood. In short, the model is used to *raise the level of debate* around a decision.

## Classifying Decision Models

We are now in a position to examine and classify the types of model previously discussed in terms of the attributes, qualities or characteristics which they possess. These attributes can then be matched to the needs of the decision maker. It is only by doing this that their potential to aid the decision maker can be judged.

The first important decision is to classify decision models as *optimizing* or *satisficing*. Optimizing models attempt to find 'the single best' solution to the decision — the maximum profit or the minimum cost, for example. Satisficing models accept that the theoretical optimum may be either just too time consuming to search for, or not recognizable as the optimum even if it were found. These models aim for a 'good sub-optimal' solution which may not be the single best, but is likely to be better than any solution reached without the aid of the model.

The second important classification distinguishes between *deterministic* and *probabilistic* models. Deterministic models use single estimates to represent the value of each variable in the decision, whereas probabilistic models use probability distributions, histograms or some other description of the range of values which a variable can take. Probabilistic models describe decisions in terms of the uncertainty inherent in them.

Viewed in one way, of course, there is nothing certain in life but death and taxes. So as everything in life is uncertain to some extent, all models ought to be probabilistic. However, this denies the modeller the normal licence in modelling to simplify elements of what is observed so as to present reality in a convenient and useful form. Decision models can be 'probabilistic' in two ways. First, there are those which model systems having elements which take different values according to an assumed or historically derived pattern and which predict a system's behaviour, the prime determinant of which is the variability itself. (Queuing models are good examples of this type.) Second, there are those models which use probability to describe the modeller's ignorance of future occurrences in a more fundamental way, where the nature of uncertainty is described much more tentatively. The decision-tree models discussed in Chapter 6 are representative of this type.

Figure 5.19 classifies some of the decision models described previously and in

|  | Deterministic | Probabilistic |
|---|---|---|
| **Optimizing** | • Linear programming | • Decision trees |
| **Satisficing** | • Most 'corporate modelling' <br> • CRAFT facilities layout technique <br> • Many heuristic models | • Queuing theory <br> • Stochastic simulations such as the stock control simulation described <br> • Risk analysis |

**Figure 5.19** Classification of some decision models

Chapter 6 in terms of these two key dimensions. It is worth stressing, however, that the fact that we select a model which optimizes does not necessarily mean that we are trying to optimize in the real decision. We could obtain an 'optimal' solution from the model, and then deliberately adapt that solution to fit the needs of reality — after all, a model does not optimize reality, it optimizes its simplified version of reality. So, using an 'optimizing' model could be a perfectly legitimate tactical ploy in the search for a satisfactory solution. Likewise, deterministic models can provide valuable assistance to the decision makers, even though their reality is probabilistic.

## Using Decision Models

What, then, should be the role of decision models? When faced with such a question managers' reactions tend to be polarized. A minority would reject modelling as having no useful role to play. After all, a good manager's judgement and intuition are worth any number of mathematical models. They would argue that many models either state the obvious about trivial problems or fail to grasp everything but the bare quantifiable skeleton of more important decisions. How is it possible, they would argue, to devise a model that can compete with years of accumulated background knowledge and experience in making similar important decisions? On the other hand, those who firmly believe in mathematical models, or have a vested interest in their use, know that the hard discipline and rigorous logic of the modelling process can cut through some of the half truths and unjustified assumptions of much management debate. There is no greater danger than applying the seductive simplicity of 'good old plain common sense'. A well-developed model can provide surprises by showing up a solution that would not have been thought of otherwise. Furthermore, the models are there, or can be developed, so why not use them?

Now while it is true that it would be foolish to refuse the assistance of something that can aid decision making, it would be a very weak or exceptionally lazy manager who followed slavishly and exclusively the pronouncements of a mathematical model. In fact, contained within this argument are two separate but related questions: when can decision models be useful to managers? and when is it worthwhile to build a decision model? We would contend that a decision model can almost always be useful to decision makers, but different types of model are useful in different ways. The large linear programming models, for example, can lay out the bones of a decision in a simple and elegant way, although the 'answer' produced will probably have to be adjusted to take account of some of the factors that were omitted from the model. Alternatively, the strategic financial model will possibly do nothing more than the manager could do 'on the back of an envelope', but it will do it very quickly. This enables alternatives to be roughly evaluated at a speed which enhances the creativity of the decision maker. Different models and different ways of using them, but both having potential to help in management decision making.

## When Can Decision Models Help?

The use of decision models is rarely as straightforward as is implied by a bold statement of the techniques. Various studies have shown that many projects intended to help managerial decision makers by developing decision models have proved singularly unsuccessful.[10]

Part of the problem stems from many managers' misunderstanding of the nature of decision modelling — both its strengths and its limitations. Raitt, among others, has pointed out that management science is not the hard science of physics and chemistry:

> The models developed in management science are generally further removed from the real world than those developed in the physical sciences. In some ways it is a clinical science. Our models of the behaviour of systems, or our models of sensible or rational ways to approach problems, give us the underlying understanding necessary for diagnosis which remains essentially practical and pragmatic. Further, management science has no distinctive subject matter in the way that physics has, and does not provide an accumulation of theoretical knowledge about the world.[11]

Before deciding whether it is worth using a decision model to help with the decision process, four questions should be addressed.

1. *How much will it cost?* The labour of developing or adapting models can be costly — few experts come cheap. The exception is now the well-developed field of off-the-shelf packages for personal computers, especially in the financial modelling field.

2. *How long will it take?* The time scale of model building is usually longer than managers (and often model builders) realize. The time scale of decisions is often short. No matter how potentially useful a model might be, it is no use if the decision deadline precedes the model's completion.

3. *To what extent could a model improve an unaided judgement?* There is little point in developing a model if the cost of doing so is large compared with the maximum benefit.

4. *Is the decision amenable to modelling?* In attempting to answer this, probably the most important question, the circumstances of the decision itself must be considered. McClelland[12] distinguishes three features of the decision situation which influence the ability of models to help the decision maker:

(a) The scale of resources at stake. The more that is at stake, the more important it is to reach a decision which is considered acceptable, and therefore the more aids (such as decision modelling) should be used. Conversely, if little is at stake, then it is unlikely that the time, effort and expense of model construction is going to be worthwhile.

(b) The complexity of the problem. The ability of mathematically based models to handle a large number of complex interrelated issues is well known. However, many managerial problems are so large and complex, and have so many feasible solutions, that they are beyond the help of even the most sophisticated model.

(c) The adequacy of the data. If it is desired to get an 'answer' from a model, the answer will be only as good as the data which the model uses. So, in these terms, models operate better where the data are certain and comprehensive.

These three features can be represented as the three dimensions of a cube, as shown in Figure 5.20. At corner A, models are useful since the decision is an important one. They are also relatively straightforward to apply because the complexity of the decision is low and the data are adequate. As we move along the edge of the cube from A to B, the increasing complexity of the problem makes modelling more necessary, so that at corner B a model would probably be greatly appreciated by the manager because the decision is important and the data which the model would be using are reliable. But for decisions of a very high complexity, the model itself might include simplifications of which the decision maker should be aware. Moving from corner B towards corner C, models remain as important and as necessary as before, but become less competent because the data they use are less adequate. It is at corner C that the maximum usefulness of models coincides with the maximum difficulty of using them successfully. From C towards D it becomes

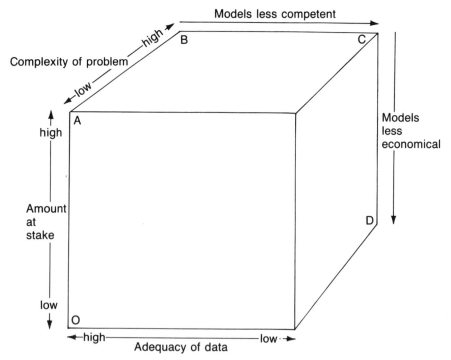

**Figure 5.20** Three dimensions of management problems[13]

economically less worthwhile to model, since the importance of the decision diminishes. At some point between C and D a manager should decide to forgo the use of any decision model because the pay-off from such a model would just not outweigh the problem of building it.

The traditional area for decision modelling and operational research has been along the edge O−A (intendedly close to A, but often closer to O). Many stock control computer packages, for example, are in this area. Corner B can be represented by some of the applications of linear programming. For example, the early applications in the petrochemical industry for either blend mixing or tanker scheduling were obviously important and had relatively straightforward data, but could at times be very complex. The side of the cube whose three visible corners are O, A and B represents the type of problem where optimization can often be achieved. As we get closer to corner C, the whole concept of an optimal decision becomes less useful. This part of the cube is best represented by the corporate financial models, where decisions can be vitally important to an organization, their complexity can be extremely high, and much of the data are little short of intelligent guesses.

## What Makes for Successful Modelling?

There have been several studies which have attempted to discover which elements in the process of model building influence the 'success' of a model. Generally, success means that at least implementation of the model has been reached. Taken together, these studies present a somewhat confusing and occasionally contradictory picture.[14] There are a multitude of factors which appear to affect the chances of success in decision modelling. Some of these are to do with the organizational environment in which the decision-modelling process is taking place, some are to do with the conduct of the modelling process itself, and some are to do with the nature of the model being built.

### The Right Organizational Setting

1. *The extent of top management support.* We would expect the extent of support received by the decision modellers from top management to influence their own confidence within the organization, their reception by decision makers, and therefore their success. Support includes not only sufficient resources to do the job (it will presumably be a continuing argument as to what level of resources is really necessary!), but also a sympathetic understanding of the time scale involved in decision modelling.

2. *The meaningful involvement of the decision makers.* One of the few factors on which most studies seem to agree is that the more the decision makers are involved with the decision modellers (sometimes to the extent of being one and the same person), the greater is the likelihood that a decision model will be used.

The extent of the involvement can include a number of different organizational linkages. Figure 5.21 shows some of the links between individuals within an organization who might work together during the decision-modelling process.

On the client (in our terms the decision maker) side of the diagram, there are three sets of people: the operational executive, to whom the decision maker is ultimately responsible; the manager (decision maker); and the users of the model (in the case of routine programmed decisions). On the other hand, the consultant (in our terms the decision modeller) side again includes three groups: the management science executive, who is responsible for decision-modelling policy within the organization; the decision modeller; and the modelling technician (for example, a computer programmer if the decision model is computer based). Figure 5.21 does not imply that these six sets of individuals always exist, or are always involved in the decision-modelling process. In the case where a single manager is solely responsible for making a one-off decision, and the manager is aided by the only decision modeller in the organization, then only the manager–modeller linkage is possible. The linkages which are formed, and the extent to which they are used, should depend on modelling need, and on the number of managers who will be directly affected by or ultimately responsible for the decision.

3. *The organizational position of the modelling function.* Two factors which appear to influence success, but can themselves be contradictory, are the extent of the solid power base which the modelling function has in an organization, and the extent to which decision modellers work with individual decision makers as

**Meaningful involvement**

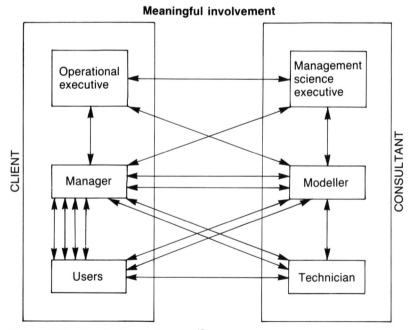

**Figure 5.21**  Meaningful involvement[15]

part of a decentralized team. The modelling function's power base within the organization means the existence of a legitimate home in the organization, to act as a base from which central policies for effective modelling can be planned and where the decision modellers can learn from each other's experience. However, modellers often can only get sufficiently close to an operating team of decision makers by working with them over relatively long periods of time. Thus, there is often a need to 'sprinkle' decision modellers throughout the organization.[16]

4. *The reputation of the modellers.* Whatever the support from top management, the ease with which decision modellers will be accepted by managerial decision makers will be influenced by the record of success or failure of the modellers. Because of this, it is particularly important to choose projects with a high expected degree of success when a modelling team is trying to establish itself.

## *The Right Modelling Process*

1. *The competence and experience of modellers and managers.* Again we must dispose of the most obvious factor affecting the success of the modelling process first. An experienced, tactful and skilled designer, together with an open-minded, competent manager who is on top of the job, can successfully use decision models even in the face of the most formidable adverse conditions. Conversely, no amount of understanding of the 'success factors' of decision modelling implementation can compensate for an incompetent modeller working with an inexperienced manager.

2. *The extent of mutual understanding between modeller and decision maker.* Mutual understanding means that the manager understands the creative aspects of the modeller's work, and the modeller understands the organizational and political context of the decision. A decision maker—modeller relationship exhibiting this type of understanding provides a basis for sharing perceptions of the decision and enables an adaptive approach to the modelling process. Such an understanding also helps to ensure that the goals of the decision maker and the decision modeller are compatible from an early stage.

As to who should move furthest towards the other, it is an old argument as to whether the cause of successful model implementation is best achieved by developing managers who have an understanding of the model-building process, or by training systems modellers in management. Clearly, by including modelling topics in a book which is primarily intended for managers and students of management, we believe in the former. However, having a knowledge of each other's jobs is unlikely to hinder the process, providing each has a respect for the other's specific skill.

3. *The closeness of the manager during modelling.* Again, we have a dilemma. While it is held to be advantageous for a manager to be closely involved with the modeller during model building, the nature of managerial work means that the manager will probably be unable to spend large amounts of time with the modeller. Any decision modeller who expects to be given continuous attention is likely to be disappointed. If the manager's time is limited, then two stages in the modelling process are crucial: setting the initial objectives and validating the model. Validation,

in the way we use the term here, involves in effect gaining final managerial acceptance of the representativeness and appropriateness of the model.

### The Right Model

Six characteristics which enhance the usefulness of a model have been proposed by Little.[17] They are as follows.

1. *The model should be 'simple'*. Simplicity aids understanding. Furthermore, it imposes a useful discipline on the model builder and the manager to include only the important issues.

2. *The model must be 'robust'*. By this it is meant that the model is 'user proof'. It should be difficult to get ridiculous answers out of the model.

3. *The model should be 'easy to control'*. The manager should have a reasonably good idea of what input data adjustments have to be made to achieve a particular range of output values in the model. If the output of the model comes as a complete surprise to the manager, he is less likely to trust the internal workings of the model, and will therefore be less likely to use it.

4. *The model must be 'adaptive'*. As new information becomes available, the model should be capable of change, so as to incorporate both new data and, as far as possible, new decision structures.

5. *The model should be 'complete'*. It should include those issues within a decision which a decision maker regards as being important. There is an obvious conflict between the need for model completeness and the need for model simplicity, and to some extent one must be traded off against the other. It is often possible to incorporate many factors in a model, yet treat them in a straightforward manner; but there is no doubt that this balance of simplicity and completeness can severely test the decision modeller's skill.

6. *The model should be 'easy to communicate with'*. Where possible the data required by a model should be in the same terms as those with which the manager is familiar. The output from the model should be in the language of management, rather than in the language of mathematics.

## Practical Prescriptions

Decide whether a formal decision model is likely to be worth formulating by considering:

1. If sufficient data are available to build a model.
2. If the decision is complex enough to warrant a model.
3. If the decision is important enough to warrant a model.

Decide whether the model should be:

1. Optimizing or satisficing.
2. Deterministic or probabilistic.

Build decision models in three steps:

1. List the input variables to the decision, some of which are controllable and some uncontrollable, and list the relevant output variables that will be used to evaluate the decision.
2. Indicate existence of relationships between variables by means of a cause—effect model.
3. Describe the form of those relationships in mathematical terms.

Check to see if any of the 'standard' operational research models are appropriate. For example:

1. Linear programming.
2. Queuing models.
3. Competitive models.
4. Heuristic models.
5. Simulation models.

Make sure that the right conditions exist for successful modelling:

1. Top management support it.
2. Modellers are involved in the decision process.
3. Modellers are seen as having a real position in the organization.
4. Modellers retain their credibility in the organization.

Make sure the modelling process is right:

1. Modellers are experienced.
2. Modellers and decision 'owners' understand each other.

Check that any decision model is:

1. Simple.
2. Robust.
3. Controllable.
4. Adaptive.
5. Complete.
6. 'User friendly'.

## Case Exercise

### Northern Home Stores Limited

Northern Home Stores Limited (NHS) was a Scottish-based retail store group. Founded in the 1920s by the McKenzie family, it has remained a family controlled business ever since. The group started operations in its Edinburgh store. This now occupies an area of 20 000 square feet, in a high street location with very much of a variety chain philosophy: that is, it trades in a high variety of goods.

The major change for the company came during the early 1970s when NHS was approached by Caledonian Developments and offered three out-of-town locations in Glasgow, Aberdeen and Newcastle. Caledonian offered NHS an exceptionally low lease for the 'package', and NHS accepted the deal and moved into the new locations over a three-year period. The move was completed remarkably smoothly in spite of the substantial increase in trading activity and personnel. 'On the face of it', wrote the *Financial Times*, 'NHS in the 1980s looks quite a different company from the small Edinburgh firm of ten years ago.'

## The Decision

Recently it had become clear to NHS that its variety chain concept was under pressure. While the Edinburgh store continued to return satisfactory profits, the new stores had proved disappointing — in fact NHS's profits had begun to fall, and this was causing concern to the family.

At a board meeting called to discuss the problem, it was decided to make some changes for the future. A consultancy company had investigated the business on behalf of NHS. Its report had suggested that the variety store was becoming an out-of-date concept in the eyes of the consumer and that some attention to product specialism should be considered.

Based on their research, they suggested that NHS should focus on four product groups which offered particularly attractive prospects, given present levels of competition and growth prospects in the NHS trading areas. The product groups suggested were gardening/horticulture; DIY; audio and TV; and toys.

The consultants' report suggested that NHS should not attempt to change its image at once. Rather, it should build expertise in selected product areas, gain consumer recognition and confidence in these areas and then, over time, move away from its variety chain store image. They further suggested that to do so would require a far larger participation by one, some or all of the four suggested product groups.

The board concluded that much of the consultants' report was sound and that NHS should seek to reposition itself in its markets. Accordingly, the buying controllers were requested to examine the four product groups suggested by the consultants, and to present their recommendations to the Board.

The directors of NHS were particularly interested in exploring the financial consequences of any decision to specialize in the suggested product areas. In particular, they wanted to know the following:

1. The effects on profitability.
2. The effects on the cash flow of the company (especially since some considerable initial promotion expenditure would be required).
3. The likely risks they would be running in switching from their present low-profit but stable operation, to the unknown of the consultants' recommendations.

## Questions

1. What type(s) of model do you think could help the decision makers?
2. What could be (a) the input variables, (b) the output variables and (c) the assumptions of the model?
3. How do you think the model would help the managers to make a decision?

---

## Bibliography

Bryant, J.W. (ed.), *Financial Modelling in Corporate Management*, Wiley, 1982. A comprehensive book which deals with both the theory and the practice of corporate modelling.

Van Gigch, J.P. (ed.), *Decision Making about Decision Making*, Abacus, 1987. Strictly for academic interest.

Jones, G.T., *Simulation and Business Decision*, Penguin, 1972. A simple introduction to simulation modelling.

Rivett, P., *Model Building for Decision Analysis*, Wiley, 1980. An excellent book which deals with the same area as this chapter.

The following books all contain a useful and wide-ranging collection of articles on the use of decision models:

Collcut, R.H. (ed.), *Successful Operational Research: A selection of cases for managers*, Operational Research Society, 1980.

Doktor, R., Schultz, R.L. and Slevin, P.D. (eds.), *The Implementation of Management Science*, North-Holland Publishing, 1979.

Gordon, G., Pressman, I. and Cohn, S., *Quantitative Decision Making for Business*, Prentice Hall, 1990.

## References

1. In *The Economist*, 22 July 1989.
2. *Ibid.*
3. It is not the intention of this book to instruct the reader in all the techniques of OR. There are many excellent publications which can be consulted for that purpose. See, for example, Samson, D., *Managerial Decision Analysis*, Irwin, 1988.
4. Armour, G.E. and Buffa, E.S., 'Allocation of facilities with CRAFT', *Harvard Business Review*, March/April 1965, pp. 136–58.
5. Weist, J.D., 'Heuristic programs for decision making', *Harvard Business Review*, September/October 1966, pp. 129–43.
6. Grinyer, P.H. and Wooler, J., *Corporate Models Today*, Institute of Chartered Accountants, UK, 1975.
7. These evaluation measures are explained in detail in Chapter 11.

8. There are several programming languages available written specifically for corporate modelling.

9. In fact, many corporate modelling languages have a 'WHAT IF' command to facilitate the decision maker assessing the consequences of changes to the original levels of exogenous variables.

10. For example, see Grayson, C., 'Management science and business practice', *Harvard Business Review*, vol. 51, 1973, pp. 41−8.

11. Raitt, R.A., 'OR and science', *Viewpoints* (Journal of the Operations Research Society), vol. 30, 1979, pp. 835−6.

12. McClelland, W.G., 'Mathematics in management: how it looks to the manager', *OMEGA* (International Journal of Management Science), vol. 3, no. 2, 1975, pp. 147−55.

13. Adapted by permission from McClelland, *op. cit*.

14. A comprehensive review of the literature in this field is provided in Hildebrandt, S., 'Implementation: the bottleneck of operations research: the state of the art', *European Journal of Operational Research*, vol. 6, no. 4, 1980, pp. 289−94.

15. Reproduced by permission from Lockett, A.G. and Polding, E., 'Organisational linkages and OR projects', *European Journal of Operations Research*, vol. 7, 1981, pp. 14−21 (North-Holland Publishing).

16. Hildebrandt, *op. cit*.

17. Little, J.D., 'Models and managers: the concept of a decision calculus', *Management Science*, vol. 16, no. 8, 1970, pp. B466−85.

# 6 Modelling uncertainty with decision trees

## Introduction

### Certainty, Uncertainty and Risk

One of the dimensions that we used to classify quantitative models in Chapter 5 was the probabilistic deterministic dimension. This dimension reflects the fact that we can choose to model decisions as having a particular degree of uncertainty. Managers sometimes have to take decisions 'in the dark', with little knowledge of the ultimate consequences of their action. We can imagine a scale on which the amount of uncertainty present in a decision can be represented. At one end of the scale, decision making can be said to be taking place under conditions of *certainty*. At the other, decisions take place under conditions of *total uncertainty*.

Under conditions of certainty only one state of nature is possible or, alternatively, any variation which is possible will not affect the consequences of choosing a particular option. Either way, the decision is judged to be insensitive to any uncontrollable factors present.

Under conditions of total uncertainty, not only can we not predict the consequences of a decision, but further we will have very little confidence in our view of either what states of nature are possible, or the likelihood of their occurrence; our understanding of the structure of the decision will be poor, and our information will be limited or ambiguous.

In reality, each of these extremes is unlikely to occur. Certainty is, perhaps, a philosophical possibility but rarely a practical one. Few decisions, however well structured and programmable, and few decision makers, however confident, can be totally and utterly certain that the consequences predicted will, in fact, occur. Nevertheless, a decision maker may deliberately choose to *model* a decision as occurring under conditions of certainty if it is believed that modelling it in a probabilistic manner will add nothing to the analysis of the problem. Indeed, it may be a perfectly legitimate ploy to assume, for example, that sales figures will have a certain value, and to assume that the costings will take a certain level, even though we know that these figures are merely 'best guesses'. Conversely, conditions of total uncertainty are also extremely rare. Managers can usually make some kind of estimates as to which consequences are most likely to occur even in the vaguest of decision situations.

When conditions of certainty are not present but we are able to make confident predictions regarding the probabilities that any particular state will occur, then decision making is said to be occurring under conditions of *risk*. So, for example, in any game involving coin tossing, the number of states is predictable and the probability of heads or tails is confidently put at 0.5. However, as we shall explain later, the type of probability illustrated by tossing a coin is not normally the type of probability which is particularly useful in management decisions. Most management decisions lie somewhere between total uncertainty and risk, in an area usually referred to as plain *uncertainty*. Here we can usually identify the states likely to occur (even if we are aware of, but disregard, some fringe possibilities). Furthermore, we have sufficient knowledge to make some estimate of how likely each possible state of nature is to occur. Under such conditions, it is generally held to be useful for decision makers to proceed as if they have confidence in their probability estimates, even if they do not. However, the important proviso is that this is done only on the grounds that it is a useful way to proceed, rather than implying a spurious confidence; furthermore, the sensitivity of the decision to the probability estimates must be well understood.

## Incorporating Uncertainty

In practice, when faced with a decision that is clearly to be made under conditions of uncertainty, there are only three possible ways to proceed:

1. Take single point estimates. In other words, make the best possible guess on the strength of the information available in the decision, and carry on with the evaluation as though uncertainty does not exist.

2. Proceed the same as in 1, but build in a 'contingency' allowance to account for the possibility of estimates being optimistic.

3. Incorporate uncertainty into our modelling.

The remainder of this chapter looks at how uncertainty can be incorporated into models.

## Quantifying Uncertainty

The likelihood of something happening is usually quantified either as a probability figure or as a set of odds. The two methods are quite simply related: if someone says that the odds of an event occurring are $X$ to $Y$, then the probability is $X/(X + Y)$.

For example, odds of 10 to 1 against a horse winning a race indicate that for every one chance of the horse winning there are ten chances of it losing. Or expressed in another way, out of eleven chances only one is for winning. The probability of the horse winning is, therefore, 1/11 or 0.091. Odds express the chance of an occurrence as a measure relative to its non-occurrence, whereas probability expresses chance relative to the total span of possibilities. The basis of the odds method has disadvantages when the chance of an event occurring becomes either very unlikely or almost certain. Using the probability method, the limits to quantifying uncertainty are 0 (impossible) to 1 (certain). Expressing these limits as the odds 'infinity to 1' is clumsy. In fact, the major advantage of using probabilities as opposed to odds is that they are far more easily and practically manipulated when they are incorporated into any calculations.

## Discrete and Continuous Probabilities

Suppose a manager is asked to estimate the chances of a development project being finished by the date originally forecast at the start of the project (the due date). After looking at the work in hand the manager makes an estimate — 'The chance of making it by the due date is 60 per cent.' Now implicit in what the manager is saying are two very important things.

1. Only two states are possible: finishing before the due date or not finishing before the due date. In other words, the two events are *exhaustive* — nothing else is possible outside them.

2. If one state occurs, the other cannot: the two possible states are *mutually exclusive* — it is not possible for both states to happen at the same time.

Suppose that the manager is now asked to refine his estimate by including a third possibility: namely, the project finishing in the month after the due date. The manager's assessment could be that there is a 30 per cent chance of this happening. So now the possible states and their chances are as follows:

| | |
|---|---|
| Project completed prior to the due date | = 60% |
| Project completed in the month after the due date | = 30% |
| Project completed more than 1 month after due date | = 10% |

(with 30% and 10% bracketed as } 40%)

Similarly, the manager could estimate the probability of finishing in the month prior to the due date, say 35 per cent. The states and their probabilities would then be:

| | |
|---|---|
| Project completed before 1 month prior to the due date | = 25% |
| Project completed in the month prior to the due date | = 35% |

(with 25% and 35% bracketed as } 60%)

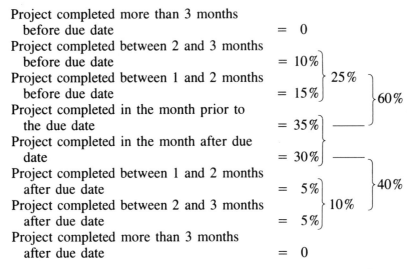

Project completed 1 month after due date = 30%
Project completed more than 1 month after due
     date = 10%   } 40%

It might be possible to break the probabilities down further on a month-by-month basis. For example:

Project completed more than 3 months
     before due date                          =  0
Project completed between 2 and 3 months
     before due date                          = 10%
Project completed between 1 and 2 months                    } 25%
     before due date                          = 15%          } 60%
Project completed in the month prior to
     the due date                             = 35%
Project completed in the month after due
     date                                     = 30%
Project completed between 1 and 2 months
     after due date                           = 5%
Project completed between 2 and 3 months                    } 10%   } 40%
     after due date                           = 5%
Project completed more than 3 months
     after due date                           =  0

Figure 6.1 shows these successive refinements in the manager's estimates in the form of probability distributions.

The minimum interval in Figure 6.1 is one month. By narrowing the interval further it may be possible to approach a smooth curve which gives the manager's probability of finish time occurring. Thus the manager has discretion over how the events are categorized. At one extreme only two categories are defined (finish before due date, and finish after due date); on the other hand, an infinite number of categories can be used by adopting a continuous probability distribution.

When the variable being forecast is not continuous itself, the choice between discrete and continuous probabilities does not exist. So, for example, a firm's bid is either accepted or it is not, the bank supports a proposal or does not, and so on.


## Cumulative Probability Distributions

The manager started by giving probability estimates as to the chance of the finished date occurring on each side of one particular point in time (the due date). This type of information is often more valuable than knowing the probability of an occurrence between two intervals. The cumulative probability distribution format shows the total probability of an event occurring by a particular point — in this case, the probability of the finish date being less than any particular time.

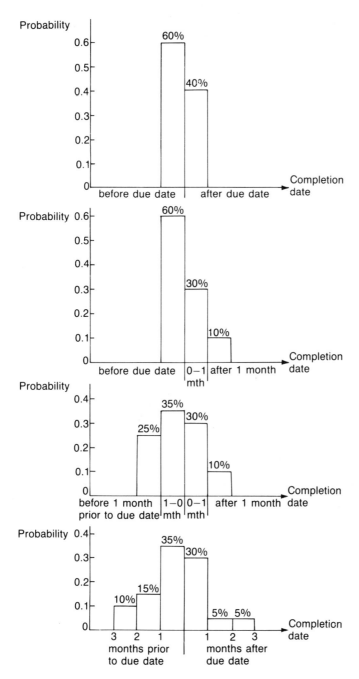

**Figure 6.1** Successive refinements of a manager's probability estimates for the completion of a project

The manager's estimates of the finish time for the project can be expressed cumulatively as follows:

| | | |
|---|---|---|
| Project completed before 3 months prior to due date | = | 0 |
| Project completed before 2 months prior to due date | = | 10% |
| Project completed before 1 month prior to due date | = | 25% |
| Project completed before due date | = | 60% |
| Project completed before 1 month after due date | = | 90% |
| Project completed before 2 months after due date | = | 95% |
| Project completed before 3 months after due date | = | 100% |

Figure 6.2 shows how the cumulative probability distribution is built up.

## Manipulating Probabilities

If including probabilities is to be useful when modelling uncertainty, we must be able to manipulate the probability estimates. Probability estimates of single events are the building blocks of modelling uncertainty, but real management decisions are often more complex. At the heart of probability theory lie three laws which allow us to combine probabilities of separate events and calculate the probabilities of further events.

### *Law 1*

If $X_1$ and $X_2$ are exclusive events, then the probability of $X_1$ *or* $X_2$ occurring is the sum of the probability of $X_1$ and the probability of $X_2$ occurring, i.e.:

$$P(X_1 \text{ or } X_2) = P(X_1) + P(X_2)$$

As an example, examine the project finishing time probabilities given in Figure 6.1. Suppose we were asked from this information to calculate the probability of the project finishing within one month of the due date. From the probability distributions we can see that the probability of the project finishing in the month prior to the due date is 35 per cent and the probability of it finishing in the month immediately after the due date is 30 per cent. Now these two events are mutually exclusive — they cannot both occur at the same time. Therefore, if:

$$P(\text{finish month prior}) = P(X_1)$$
$$P(\text{finish month after}) = P(X_2)$$

then:

$$P(X_1 \text{ or } X_2) = P(X_1) + P(X_2)$$
$$P(X_1 \text{ or } X_2) = 0.35 + 0.30 = 0.65$$

Thus the probability of the project finishing within one month of the due date is 65 per cent.

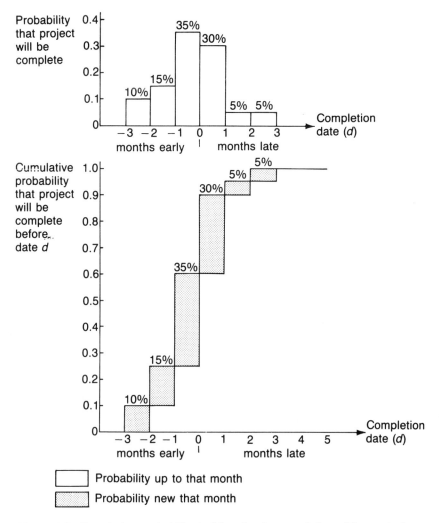

**Figure 6.2** Cumulative probability build-up for the completion of the project

This law can be extended to more than two exclusive events, so:

$$P(X_1 \text{ or } X_2 \text{ or } X_3 \ldots \text{ or } X_n) = P(X_1) + P(X_2) + P(X_3) + \ldots + P(X_n)$$

So, for example, the probability of the project being late is equal to the probability of it finishing in the first or the second or the third month after the due date:

$P(\text{late}) = P(\text{1st month}) + P(\text{2nd month}) + P(\text{3rd month})$
$P(\text{late}) = 0.30 + 0.05 + 0.05$
$P(\text{late}) = 0.40$ (which is consistent with the manager's original estimate)

A special case of this law occurs when $X_1$ and $X_2$ are exhaustive: that is, together they completely define all possibilities. Then since:

$$P(X_1 \text{ or } X_2) = 1(\text{certainty})$$
$$P(X_1) + P(X_2) = 1$$

or

$$P(X_1) = 1 - P(X_2)$$

In other words, the probability of something occurring is 1 minus the probability of it not occurring.

## Law 2

If $X$ and $Y$ are uncertain events, then the probability of *both* occurring is given by the probability of one occurring multiplied by the probability of the other occurring, given that the first event occurs, i.e.:

$$P(X \text{ and } Y) = P(X) \times P(Y|X)$$

where $P(Y|X)$ means the probability of $Y$ occurring given $X$.

For example, suppose the manager who is making probability estimates of the project finishing time is also asked to consider the probability of the project staying within its financial budget. The question might be 'What are the chances of the project finishing in time and within budget?'

The manager's estimate of the chance of keeping within budget, given that the project finishes before the due date, might be, say, 0.5, and since the chance of finishing on time has already been estimated as 0.6, then:

$$P(\text{on time and within budget}) = P(\text{on time}) \times P(\text{in budget given on time})$$
$$= 0.6 \times 0.5$$
$$= 0.3$$

The answer to the question is that there is a 30 per cent chance of the project finishing on time and within budget.

## Law 3

If $X_1$ and $X_2$ are exhaustive and mutually exclusive events, then the probability of any other event, $Y$, occurring is given by:

$$P(Y) = P(Y|X_1) \times P(X_1) + P(Y|X_2) \times P(X_2)$$

remembering that:

$$P(X_1) = 1 - P(X_2)$$

This law is a combination of the first two laws and can be illustrated by returning to the project example.

Suppose the manager assesses the probability of remaining within budget should the project finish later than the due date as being 10 per cent.

If $Y$ denotes the project remaining within its budget
   $X_1$ denotes the project finishing on time
   $X_2$ denotes the project finishing late

then:

$$P(X_1) = 0.6$$
$$P(X_2) = 0.4$$
$$P(Y|X_1) = P(\text{in budget given that the project finishes on time}) = 0.5$$
$$P(Y|X_2) = P(\text{in budget given that the project finishes late}) = 0.1$$

then:

$$P(Y) = 0.5 \times 0.6 + 0.1 \times 0.4$$
$$P(Y) = 0.34$$

So the probability of remaining within budget is 34 per cent. Figure 6.3 shows this example as a probability tree.

## The Decision Matrix

As we originally discussed in Chapter 1, a decision matrix is a method of modelling relatively straightforward decisions under uncertainty in such a way as to make

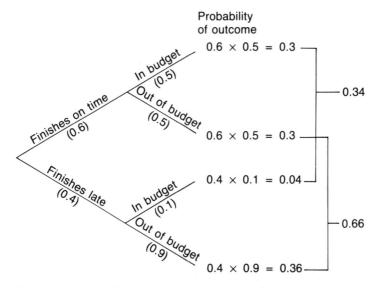

**Figure 6.3** Probability tree for the project remaining within its budget

explicit the options open to the decision taker, the states of nature pertinent to the decision, and the decision rule used to choose between options. Its usual form is as shown in Figure 6.4. Thus option $S_i$ and state of nature $N_j$ will produce a consequence or outcome $O_{ij}$.

The following example will illustrate how such a matrix can be used.

*Example: Trailaid Limited*

Trailaid Limited manufacture medically equipped trailers for the European and North American health-care markets. These trailers are widely used in developed countries for carrying out programmes of immunization, blood collection, radiology and general health care. Trailaid do not make the complete trailers themselves, but buy out the chassis and basic shell from a larger trailer manufacturer and then fit them out with the necessary internal equipment.

Recently, the company had been considering entering what was a fast-growing sector of the market — that of making trailers for Third World countries. Such trailers would have to be slightly different in construction and more robust, with extra air-conditioning equipment and a more general-purpose set of basic medical equipment.

The sales agencies which operate in these regions were convinced that, if Trailaid went into the business, they could sell about 1000 trailers a year to various developing countries. However, the major inducement for Trailaid was that it was well known that a United Nations development agency was considering placing a contract for a very large programme of medical aid equipment of this type. If Trailaid were included as a major contractor in this programme, it would mean that its total annual sales would be almost guaranteed at 3000 trailers. The company had a wealth of experience in manufacturing medical trailers and also enjoyed a

| | | States of nature | | | | |
|---|---|---|---|---|---|---|
| | | $N_1$ | $N_2$ | $N_3$ | — — — — — | $N_n$ |
| | $S_1$ | $O_{11}$ | $O_{12}$ | $O_{13}$ | — — — — — | $O_{1n}$ |
| | $S_2$ | $O_{21}$ | $O_{22}$ | $O_{23}$ | — — — — — | $O_{2n}$ |
| | $S_3$ | $O_{31}$ | $O_{32}$ | $O_{33}$ | — — — — — | |
| Options | \| | | | | | |
| | \| | | | | | |
| | \| | | | | | |
| | $S_m$ | $O_{m1}$ | $O_{m2}$ | $O_{m3}$ | — — — — — | $O_{mn}$ |

$S_1 - S_m$ = The options
$N_1 - N_n$ = The uncertain events
$O_{11} - O_{mn}$ = The outcomes

**Figure 6.4** The outcome matrix

good reputation, so it was confident that it stood a fairly good chance of becoming a major contractor.

Trailaid's production team had come up with two alternative ways to make the new product. Method 1 was to subcontract most of the manufacture. All that Trailaid would need to do 'in house' would be to assemble the trailer — a brief operation. This option would incur little fixed cost, giving relatively good profits at low levels of sales but relatively poor profits at high levels. Method 2 entailed taking an existing shell from a trailer manufacturer and modifying it in Trailaid's own workshops. Fitting out of the trailer would then be identical to method 1. Figure 6.5 shows the estimated profit for the two alternative manufacturing processes, at the 'low' sales volume, and at the 'high' sales volume.

When deciding which production facility to choose, the company will obviously want to take into account the likelihood of getting the development agency contract. Now the company is reasonably optimistic about this, but by no means sure. Since prediction is by definition a rather uncertain occupation, it is not surprising that before venturing into assessing the likelihood of getting the contract any manager may well want to examine the decision independently of any predictions. In fact, a number of decision rules are commonly put forward as being helpful in under-standing the nature of the decision. We shall look at four of these, with respect to Trailaid. The first three do not involve the manager in forecasting future uncertain events, but the fourth does. The four decision rules are as follows:

1. The optimistic decision rule.

2. The pessimistic decision rule.

3. The regret decision rule.

4. The expected value decision rule.

## The Optimistic Decision Rule

This approach to selecting the preferred option is to consider all possible circum-stances and choose that option which yields the best possible outcome. For Trailaid, the best profit is 330. This occurs when method 2 is used and the annual sales volume is high. So the total optimist would choose method 2 because it provides

| | Annual sales volume | |
| --- | --- | --- |
| | Low | High |
| Method 1 | 240 | 310 |
| Method 2 | 200 | 330 |

**Figure 6.5**  Profit table for the two alternative manufacturing options (£000s)

| | Annual sales volume | | Maximum regret |
|---|---|---|---|
| | Low | High | |
| Method 1 | 240 (0) | 310 (20) | 20* |
| Method 2 | 200 (40) | 330 (0) | 40 |

*Minimum of the maximum regrets.

**Figure 6.6** Regret table for the two alternative manufacturing options (£000s)

the opportunity to achieve the best outcome. In detail, this decision rule involves examining each option, selecting the maximum profit outcome, and choosing the option which provides the highest maximum profit.

## The Pessimistic Decision Rule

A decision maker who took the very opposite view to the one described above would follow the reverse procedure. Each option would be examined, and the worst possible outcome for that option identified. The option would be selected which provided the best of the worst outcomes. In the case of Trailaid, the worst outcome would be 200 if manufacturing method 2 were chosen, whereas if manufacturing method 1 were chosen the worst outcome would be 240. The best of these two outcomes is the profit of 240 associated with method 1. Thus a pessimist would assume that the worst is going to happen, and because the worst outcome with method 1 is better than the worst outcome with method 2, would choose method 1.

## The Regret Decision Rule

The regret decision rule is based on a deceptively simple but extremely useful question: that is, 'If we decide on one particular option, then, with hindsight, how much would we regret not having chosen what turns out to be the best option for a particular set of circumstances?'

For example, suppose method 2 were chosen. If sales are low, then the wrong decision would have been made. Method 1 would have given a profit of 240. A measure of the regret at having chosen method 2 is given by the difference in profit between the two manufacturing methods at that level of sales volume. The regret at having chosen method 2 would be $240 - 200 = 40$. If method 1 had been chosen, there would have been no regret, since at this particular level of sales volume this is the best method. At the high sales volume level the position reverses. With method 2 there is no regret because this is the highest profit method. However, if method 1 had been chosen, then the regret would have been the difference between the profits, i.e. $330 - 310 = 20$.

Figure 6.6 shows the regret table for this decision; the regrets are shown in brackets. If method 1 is chosen, there is a regret of either zero or 20, and if method 2 is chosen, there is a regret of 40 or zero, depending on the level of sales. Thus the maximum regret that could be suffered if method 1 is chosen is 20, whereas the maximum regret with method 2 is 40. Under the regret decision rule, the option which gave the minimum of the maximum regrets would be chosen, i.e. method 1.

### Inconsistency in the Regret Rule

The regret decision rule is a powerful and intuitively attractive idea. It attempts to minimize the embarrassment we might feel at making the wrong decision. It is closely related to the economist's traditional concept of the 'opportunity cost' of a decision: that is, by choosing one alternative course of action, what opportunity are we forgoing by not choosing another course of action? Unfortunately, as a decision rule the concept has a major disadvantage: if we are choosing the alternative which will give us the least cause for regret when compared with another alternative, then the degree of regret will depend upon which other options are considered. This can cause problems of logical inconsistency.

Developing the case of Trailaid further will illustrate this. Suppose that, while the two options open to Trailaid are being considered, the purchasing manager of the company suggests a third alternative. This is to set up a totally new, dedicated production facility. This would be expensive but give good profits at high levels of sales: 360. However, if sales were poor, profits would be poor: 190.

If the new option, let us call it method 3, is included in the decision process, then it should be included with the other two in the decision matrix. Figure 6.7 shows all three options, their respective unit costs, and the regret values for each outcome.

For the low demand level the option with the lowest profit is the new proposal, method 3. This has a regret value of 50. If manufacturing method 2 is chosen, then the regret is 40. Likewise, if manufacturing method 1 is chosen, then the regret is zero. If the demand is at the high level, then method 3 is the best decision, and so has a regret of zero. Method 2 is 30 and method 1 is 50 more expensive than method 3. So, if method 1 is chosen, the regret will be either zero or 50,

| | Annual sales volume | | Maximum regret |
|---|---|---|---|
| | Low | High | |
| Method 1 | 240 (0) | 310 (50) | 50 |
| Method 2 | 200 (40) | 330 (30) | 40* |
| Method 3 | 190 (50) | 360 (0) | 50 |

*Minimum of maximum regrets.

**Figure 6.7** Profit and regret tables when the third option is included (£000s)

if method 2 is chosen the regret will be either 40 or 30, and if method 3 is chosen the regret will be either 50 or zero. Using the regret decision rule, method 2 could be chosen, since this is the lowest of the maximum regrets.

However, surely here is an inconsistency. By including the third option we have shifted our decision from method 1 to method 2. Yet, even when it is included, method 3 is not the preferred option by the regret decision rule! Herein lies the major problem with opportunity costing — against what other opportunity are you going to evaluate a particular option?

## The Expected Value Decision Rule

The three criteria so far described may go some way towards clarifying the decision for us, but they do not use one of the potentially most useful factors within any management decision. That is our estimate of the likelihood of a particular situation occurring.

The principle of expectation *weights* each outcome by the likelihood of it occurring. Suppose that, as yet, Trailaid is unwilling to put a definite figure on its chances of gaining the developing agency contract. It can still explore the decision further by calculating the expected profit associated with each method as the probability of gaining the contract varies.

Let us call the probability of gaining the contract $p$. Then the probability of not gaining the contract will be $1 - p$.

> For method 1: Expected profit $= 240(1 - p) + 310p$
> For method 2: Expected profit $= 200(1 - p) + 330p$
> For method 3: Expected profit $= 190(1 - p) + 360p$

Figure 6.8 shows the graph of these three equations. The point at which the expected unit-cost lines for methods 1 and 3 cross is when the value of $P$ is 0.5. This means that method 1 yields a higher expected profit than any of the other two methods, if it is believed that the chance of gaining the development contract is less than 0.5. If the company assessed the chances of gaining the contract at more than 0.5, then method 3 would be the preferred option.

Perhaps a more useful way of interpreting the graph is to say that, if the probability of high demand is between 0.4 and 0.6, then all three methods show fairly similar unit-cost figures. Below 0.4 and above 0.6 real differences start showing. So, if Trailaid's assessment of its chances of getting the development contract fall between 0.4 and 0.6, then perhaps it ought to be using a criterion other than expected profit on which to base its decision, since no preference for one of the methods is clear using this criterion.

After speaking further with the development agency and reviewing the possible competition, the company at last attempts to assess the likelihood of it gaining the development contract. It reckons that its chances are somewhat better than evens, and places a probability figure of 0.6 on getting the contract. So:

The expected profit for method 1 = 240 × 0.4 + 310 × 0.6 = 282
The expected profit for method 2 = 200 × 0.4 + 330 × 0.6 = 278
The expected profit for method 3 = 190 × 0.4 + 360 × 0.6 = 292

It must be emphasized that expected profits are in themselves totally hypothetical figures. In reality, the profits of 282 and 278 for methods 1 and 2 will never actually occur. The profits will be any of the figures illustrated in Figure 6.6 but not *ever* the 'expected' figure. The expected values are merely an indication of the worth of each option.

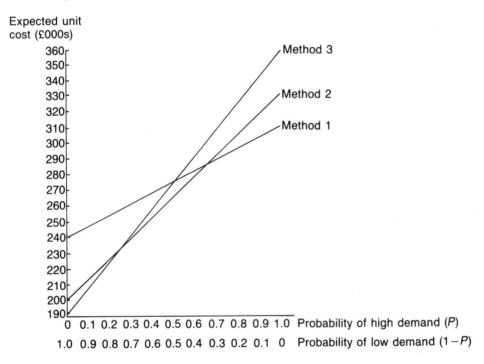

**Figure 6.8**  The expected unit cost of the three methods as the probability of achieving the high demand level varies

## Decision Trees

One limitation of the decision matrix model is the simplistic way in which it treats the options open to the manager. Many management decisions are in reality a series of related sequential decisions, where choices made at one point in time can change the probability of their decisions happening or alter their consequences. The decision tree format enables sequential decisions to be represented and the consequences of *future* decisions to be traced back to assess their influence on the present decision.

In fact, a decision matrix can be represented as a decision tree. Take the matrix shown in Figure 6.6: described another way, it has two options, each of which is followed by an uncertain event which can take two possible forms. Figure 6.9 shows the matrix in the form of a decision tree. This tree represents a simple single-stage decision. However, the procedure can be extended to incorporate future decisions, as is demonstrated in the following example, which shows how a decision tree can be constructed and analysed.

### Example: The Metropole-Royal

Hotel rooms are an extremely perishable product, and letting them is always an uncertain business. Mike Robinson, the manager of the Metropole-Royal, a large London hotel situated in the West End, was worried. This year had been exceptionally bad and the coming 12-month period looked like offering no improvement. The drop in tourism to London was not something that was likely to last for more than the next couple of years, but his problem was, how was he to run a hotel where 25 per cent of the bedrooms were forecast to be empty over a two-year period?

By far the most reliable part of Mike's business was his 'crew contract'. A crew contract is a contract with an airline for a fixed number of rooms every night, for which it pays a fixed sum per year. Presently, Mike had a contract with one

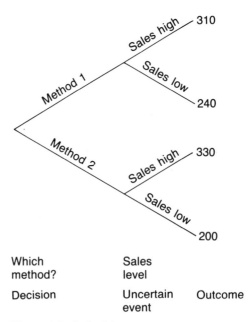

Figure 6.9  A decision tree

of the largest Middle Eastern airlines, Arabia Airlines, for ten rooms a night. This contract was entering its final year of a five-year period. Currently, the worth to the hotel was about £100 000 per year.

Most airlines were well aware of the over-capacity in the hotel market in London, and, taking advantage of this, Americal Airlines had recently approached Mike with a proposal for a crew contract of the similar size to his existing contract with Arabia. However, it insisted that it would only place the contract with him if he could give Americal a substantial discount on the price he was currently charging Arabia. Americal was adamant that the most it would pay was £60 000 for a one-year-only contract. Although this price was well below what Mike would normally offer, he knew that, given the current state of the market, he would be well able to offer the extra ten rooms to Americal with only a marginal increase in his costs.

The major danger lay in the chance of offending his longstanding Middle Eastern customer. Of course, the deal would be theoretically confidential, and therefore Arabia would not hear of it. However, Mike knew as well as anybody that crews do talk in the bar at night, and there was a chance that eventually Arabia would find out. Mike also guessed that, if Arabia had no cause for complaint at the end of the year, they would almost certainly renew the contract for a further five years at the existing price. However, if they realized that substantially better terms had been offered to one of their competitors, then there was a small chance that they would cancel the contract straight away (or, more likely, not renew) unless they got the same terms as Americal had obtained when the next five-year contract was negotiated.

Mike summed up his dilemma thus:

> It all depends upon whether they find out about our deal with Americal Airlines. You can never tell what will happen. They might be so offended that they immediately cancelled the contract. Of course, they would have to pay us a half rate under our agreement, which means that we would get £50 000 for the next year, but they would have no difficulty in getting accommodation elsewhere, and we would certainly not get the contract for the next five years. If they find out, and don't cancel the contract immediately, then the ball is back in our court. We can either keep our prices as they are, in which case our chance of getting the next five-year contract would be substantially reduced. Alternatively, we could offer them the same terms as we offered to Americal Airlines, in which case, given that they hadn't already cancelled, we would stand a reasonably good chance of getting the contract, but obviously with reduced profits.
>
> My problem is that there are quite a lot of unknowns in this. For example, I don't know for sure that the airline would find out about the Americal deal. I guess on the whole it's more likely that they don't, but there is still a good chance that they might — say, 6 to 4 against them finding out. Similarly, we don't know whether they would immediately be so offended that they would cancel the contract straight away. It's fairly unlikely, but there is a finite possibility — I wouldn't give it more than one in ten chance of happening though. If they don't immediately cancel, at least it means that they are not gravely offended. However, they are almost certainly likely to take a closer look at the terms we offer them than they would otherwise have done. If we offer the same terms as we offered to Americal, it would represent a 40 per cent reduction in price,

and therefore I feel that they would almost certainly be inclined to accept our offer — say, only a one in ten chance of not accepting it. However, if we keep our original price, our chances of getting the contract will be substantially reduced — I would guess no better than 50:50.

Given this information, Mike drew a preliminary decision tree to try and represent his decision. This is shown in Figure 6.10.

The first decision is whether to accept Americal Airline's offer or not. The second decision will only be necessary if the Americal contract is accepted, Arabia find out, and they do not immediately cancel their existing contract. This decision is:

Do we offer Arabia the same price as we offered Americal, or do we keep the price the same as it was for the five-year contract which has just ended?

We can see from the decision tree that there are seven possible final outcomes to the decision. They are as follows:

1. Americal's offer is accepted, Arabia find out and immediately cancel. The financial consequence of this chain of events would be for the hotel to get the £60 000 from Americal, but only get half of the remaining payments due from Arabia, i.e. £50 000. The total financial payment then is £110 000.

2. Americal's offer is accepted, Arabia find out, they don't immediately cancel the contract, at the end of the year the hotel offers them the same terms as they offered Americal, and they obtain the new contract. The financial consequences of this would be to get £100 000 from Arabia for this year's rooms, £60 000 from Americal and a reduced five-year fee of £300 000 for the next five-year contract with Arabia. This gives a total of £460 000.

3. Americal's offer is accepted, Arabia find out, they continue for this year, the hotel offers the low rate, but in spite of that loses the contract. The financial outcome of this would be to get the £100 000 from Arabia for this year, plus the £60 000 from Americal for this year, giving a total of £160 000.

4. Americal's offer is accepted, Arabia find out, they continue for this year, the hotel offers them the same high rate as before, but in spite of this the hotel gets the new five-year contract. In this case the hotel would be getting £100 000 from Arabia for this year, plus £60 000 from Americal for this year, plus £500 000 for the new five-year contract. This gives a total of £660 000.

5. Americal's offer is accepted, Arabia find out, they continue for this year, the hotel offers them the same high rate as before and, not surprisingly, the hotel loses the contract. In this case the hotel would get £100 000 for this year from Arabia, plus £60 000 from Americal, making a total of £160 000.

6. Americal's offer is accepted, and Arabia don't find out. In these circumstances the hotel will get £100 000 from Arabia for this year, £60 000 from Americal

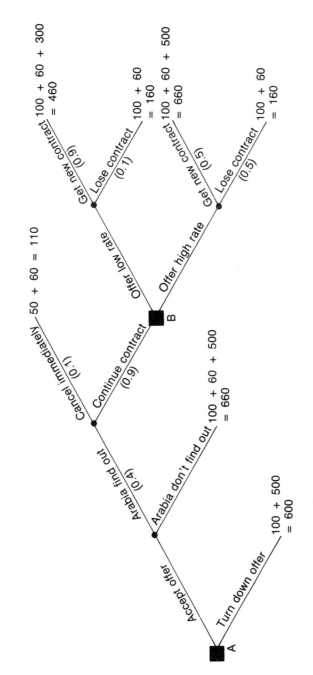

**Figure 6.10** The Metropole-Royal decision

for this year, plus £500 000 from Arabia for the new five-year contract, giving a total of £660 000.

7. American's offer is rejected. In this case the hotel would get £100 000 from Arabia for this year, plus £500 000 from Arabia for the new five-year contract, making a total of £600 000.

Let us first assume that we have reached decision point B and take the decision from there (Figure 6.11). The two alternatives are to offer the low rate to Arabia or to offer the old high rate. If the hotel offers the low rate, then it enters a lottery with a 90 per cent chance of gaining £460 000 and a 10 per cent chance of gaining £160 000. If the hotel offers the high rate, then the gamble is between a 50 per cent chance of gaining £660 000 and a 50 per cent chance of gaining £160 000. Following the principle of expectation, the expected outcome of offering the low rate is:

$$460\ 000 \times 0.9 + 160\ 000 \times 0.1 = £430\ 000$$

whereas the expected outcome from offering the high rate is:

$$660\ 000 \times 0.5 + 160\ 000 \times 0.5 = £410\ 000.$$

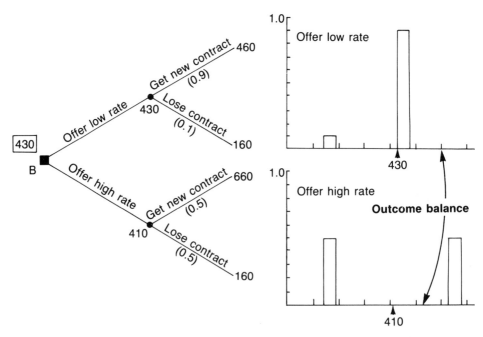

**Figure 6.11** The Metropole-Royal decision tree and outcome balance from decision point B

## The Outcome Balance

Figure 6.11 also shows the outcome balance for these two alternatives. The outcome balance is simply a diagrammatic method of showing the magnitude and likelihood of the outcomes from a decision point. If our objective is to choose the alternative that yields the highest expected monetary value, then the hotel would decide to offer the low rate since this has a higher expected value. Thus, if we reach decision point B in the tree, we can expect to gain £430 000. The decision tree then reduces to that shown in Figure 6.12, and the decision comes down to the fundamental one of whether to accept American's offer or not.

If American's offer is accepted, one of three outcomes is possible:

1. Arabia will find out and cancel immediately.
2. Arabia will find out but continue the contract.
3. Arabia will not find out.

The probability of Arabia finding out *and* cancelling immediately will be 0.4 (the probability of them finding out) multiplied by 0.1 (the probability of them cancelling immediately), i.e. the combined probability is 0.04. The probability of them continuing the contract, given that they find out, will be 0.4 (the probability of Arabia finding out) multiplied by 0.9 (the probability of them continuing the contract), i.e. 0.36. The probability of Arabia not finding out is 0.6. So the expected outcome for this option is:

$$0.04 \times 110\ 000 + 0.36 \times 430\ 000 + 0.6 \times 660\ 000 = £555\ 200.$$

The alternative option, to turn down the offer, has only one outcome, i.e. there is certainty. The outcome in this case would be £600 000. Thus, we have a choice between an expected monetary value of £550 200 and a certainty of £600 000. Not unnaturally, if the hotel followed the principle of expectation, it would choose the latter.

This process of starting with the decisions 'further away' from the initial decision, treating them as independent decisions and then substituting the expected value of the decision is called the *roll-back* technique.

## Including Extra Information in Decision Trees

When drawing decision trees managers can incorporate their subjective assessments of the probabilities of each uncertain event occurring. It may be, though, that extra information can be obtained which will influence the manager's subjective estimates of the probabilities.

The probability law which enables us to incorporate the effects of further information is called *Bayes law*,[1] and it is best illustrated with an example.

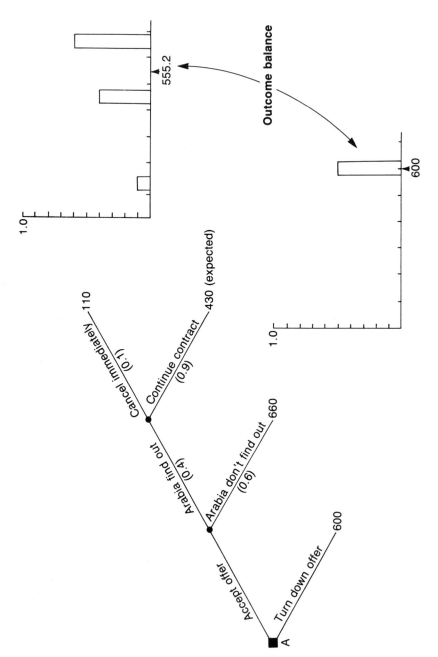

**Figure 6.12** The Metropole-Royal reduced decision tree and outcome balance

> ## Box 6.1[2]
>
> Looking forward and including uncertainty formally in decision modelling can have remarkably beneficial results. In the oil business, Shell spends considerable effort in looking at what could affect its business up to twenty years ahead. In the turbulent oil world Shell regards incorporating future uncertainty as a central part of its decision processes. For example, in the early 1980s many oil companies were counting on even higher oil prices, but Shell had examined what its future would be like if the oil price dropped to $15 a barrel. Shocked by what its position would be, it started to use higher technology to cut its costs. The result was an oil and gas exploration cost of about half the industry average. When the oil price dropped the company was more able than its competitors to withstand the price downturn. By the time the oil price actually did drop to $15 a barrel, Shell could make profits of £2.9 billion on sales of £55.8 billion. That was only £84 million less profit than when the oil price was $28 per barrel and sales were £73.1 billion. By the end of the 1980s Shell was achieving twice the return on its assets of many of its largest competitors. Ten years earlier it had looked ahead to what *might* happen.

### Example: Wallingford Foods Limited

Wallingford Foods Limited is a small company which manufactures and sells cheese-flavoured biscuits in the south of England. The company has been offered the opportunity to manufacture, under licence, a new garlic-flavoured biscuit, presently made and sold only in France. The company is very interested in this opportunity because it would enable it to expand its sales area throughout Britain, but it has reservations about this particular product. The French company has specified that the licence would only be granted if the company guaranteed a high expenditure on promoting the product. In addition, the manufacturing plant required for the product would involve a high capital outlay. This means that the fixed costs of the operation would be relatively high, and unless the product succeeded on a national level the company would lose heavily on the project. However, if the product were successful, then the profits would be potentially large.

The marketing manager of the company thinks the chances of the product being a success are very good on the grounds that it is an interesting product and has proved highly successful in France. After some discussion the marketing team reckons that the chances of the product being a success are about 70 per cent, and the profit to the company over the licence period, if sales were good, would be around £2 million. The management team, however, are hesistant to commit themselves. Should the sales be poor, the losses would amount to around £1 million, which is a serious loss to a company of Wallingford's size. The marketing manager sketched a decision tree to show the rest of the team the decision as she saw it. This tree is shown in Figure 6.13.

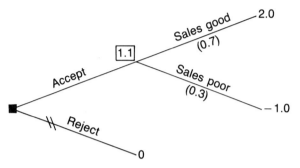

**Figure 6.13** Decision tree for accepting or rejecting the licence

In her presentation to her colleagues, she explained her reaction to the dilemma:

> I know that according to the decision tree we should definitely go ahead and accept the licence, but I am hesitant to recommend that we do that at the moment, largely because such a move would imply a great deal more confidence in my own estimate of our chances in the market than I feel is justified. Personally, I feel that we should test market the product by hiring a specialist firm and getting samples of the product over from France. I know of a firm who would conduct this market research for us, and who claim 90 per cent reliability of their forecasts.

The rest of the management team agreed to delay a decision until the market research company could be contacted to give estimates for the job. When the estimates came through, they quoted a price of £50 000 for information which should be, as the marketing manager suggested, 90 per cent reliable. The question then facing the management team is, would it be worth £50 000 to obtain information of this type?

Putting the question another way, 'How much should my original estimate of the chance of success be influenced if I choose to go ahead with a test market?'

Let $X$ represent the line being a success nationwide
and $\check{X}$ represent the line not being a success nationwide.
Let $Y$ represent the test market indicating 'successful'
and $\check{Y}$ represent the test market indicating 'unsuccessful'.

From Law 2:

$$P(X \text{ and } Y) = P(X) \times P(Y|X)$$

and

$$P(Y \text{ and } X) = P(Y) \times P(X|Y)$$

but the probability of $X$ and $Y$ happening must be the same as the probability of $Y$ and $X$ happening. Therefore:

$$P(X) \times P(Y|X) = P(Y) \times P(X|Y)$$

Thus

$$P(X|Y) = \frac{P(X) \times P(Y|X)}{P(Y)} \tag{7.1}$$

Now from Law 3:

$$P(Y) = P(Y|X) \times P(X) + P(Y|\bar{X}) \times P(\bar{X}) \tag{7.2}$$

remembering $X$ represents the product being unsuccessful, where:

$$P(X) = 1 - P(\bar{X})$$

So substituting equation 7.2 into equation 7.1:

$$P(X|Y) = \frac{P(X) \times P(Y|X)}{P(Y|X) \times P(X) + P(Y|\bar{X}) \times P(\bar{X})} \tag{7.3}$$

Equation 7.3 is Bayes law, where in this example:

$P(X|Y)$ is the probability of the product being a success, given that the test market indicates a success.

$P(X)$ is the original estimate of the probability that the product will be successful.

$P(Y|X)$ is the likelihood that the test market will indicate a success, given that the product would be a success nationwide. (This is the confidence we have in the accuracy of the test market.)

$P(Y|\bar{X})$ is the likelihood that the test market will indicate a success, given that the product would not be successful nationwide.

Now:

$$P(X) = 0.7$$

Therefore:

$$P(\bar{X}) = 0.3$$

and

$$P(Y|X) = 0.9$$
$$P(Y|\bar{X}) = 0.1$$

Therefore:

$$P(X|Y) = \frac{0.7 \times 0.9}{0.9 \times 0.7 + 0.1 \times 0.3} = 0.96$$

Thus, if the market research indicates that the line will be successful, the marketing manager could raise her estimate of nationwide success from 0.7 to 0.96.

This process of revising our original or *prior* probability given further information is illustrated diagrammatically in Figure 6.14. If we represent all possible events

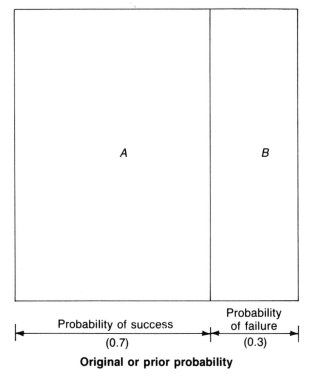

Probability of success
(0.7)

Probability
of failure
(0.3)

**Original or prior probability**

**Figure 6.14** Using only the original (prior) probability estimates there are two states

by the area bounded by a square, our original estimate divided the area into two possibilities: $A$ representing the line being successful and $B$ representing the line being unsuccessful.

So the probability of success $P(X)$ can be expressed as:

$$P(X) = \frac{A}{A + B} = \frac{\text{The event in question}}{\text{All possible events}}$$

Holding a test market, in effect, sub-divides the two original possibilities. There are now four possible states as shown in Figure 6.15:

1. Research indicates 'successful' and the line is successful ($A_1$).
2. Research indicates 'successful' and the line is unsuccessful ($B_1$).
3. Research indicates 'unsuccessful' and the line is successful ($A_2$).
4. Research indicates 'unsuccessful' and the line is unsuccessful ($B_2$).

Information from the test market, however, again restricts the possible events to two. So, for example, if the test market indicated 'successsful', the only two possible events are those represented by areas $A_1$ and $B_1$. This means that the probability of the line being a success nationwide, given that the test indicated 'successful' $P(X|Y)$, is:

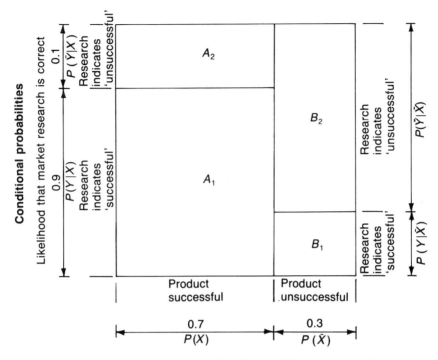

**Figure 6.15** Using both prior and conditional probabilities there are four states

$$P(X|Y) = \frac{A_1}{A_1 + B_1} = \frac{P(X) \times P(Y|X)}{P(Y|X) \times P(X) + P(Y|\check{X}) \times P(\check{X})}$$

Similarly, the probability of the line being successful, given that test indicated unsuccessful, is:

$$\frac{A_2}{A_2 + B_2} = \frac{0.7 \times 0.1}{0.7 \times 0.1 + 0.3 \times 0.9} = 0.21$$

The probability of the line being unsuccessful, given that the test indicated unsuccessful, is:

$$\frac{B_2}{A_2 + B_2} = \frac{0.3 \times 0.9}{0.7 \times 0.1 + 0.3 \times 0.9} = 0.79$$

The probability of the line being unsuccessful, given that the test indicated successful, is:

$$\frac{B_1}{A_1 + B_1} = \frac{0.3 \times 0.1}{0.7 \times 0.9 + 0.3 \times 0.1} = 0.34$$

So, if the market research indicates that sales will be good, the marketing manager's estimate of the probability of, in fact, achieving good sales, will rise to 0.96. If the market research indicates poor sales, then the probability of sales being, in fact, poor, rises to 0.79.

## The Value of the Information

Armed with the revised probabilities from Bayes theorem, we can now draw a revised decision tree where the initial decision is whether or not to seek the market research data. This revised decision tree is shown in Figure 6.16.

If it is decided to buy the market research, the results could predict either 'good' or 'poor' sales. The next decision is whether to accept or reject the licence offer. Rejection would result in a net pay-off of −£0.05 million (the market resarch costs). If the research indicates good sales, accepting the licence results in a higher expected pay-off of £1.83 million, but if the research indicates poor sales, rejection results in a better (though negative) expected pay-off. If the market research

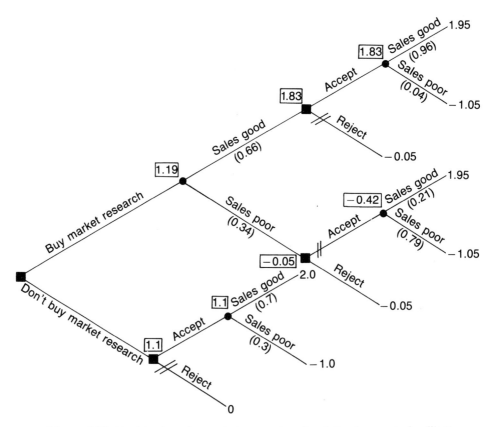

**Figure 6.16** Decision tree for market research option (all outcomes in £ million)

information is not taken, accepting the licence gives the higher expected pay-off as before.

But notice the spread of possible outcomes for the two initial options. By taking the market research we have reduced both best and worst outcomes by £50 000, but the probabilities have been changed sufficiently for the *expected* pay-off to be enhanced.[3] Thus, the net benefit of the information after paying for the market research is:

$$£1.19 \text{ million} - £1.1 \text{ million} = £90\ 000$$

## The Value of Perfect Information

To perform a quick check on the value of potential information, without resorting to Bayesian revision of prior probabilities, it is useful to determine the value of *perfect* information. This involves accepting a hypothetical gift of information which is guaranteed to be accurate, then determining the increase in expected pay-off as a result of this 'gift'. Figure 6.17 shows the decision tree for the previous example, with the option of accepting perfect information.

If the perfect information is accepted, there is still a 0.7 probability that it will indicate good sales and a 0.3 chance of it indicating poor sales. But if good sales are indicated, we can decide to accept the licence with total confidence that it is the better of the two options. Likewise, if poor sales are indicated, the offer should definitely be rejected. Rolling back this branch of the tree gives an expected pay-off for perfect information of £1.4 million. This is compared with an expected pay-off of £1.1 million when using no extra information. Since perfect information cannot be improved upon, the maximum value of any market information is, in this case:

$$£1.4 \text{ million} - £1.1 \text{ million} = £300\ 000$$

## Practical Prescriptions

Uncertainty need not be incorporated in decision models. Only build uncertainty into the model if uncertain events have a significant influence on the outcomes of the decision. Alternatives to using uncertainty models include:

- Using deterministic estimates.
- Building in contingency allowances for uncertain events.

If uncertainty is important in the decision, try to quantify the likelihood of uncertain events occurring by using subjective probabilities.

Even though the probability estimates are subjective, they can be manipulated according to the basic laws of probability. Remember, though, that they are still

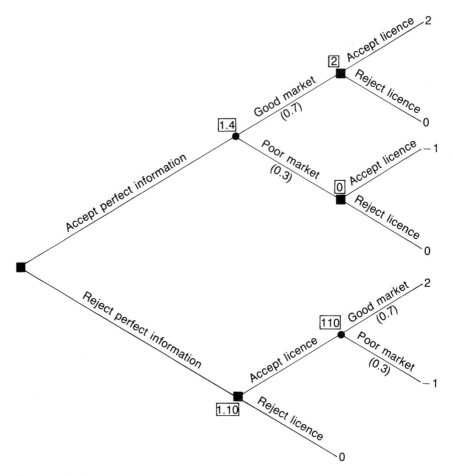

**Figure 6.17** Determining the value of perfect information

estimates or 'best guesses'; manipulating them does not make them any more accurate.

Use the decision matrix format as a starting point for building a model. Before assigning probabilities, examine the decision by using optimistic, pessimistic and regret rules.

After assigning subjective probabilities to each uncertain event, calculate the expected value of each option.

If confidence in the probability estimates is not high, test the sensitivity of the outcomes to changes in the probability estimates.

Use decision trees to model decisions with more than one stage: that is, where a further decision follows the occurrence of uncertain events.

Use the concept of the 'outcome balance' to assess the risk associated with expected outcomes.

If there is a possibility of extra information being made available, test whether it is worth having by incorporating the 'extra information' option in the decision tree.

---

# Case Exercise 1

---

## Orient Trading Company

The Orient Trading Company was started by Richard Geraldson after he spent a summer vacation as a student in India. The contacts he made during his time in Bombay became the suppliers for his import business. Richard specialized initially in dress fabrics, but expanded later into carpets, furniture and household goods. He sold most of his goods directly to three or four major retail chains, but on a few lines dealt exclusively with one large household chain, Household Limited.

Two years ago Richard had entered into partnership with an old friend of his to form a direct trading company. Orient-Direct, which promoted both his and other goods in national newspapers and magazines. The direct selling operation had been slower to take off than Richard had anticipated, and had required considerable capital to set up its two warehouses, but it was now slowly moving towards profitability. Even so, the direct trading company had more debt than either of its owners would have liked.

This was one reason why Richard was so undecided over the latest offer from one of his agents in Bombay. The prospective deal involved a large quantity of hand-woven rugs. The transportation costs involved were higher than usual, but the unit price of the rugs was very low indeed. This meant that, if Richard sold the rugs through his normal retail channels, his profit would be dependent on how well the merchandise sold. High sales would result in a total profit of about £90 000 to Orient Trading. Normally Richard would have checked out with his contacts at Household and other retail chains to see how attractive they thought the rugs deal would be, but the time scale involved did not allow him to sound out opinion fully. The only reaction he had was from Household's chief buyer, who was less than enthusiastic about the merchandise and hinted that Household would only take a small quantity initially to see how well they sold in the shops.

If the rugs did not sell well through normal retail channels, the alternative outlet would be through Orient-Direct, the direct trading company, but this would mean expenditure in promoting the merchandise. After talking with his partner, they were pretty sure that there would be a fifty-fifty chance of selling all the rugs through the direct trading company, but the level of promotion expenditure would reduce the total profits on the deal to about £40 000. If, however, the rugs still did not sell, they would have to unload them on to the smaller discount stores and market trade at a considerable loss, probably a loss of £30 000 on the whole scheme. Alternatively, they could avoid some of this risk by immediately dumping the rugs to the discount houses should they fail to sell in the major chains, and not try promoting them through Orient-Direct at all. If they did this, they think that they could get their losses down to £10 000.

Richard summed up his dilemma:

> The decision I have to take almost immediately is, do I take the whole load of rugs or do I politely decline the offer? The problem is that, although I normally have a pretty shrewd idea of how well merchandise will sell in the big retail chains, I am uncertain about this particular line of merchandise. I think I would have to say that there is less than a fifty-fifty chance of it selling well, probably as low as a 30 per cent chance. This means that there is a 70 per cent chance of having to sell the rugs through our direct trading operation. And the last thing the company needs at the moment is losses of £30 000 on a deal!

## Questions

1.  From whose point of view should this decision be modelled, from Richard Geraldson's, from his partner's, or from their joint position?
2.  Should Richard accept the deal?
3.  If you were Richard's partner, would you be willing to take the rugs if they did fail to sell in the national retail chains?

# Case Exercise 2

## DeFrey Limited

The deFrey design company was a firm of consulting engineers, specializing in chemical plant design and based in Ontario, Canada. Although a relatively small group of engineers, they had already established themselves as innovators in the process design field. The company was particularly excited by a new design technique recently developed by one of its young engineers. She claimed that, by using the new technique, significant construction cost savings could be achieved on almost any type of plant. The technique had been reviewed by the company's senior engineers and seemed to be theoretically sound, but as yet no actual plant had been designed using the technique, and no experimental pilot rig had been constructed for verification tests.

While the senior engineers were deciding whether to sanction the expense of a pilot rig to test the new technique, the company won an order to design a chemical plant in the Vancouver area. Immediately, two design teams were started on producing preliminary designs, one using conventional design techniques and the other using the new technique. These designs became known as design 1 and design 2 respectively. At the same time, cost estimates were collected to establish the total cost of setting up an experimental pilot rig to test some of the assumptions involved in the new design, design 2, before final plans would have to be submitted. In fact, the design 2 team produced two designs: one using the new technique, and one which was a modification of the new design, which could be used if the design did not prove successful.

When all this information had been brought together, the senior engineers were presented with the following financial summary:

Cost of pilot rig test = $80 000
Design 1 (conventional design)
  Profit = $200 000
Design 2 (experimental design)
  Profit if design successful = $400 000
  Profit if modification necessary = $50 000

The senior engineers then discussed the chances of the designs being successful. They were agreed that design 1, using tried and tested conventional theories, was sure to be successful: that is, 100 per cent success. They were less sure, however, of the experimental design. The theory looked good, but it had not been tried before, so without further information they assessed the chances of the design being successful at 60 per cent.

Discussion then turned to considering the advisability of building a pilot rig to test the new design. They had built similar rigs before, and knew that they were extremely reliable in indicating whether a design was feasible or not. Tests of this sort were generally regarded in the industry as being about 95 per cent reliable in indicating actual performance. If they decided to build the test rig, they would still have plenty of time to decide between design 1 and design 2.

## Questions

Draw a decision tree for deFrey's problem, where the first decision involves whether or not to build the test rig. Examine the following questions:

1. At a cost of $80 000, is it worthwhile building the pilot rig?
2. At what cost would the decision makers be indifferent between building or not building a test rig?
3. If the reliability of the test rig information were perfect, how much would the information be worth?

# Bibliography

## Probability

There are many excellent books which treat statistical probability. Practically any of these would be useful further reading. For example:

Berenson, M. and Levine, D., *Basic Business Statistics: Concepts and application*, Prentice Hall, 1979.

## Decision Matrices and Trees

Baird, B.F., *Managerial Decisions Under Uncertainty*, Wiley, 1989. A good thorough treatment.
Bell, D.E., Raiffa, H. and Teversky, A., *Decision Making*, Cambridge University Press, 1988. An academic but comprehensive treatment.
Cooper, D. and Chapman, C., *Risk Analysis for Large Projects*, Wiley, 1987. A view of uncertainty from the project management perspective.
Holloway, C.A., *Decision Making Under Uncertainty: Models and choices.* Prentice Hall, 1979.
Moore, P.G. and Thomas, H., *The Anatomy of Decisions*, Penguin, 1976. A very readable treatment of decision tree analysis, largely through examples.

# References

1. Bayes law has had a somewhat controversial history, since the end result clearly depends on the prior probabilities assigned. However, although the law can lead to spurious accuracy (like most manipulation of subjective probabilities), it does provide us with a useful logical structure in making probability revisions as we learn more about a decision.
2. *The Economist*, 22 July 1989, p. 75.
3. Strictly speaking, the market research costs should not be deducted from the final pay-offs, because when the secondary decision is taken, this cost has already been incurred. The method we have used, however, makes the point clearer.

# 7 Modelling preference

It has been assumed that the final result of a decision will be a single, unambiguous and clear indication of the worth of the decision to the manager. Under such circumstances the evaluation of the consequence of a decision would be a straightforward matter. Unfortunately, this conceptually neat idea of decision modelling is upset by two important questions:

- Can it be assumed that, even when a single measure is used to represent the outcome of a decision, our preference for any outcome is linearly related to the measure? Put another way, is an extra pound always worth the same to us, even when it represents the difference between assets of nothing and £1 or £1000 and £1001?
- Suppose the outcome of a decision can only be adequately represented by a whole bunch of measures, some quantifiable (cost, profit, etc.) some not (image, flexibility, etc.); how do we combine and compare several bunches of measures with each other?

The implications of these two questions are explored in the rest of this chapter.

## Modelling Single Attribute Preference

### The Utility of Money

Some of the decision tree examples in Chapter 6 used the idea of the outcome balance. This simple device described in diagrammatic form how the total spread of outcomes and their respective probabilities of occurring related to the expected value of a decision. The implication in describing the consequences of decisions in this way is that two alternatives, even though they have the same expected outcome, may not be viewed as having the same worth in the eyes of the manager making the decision. This means that *the worth of a monetary outcome is not necessarily linearly related to its numerical value*; or, to put it another way, one pound lost on a deal is not merely the negative equivalent of one pound gained. Figure 7.1 illustrates this effect.

The device of using an individual's view of risky alternatives is a powerful way of determining the worth, preference or utility[1] of amounts of money. However, the underlying concept of utility need not be relevant only when risky or uncertain decisions are being taken.[2] The concept of the utility of an outcome being different from its quantitative measure is an intuitively obvious one. The utility of a meal to a person close to starvation is more than the utility of the same meal when the same person has been well fed and restored to full vigour. Likewise, a pound has clearly a greater utility when it marks the borderline between bankruptcy

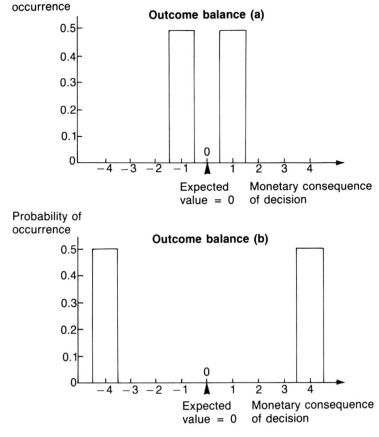

**Figure 7.1** Two outcome balance diagrams with identical expected values. If outcome balance (a) really does represent an expected value of zero to the manager, then if outcome balance (b) is not viewed as being exactly equivalent to outcome balance (a), the worth of −4 to the manager cannot be the same magnitude as the worth of 4: 0.5 × (worth of −4) + 0.5 × (worth of 4) ≠ 0

and survival, than when it merely adds another pound to already high profits. Thus, in trying to determine how much more we prefer one outcome to another, we cannot necessarily rely totally on the monetary consequence of that outcome.

Here, then, is a dilemma: since money is not necessarily a straightforward measure of preference, should managers use a utility measure which reflects more accurately the relative worth of outcomes or, alternatively, should they stick to measuring outcomes in straight money terms and leave any adjustments to the judgemental process which follows the analysis of the decision? Those who argue for using money, in spite of its limitations, generally do so on the grounds that most managers do in fact understand the value of money very well and are fully capable of using an *implicit* utility scale when they evaluate decision options. The arguments in favour of an *explicit* statement of utility tend to be similar to those for the use of explicit models in general — that only by describing our preference scale as accurately as we can are we able to discipline and structure our decision making and communicate how we have done so to others.

## Drawing the Utility Function

A utility function relates possible decision outcomes to a scale which reflects the decision maker's relative preferences. Two points which often cause confusion should be made clear at this stage:

- The utility scale itself is quite arbitrary. Some scales, however, are more widely used than others.

- The function is the decision maker's preference alone — it is entirely subjective. No 'correct' utility function for a particular circumstance is implied.

As an example, suppose the manager of a large research and development organization is putting together his yearly budget. The mix of projects awaiting investigation this year is complex and interdependent. By scheduling the starting dates and staffing assignments to the various projects in different ways, the manager can vary R & D expenditure in the coming year between £500 000 and £300 000. The organization does not operate a strict budget system, but each manager is expected to forecast his total expenditure with reasonable accuracy. Now, although there are many other criteria by which the manager's decision will be judged, he is anxious to understand his own view of the relative merits in any financial budgetary outcome between £300 000 and £500 000. He decides to draw a utility function.

The first thing he needs is a scale. Although any scale could be used, it is conventional to use one which ranges from zero to either one or a hundred. If he decides to use a 0–1 scale, his next step is to assign his least preferred outcome a utility of 0 and his most preferred outcome a utility of 1. Thus £500 000 has 0 utility and £300 000 has a utility of 1. These are the first two points on his utility function.

The manager now uses a particularly useful device known as the basic reference lottery to explore his relative preference between these two points. The basic reference lottery is a lottery in which probabilities are assigned to the best and worst possible outcomes for the decision in question, in this case £300 000 and £500 000.

So 0.5 chance of £300 000 and 0.5 chance of £500 000 is a 0.5 lottery
    0.1 chance of £300 000 and 0.9 chance of £500 000 is a 0.1 lottery
    0.9 chance of £300 000 and 0.1 chance of £500 000 is a 0.9 lottery

and so on.

The next step is for the manager to judge the certainty equivalents of the standard reference lotteries. For example, the manager considers the 0.5 lottery and asks:

> Which would I prefer: (a) a lottery on the basis of a fifty-fifty chance of either the £300 000 or the £500 000 outcome (the 0.5 lottery), or (b) the certainty of £X?

When $X$ is close to £500 000, the manager will tend to prefer the lottery since the certainty outcome is close to the worst that could happen anyway. On the other hand, when $X$ is close to £300 000, the certainty pay-off is likely to be preferred, since the possible gain on the lottery will not be much more than what is being offered for certain. Yet, he is running the risk of being considerably worse off. There will be some value of $X$ where the manager will find it very difficult to decide which is preferred. At this point the manager is said to be indifferent between the lottery and the certainty pay-off. This point is the certainty equivalent of a 0.5 lottery.

Suppose the R & D manager prefers the certainty pay-off when it is less than £450 000, but prefers the lottery above this value. At £450 000, however, he is indifferent between the two. Then:

$$0.5 \times (\text{Utility of £300 000}) + 0.5 \times (\text{Utility of £500 000})$$
$$= \text{Utility of £450 000}$$

That is:

$$0.5 \times (1) + 0.5 \times (0) = \text{Utility of £450 000}$$

Therefore:

$$\text{Utility of £450 000} = 0.5$$

We now have another point to put on the graph of the manager's utility function, as in Figure 7.2. The first thing this tells us is that in this case money and utility are clearly not linearly related. If they were, it would be £400 000 rather than £450 000 which would have a utility of 0.5. The difference between £450 000 and £400 000 is a measure of the 'price' the manager is willing to pay to avoid the risk inherent in the 0.5 lottery.

The manager can now go on to consider another basic reference lottery. For example, the 0.25 lottery. The question is now:

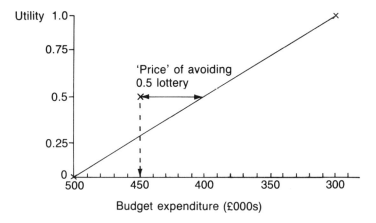

**Figure 7.2** The first three points on the R & D manager's utility function

At what monetary level would I be indifferent between (a) a certainty of that monetary outcome, or (b) a lottery of £300 000 at 0.25 probability and £500 000 at 0.75 probability?

Suppose that after consideration the manager decides that if the certainty pay-off were below £440 000 the lottery is preferred, and above this the certainty is preferred, then the certainty equivalent of a 0.25 lottery is £440 000.

$$0.25 \times (\text{Utility of £300 000}) + 0.75 \times (\text{Utility of £500 000})$$
$$= \text{Utility of £440 000}$$
$$0.25 \times (1) + 0.75 \times (0) = \text{Utility of £440 000}$$
$$\text{Utility of £440 000} = 0.25$$

If the manager finds it difficult to examine preference using a 0.25 lottery but (as is usually the case) finds the fifty-fifty chance of the 0.5 lottery easier to use, then by changing the pay-off considered, a 0.5 lottery can be achieved. We can change the question to:

At what value am I indifferent between (a) a certainty of that value and (b) a fifty-fifty (0.5) lottery between £450 000 (utility of 0.5) and £500 000 (utility of 0)?

If the manager is consistent, the answer to this question should be £440 000. Then:

$$0.5 \times (\text{Utility of £450 000}) + 0.5 \times (\text{Utility of £500 000})$$
$$= \text{Utility of £440 000}$$
$$0.5 \times (0.5) + 0.5 \times (0) = \text{Utility of £440 000}$$
$$\text{Utility of £440 000} = 0.25$$

Similarly, suppose for a 0.5 lottery between £300 000 and £450 000 the certainty equivalent is £420 000. Then:

$$0.5 \times (\text{Utility of £300 000}) + 0.5 \times (\text{Utility of £450 000})$$
$$= \text{Utility of £420 000}$$

$$0.5 \times (1) + 0.5 \times (0.5) = \text{Utility of £420 000}$$
$$\text{Utility of £420 000} = 0.75$$

We now have five points to plot on the manager's utility function, for utilities of 0, 0.25, 0.5, 0.75 and 1.0. These five points are plotted in Figure 7.3, and a provisional curve drawn through them (more points are really needed before any final curve could be drawn). A number of issues emerge from an examination of this curve:

1. Utility is not the same as monetary expectation. We would have seen all the points lie on the straight line *AB* if the manager was merely 'playing the odds' and calculating expected values. This does not mean that a manager's utility curve cannot ever be the straight line, representing the linear monetary equivalent. There could be circumstances where, between the best and worst outcomes in a decision, every pound has the same worth to the decision maker.

2. The slope of the curve changes. This implies that the manager has differing sensitivities to small changes in outcome as the outcome value changes. For example, in the range between £470 000 and £420 000 the manager's utility changes considerably. In fact, in that £50 000 range the manager's utility changes more than in the remaining £150 000 range of possible outcomes. Why is this? We do not know, of course, unless we question the manager further. It could be that the R & D budget has been nominally set at £450 000, or some near value which the manager is anxious not to exceed.

3. There is relatively little change in the manager's utility if his budget increases from £300 000 to £420 000. This does not necessarily mean that he is not worried by such an increase. All the utility curve is saying is that the increase

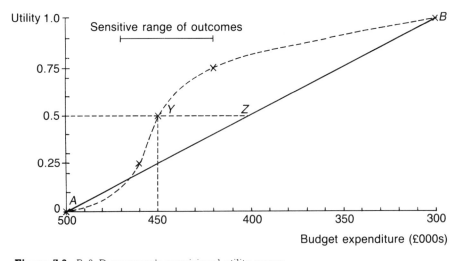

**Figure 7.3** R & D manager's provisional utility curve

is, relatively, not as important as a budget increase between £420 000 and £460 000.

4. The utility curve is concave at the worst outcome end, and convex at the best outcome end. This is because the manager is being 'risk averse' over one range of values and 'risk seeking' over the other. These two terms are fully explained in the next section.

## Some Utility Functions

The budget expenditure figure desired by the company in the previous example seemed to influence the manager's utility function, and probably would have a similar effect on any manager in the same position. The interpretation of that effect into a particular utility function, however, is something only the interaction of the manager, the decision itself and the manager's perception of the decision, can determine.

In the way we are using the term, utility functions are unique to a particular decision maker in a particular set of circumstances. Yet some forms do commonly occur. Figure 7.4 shows three of these, the risk-neutral, the risk-averse and the risk-seeking curves. It is the slope of these curves for various values of decision outcome which indicate the type of behaviour they represent.

The *risk-neutral* curve has a constant slope. This indicates that the decision maker gets equal pleasure from a unit increase in outcome or equal displeasure from a unit decrease in outcome no matter what level of outcome is being considered.

The *risk-averse* curve has a greater slope at bad outcome levels than at good outcome levels. This indicates that the decision maker is relatively happier to be getting away from a bad outcome than he is unhappy at foregoing a good one.

The *risk-seeking* curve has a greater slope at the good outcome end of the scale than it has at the bad outcome end. This indicates that the decision maker is getting relatively more pleasure at the possibility of achieving a good outcome than he is displeasured at the possibility of suffering a bad outcome.

## Expected Utility Versus Expected Monetary Value

The shape of a decision maker's utility function can totally change a decision. This is best illustrated with an example using a decision tree.

### Example: Vitlers Plating

Charles Doman had recently taken over the well-established but rather old-fashioned company of Vitlers Plating from his father. The company had been mainly concerned with silver plating cutlery and decorative tableware, and chrome plating industrial parts, on a subcontract basis. When Charles took over the company,

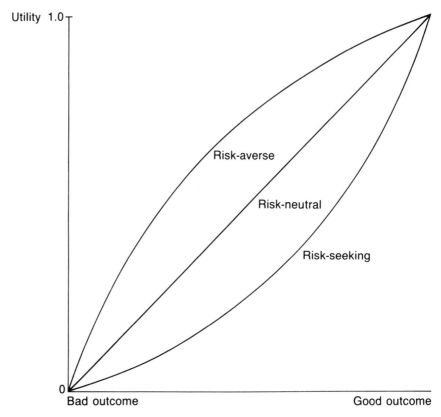

**Figure 7.4**  Risk-neutral, risk-averse and risk-seeking utility curves

he forecast (correctly) that both these markets were declining. After consideration, he decided to re-equip the whole plant and move into an expanding market which would provide a higher margin. His programme of re-equipment included closing and partially stripping his old automatic silver-plating line and buying a newer, technically more advanced, gold-plating line to get into the lucrative gold bathroom fittings market. The company's bank manager had been most helpful in providing loans for the company's capital investment programme.

Unfortunately, twelve months into the programme, the whole economy had turned down and business had become very tight indeed. The new gold-plating line had hardly been used, and even when it was working, it was giving trouble. Charles was most disillusioned:

> It's a technical problem more than anything else. The line just won't operate at the rate we had hoped. If we run the line at half the speed it is OK, but those rates of working just aren't economic. At full speed the line often requires considerable maintenance and is sometimes down for several days. Since we bought the line, business has been so bad that we haven't been under pressure, but this new order changes things.

The new order to which Charles referred was a short lead time export order for the gold plating of a large consignment of bathroom fittings. The fittings were to be delivered to Vitlers in two weeks' time, and the finished goods were due for shipment two weeks after that. At full speed the new line could cope with the order, but if the line went down for more than two days the delivery would be late, and penalties would be extracted from the company by the customer.

One way of ensuring delivery on time was available. That was to resurrect the old plating line, to take over if the new line went down. However, to make the old line operational again would be expensive. The dilemma was summed up by Charles:

> The major decision is whether to get the old line operational before the consignment arrives. If we do, delivery can be guaranteed on time, even though its operating costs are higher than the new line. If we don't activate the old line, and the line stops, we could still subcontract if we arranged it as soon as the line goes down; otherwise we could take the chance that the line would be repaired in under two days.

Charles' engineer advised him that he thought that he had the new line under better control than in the past, but that the chance of it going down during the two weeks would be about 20 per cent. Should the line go down, he reckoned on a 50 per cent chance of repairing it within two days. At this stage the decision tree looked as shown in Figure 7.5. The tree shows the profits which Charles was able to put on the six possible outcomes of the decisions.

Activating the old line straight away could result in profits of either £14 000 should the new line stop, or £16 000 if the new line was OK. If Charles did nothing,

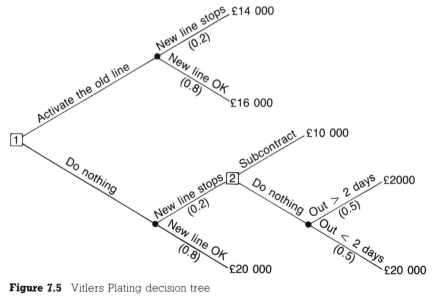

**Figure 7.5** Vitlers Plating decision tree

and the new line proved OK, then he would get the maximum possible profit of £20 000. If the new line stopped, he could either subcontract immediately, in which case his profit would be reduced to £10 000, or take a chance and do nothing. If he did nothing, and the line was down for more than two days, the penalty clauses would mean that his final profit was unlikely to be more than £2000. If, however, he was lucky, and the line was repaired in less than two days, his final profit would be the full £20 000.

*Analysis Using Monetary Values*

At decision point 1 — activate the old line:
    Expected monetary value = 0.2 × £14 000 + 0.8 × £16 000 = £15 6000
At decision point 2 — subcontract:
    Monetary value = £10 000
At decision point 2 — do nothing:
    Expected monetary value = 0.5 × £2000 + 0.5 × £20 000 = £11 000

Therefore at decision point 2 Charles should do nothing.

At decision point 1 — do nothing:
    Expected monetary value = 0.2 × £11 000 + 0.8 × £20 000 = £18 200

Therefore Charles should do nothing (expected outcome £18 200), and not activate the old line (expected outcome £15 600).

*Analysis Using Utility Values*

After posing himself lottery decisions of the type previously described, Charles was able to draw his utility curve for the range of possible outcomes in his decision. Possibly because of his bank manager's recent coolness when loan repayments got delayed, he shows a marked relative dislike of the £2000 outcome. This gives the curve the pronounced risk-averse shape illustrated in Figure 7.6.
    Using utility values in the place of monetary values gives the following analysis:

At decision point 1 — activate old line:
    Expected utility = 0.2 × 0.9 + 0.8 × 0.96 = 0.95
At decision point 2 — subcontract:
    Utility = 0.65
At decision point 2 — do nothing:
    Expected utility = 0.5 × 0 + 0.5 × 1 = 0.5

Therefore at decision point 2 Charles should subcontract.

At decision point 1 — do nothing:
    Expected utility = 0.2 × 0.65 + 0.8 × 1 = 0.93

Therefore Charles should activate the old line (expected utility 0.95), not do nothing (expected utility 0.93).

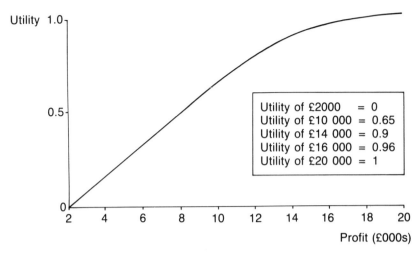

**Figure 7.6** Utility curve for Charles Doman's decision

Thus, by substituting utility values for monetary values, we have changed Charles' decision at both decision points.

## Modelling Multi-attribute Preference[3]

One of the things which has characterized our discussions up to this point is that each alternative decision had consequences which could be described fairly clearly in terms of one attribute. All outcomes have been expressed in monetary terms. Yet this is a simplification of many management, and even domestic, decisions. For example, when choosing a house we do not consider only the purchase price. While money may be the attribute of a house which most constrains our choice, other factors such as the number of bedrooms, the size of the garden, the desirability of the neighbourhood, the distance from work and the proximity of shops will exercise an important influence on our choice. The theory which treats modelling decisions such as this is called *multi-criteria* decision theory.

The problem of modelling multi-criteria preference may be summed up in the following manner. How can a manager be helped to determine his or her own preferences between many different options, when each option has an outcome which is characterized by several heterogeneous factors? This problem can be treated by two methods:

- Those which attempt to establish an overall preference scale, incorporating all the attributes into one composite measure.

- Separate preference methods, which treat each attribute separately, but use preference scales to exclude or eliminate certain options.

## The Three Modelling Conditions

Whichever of the two approaches, overall preference or separate preference, is chosen, will depend largely upon the characteristics of the multi-criteria decision that is being modelled.[4] The three most important characteristics of the decision are as follows:

1. Whether meaningful quantitative measures of progress towards the achievement of each decision objective can be established.

2. Whether the measures established for the objective can be expressed in terms of the same unit.

3. Whether relative priorities for achievement of the objectives can be expressed, either in terms of numeric weighting factors or in terms of ranked preferences.

If these characteristics are regarded as conditions, then in order to apply any of the methods which adopt an overall preference approach, all three conditions generally must be met. There would be little point in trying to establish a composite measure of preference if we could not directly quantify each attribute in which we were interested, or if those attributes were measured in quite different units, or if we were unable to decide which of the attributes is the most important.

Separate preference methods, on the other hand, need only some indication of the relative importance of each criterion.

## Overall Preference Methods

### Multi-Attribute Utility

Just as utility theory determined the relationship between utility and some single attribute of a decision (in all the previous examples, money) multi-attribute utility does the same for several attributes. However, now one further condition must be met. This is the condition of *preferential independence*. Preferential independence means that the relative preferences of attributes are not altered by changes in other attributes. For example, suppose we are trying to choose between two makes of truck. Model A has a carrying capacity of 30 tons and a total length of 25 feet. Model B has a carrying capacity of 32 tons and a total length of 21 feet. Both models cost £40 000. If model A is preferred to model B at this particular price, then the condition of preferential independence will be satisfied if model A is still preferred to model B *at any other price*. In other words, our preference based on the two attributes (carrying capacity and length) is independent of changes in the other attribute (purchase price), which is the same for both options.

This example can be extended to show how utilities can be combined into an overall measure. Suppose the manager making the decision is primarily interested in two factors: the purchase price of the truck, and its fuel consumption. After consideration, the manager draws utility curves for them both. These curves are

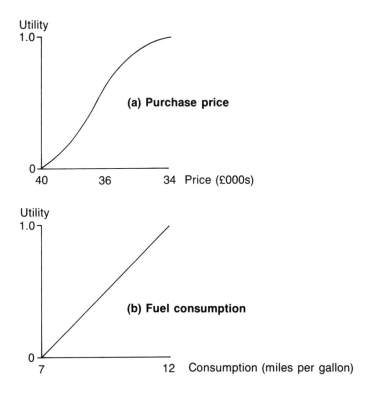

**Figure 7.7** Utility curves for the two attributes: price and fuel consumption

shown in Figure 7.7. We can see that, whereas the utility curve for fuel consumption is linearly related to the consumption, measured in miles per gallon, the utility curve for the purchase price of the vehicle shows that there is a distinct preference for a vehicle costing less than £36 000. One way of combining these utilities would be by straight addition:

Combined utility $= U(P) + U(F)$

where $U(P)$ is the utility of purchase price and $U(F)$ is the utility of fuel consumption. This simple addition assumes that both criteria are of equal importance. If this is not so (and there is no reason to suppose that it should be), then a combined utility measure using the weighted sum of the individual utilities could be used:

Combined utility $= W_1 \times U(P) + W_2 \times U(F)$

where $W_1$ is the weighting factor applied to the purchase price criterion and $W_2$ is the weighting factor applied to the fuel consumption criterion.

Combining these two utility functions would give us a utility surface as shown

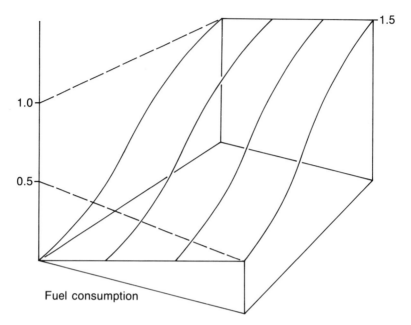

**Figure 7.8**  Combined utility for purchase and fuel consumption

in Figure 7.8. In this combined utility diagram we have assumed that fuel consumption is half as important as purchase price. The relative importance weightings of each attribute's utility function can be obtained by using indifference lotteries. Thus the weight of attribute $A$ is obtained by an indifference decision between, on the one hand, $A$ at its most preferred level and all other attributes at their least preferred level and, on the other hand, a lottery of either all attributes at their most preferred level with the probability $p$, or all attributes at their least preferred level with a probability of $(1-p)$. The value of $p$ is found for which the person is indifferent between the lottery and the certain outcome; $p$ is then the weight assigned to attribute $A$.

Note that we have made assumptions regarding all three multi-attribute modelling conditions. The manager's preference for different purchase price levels and fuel consumption figures have been quantified, these preferences have been made in the same units (utility units) and we have been able to assign weights denoting the relative importance of the two attributes. In addition, the manager has assumed preferential independence which allows us to obtain a combined measure of utility by a weighted sum of the individual utilities.

Of course, we can extend our simple example to include as many attributes as we need to describe each option satisfactorily. It does, however, get more difficult to derive weights for each attribute which genuinely reflect their importance as the number of attributes becomes large.

*Weighted Scoring*

Closely related to multi-attribute utility are the techniques of weighted scoring. Whereas in multi-attribute utility theory we are attempting to establish the ground rules which govern our preferences between various options, in weighted scoring we are directly comparing specific alternative options.

The procedure involves, first of all, identifying the attributes which will be used to evaluate the various options; secondly, establishing the relative importance of the criteria governing the attributes and giving weighting factors to them; thirdly, sorting each option on each criterion — the scale of the score is arbitrary, as it is in utility analysis. Here we shall use 0−100, where 0 represents the worst possible score and 100 the best.

Extending the example used to illustrate multi-attribute utility, suppose that the manager is interested not only in the purchase price of the trucks and their fuel consumption, but also in the carrying capacity of the trucks (in terms of both the weight they can carry and also their maximum volumes). In addition, the reported reliability of each model, and the likely repair and servicing costs, are to be considered. Three models of truck, X, Y and Z are being compared. After consultation with the drivers and a thorough reading of the sales literature and available consumer reports, the manager draws up a weighted score table as shown in Figure 7.9. It is important to remember that the scores shown in Figure 7.9 are those which the manager has given as an indication of how each model meets the *manager's needs* specifically. As with multi-attribute utility, nothing is necessarily being implied regarding any intrinsic worth of the options. Likewise, the weighted scores are an indication of how important the manager finds each criterion in the decision circumstance in which he finds himself.

Figure 7.9 indicates that model Z has the highest overall score and therefore would be the preferred choice. It is interesting to note that, in fact, model Z has

| Attributes | Importance weighting | Scores | | |
|---|---|---|---|---|
| | | Models | | |
| | | X | Y | Z |
| Purchase price | 4 | 80 | 65 | 60 |
| Fuel consumption | 2 | 20 | 50 | 80 |
| Capacity — weight | 1 | 80 | 60 | 40 |
| Capacity — volume | 1 | 50 | 60 | 40 |
| Reliability | 1 | 20 | 60 | 70 |
| Servicing costs | 1 | 75 | 40 | 55 |
| Total scores | | 585 | 580 | 605* |

*Preferred option.

**Figure 7.9**  Weighted score method for truck purchase example

the lowest score on what is, by the manager's own choice, the most important criteria — purchase price. The high scores which model Z achieves in other criteria, however, outweigh this deficiency. If, on examination of this table, a manager cannot accept what appears to be an inconsistency, then either the weights which have been given to each criterion or the scores that have been allocated do not truly reflect the manager's preference.

*Vector Methods*

If a multiple-attribute decision has *m* attributes, and each attribute is represented by a dimension in *m*-dimensional space, then all options to be considered can be described by a point in this *m*-dimensional space. The overall merit of an option could then be taken as being the weighted distance from some particular point. So, for example, if three attributes are considered, two options could be placed as in Figure 7.10. The overall merit values for the two options would then be the vectors **OX** and **OY**.

More generally, for *M* attributes:

$$\text{Overall merit value for option} = \left[ \sum_{j=1}^{M} (w_j a_j)^2 \right]^{\frac{1}{2}}$$

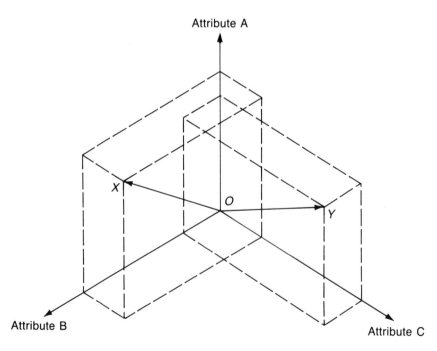

**Figure 7.10** Vectors **OX** and **OY**, describing two options X and Y which are scored on three attributes A, B and C

where $w_j$ is the importance weighting of attribute j and $a_j$ is the score for attribute j.

In this case, the vector length has been measured from the origin of the m-dimensional space. This point can be taken as representing the score for the worst possible option imaginable, and for this reason the method is sometimes called the *furthest from the worst* rule. In a similar way, a vector connecting the option point with the point representing the best possible option can be used. So, if each attribute is being scored on a 0−100 scale, this *furthest from perfection* overall merit value would be:

$$\text{Overall merit value for option} = \left[ \sum_{j=1}^{M} w^2 (100 - a_j)^2 \right]^{\frac{1}{2}}$$

### Ideal Profile Method

In the vector methods we always used the same point to calculate the distance along a particular attribute axis, but there is no reason why we should not use different points for each attribute. If we choose target scores for each attribute, which when put together represent the profile of the ideal option, then we can derive an overall merit value which is the weighted sum of the distances of each attribute from the ideal score. This overall merit value would then be:

$$\text{Overall merit value for option} = \left[ \sum_{j=1}^{M} w_j^2 (a_j - t_j)^2 \right]^{\frac{1}{2}}$$

where $t_j$ = the target score for attribute j.

If we simply want to maximize the score on all the attribute scales, $t_j$ would always be 100, and the overall merit value would be equivalent to the distance from the best rule.

## Modelling Separate Preference

The general requirement of overall preference methods for the quantification of attributes, and the expression of them in homogeneous units, is in fact quite restrictive. Even though, in the last example, we were dealing in different kinds of unit (pounds, square feet and a 'goodness' score), we still had to convert our descriptive verbal judgement of good, fair, mediocre, etc. into a numerical value. As soon as we abandon any attempt to achieve an overall measure of merit, this restriction no longer applies.

### Simple Elimination

Using simple elimination procedures, we set minimum acceptable standards for each attribute and then eliminate any option that does not meet the standard, starting with the most important criterion, going on to the next important and so on.

For example, suppose a company is evaluating four possible products for further development, but can only choose one. It has decided to rate each product against five criteria: the total cost of developing the product to a production stage, the likely gross margin which the company could command per unit, the likely sales potential per year for the product, the degree of marketing fit with the company's other products and the technical similarity to the company's existing products. These last two criteria reflect the company's desire to avoid either product proliferation with many dissimilar products on its catalogue or, alternatively, stretching its production capacity in too many directions at once. The four products have been rated as shown in Figure 7.11.

The manager who is faced with making the decision then considers the minimum requirements which need to be met for each criterion:

Development cost — not more than £250 000 (the maximum that the company could borrow at the moment).

Likely gross margin per unit — at least £2000 (longstanding company policy to operate only in high-margin products).

Sales potential per year — at least 100 units per year (the manufacturing managers always argue strongly for this, as a minimum annual production quantity).

Degree of fit with marketing strategy — to be rated at least fair (marketing manager's insistence!).

Technical similarity to other products — to be rated at least fair (manufacturing manager's insistence!).

These criteria have been listed in order of importance. Note that in this method no explicit importance weighting is necessary, only a simple ranking. Figure 7.12 shows how the four products rate against the criteria.

Let us take the criteria in Figure 7.12 in order. All four products pass the first test of having a development cost of less than £250 000. Product C fails the second test and is therefore eliminated. Product B fails the third test and is likewise eliminated. The two remaining products, A and D, both pass the fourth test, but D fails on the fifth test, leaving product A as the only surviving option.

If two or more alternatives survive the test. Easton[5] suggests that the standards can be raised progressively in small increments until only one alternative survives.

| Attributes | Alternative products | | | |
|---|---|---|---|---|
| | A | B | C | D |
| Development cost (£000s) | 200 | 250 | 175 | 220 |
| Gross margin/unit (£) | 2000 | 3000 | 1500 | 2500 |
| Sales potential (units/year) | 100 | 70 | 150 | 100 |
| Degree of fit with market strategy | Good | Poor | Good | Fair |
| Degree of technical fit with other products | Good | Excellent | Poor | Bad |

**Figure 7.11** Attributes of the four possible products for further development

| Criteria in ranked order of preference | Alternative products | | | |
| --- | --- | --- | --- | --- |
| | A | B | C | D |
| Development costs < £250 000 | Yes | Yes | Yes | Yes |
| Gross margin ≥ £2000 | Yes | Yes | No | Yes |
| Annual sales ≥ 100/year | Yes | No | Yes | Yes |
| Marketing fit ≥ fair | Yes | No | Yes | Yes |
| Technical fit ≥ fair | Yes | Yes | No | No |

**Figure 7.12** Criteria for simple elimination

Furthermore, recognition should be given to the relative importance of the criteria. Standards for the more important criteria should be raised more rapidly than for the less important criteria.

### Complex Elimination Method

Using criteria as we did in the previous example is somewhat simplistic. It did not convey the subtleties of many decision situations. For example, when questioned about total development costs, the manager might say that under no circumstances would he be prepared to sanction a product which required more than £250 000 development. Furthermore, he would only sanction a product requiring more than £200 000 development provided other conditions were met, such as 'the gross return for the first year must be at least as much as the development cost' (note that gross return is considerably more important for this company than net return on investment). To express the criteria another way, the development cost must be less than or equal to the product of the likely gross margin per unit and the sales potential per year.

Similarly, when questioned further, the manager might admit that a poor classification in one of the last two criteria would be accepted *if* the gross return in the first was greater than the development cost *and* it was accompanied by at least a good grading in the other 'degree of fit' criteria. Figure 7.13 shows the new criteria applied to the same four products. While products B and D are eliminated as before, product C survives this set of tests with product A. This is because, using these more complex criteria, the product's good points have been allowed to outweigh its drawbacks. Although these methods are clearly normative, they are probably a far more realistic description of preferred managerial behaviour than using the simple criteria alone.

## Practical Prescriptions

It is important to form some view on your own preference scale if:

(a) the value of each extra pound or dollar is not constant, or

| Criteria | Alternative products | | | |
|---|---|---|---|---|
| | **A** | **B** | **C** | **D** |
| Development costs not more than £250 000 | Yes | Yes | Yes | Yes |
| Development costs not more than £200 000 unless gross return > development costs | Yes | No | Yes | Yes |
| Degree of fit with product strategy at least *fair* unless gross return > development costs *and* technical fit *good* or better | Yes | No | Yes | Yes |
| Degree of technical fit at least *fair* unless gross return > development costs *and* product strategy fit *good* or better | Yes | Yes | Yes | No |

**Figure 7.13** Elimination with complex criteria

(b) outcomes from the decision can not be adequately represented by a single measure, such as cost.

Draw a utility curve for the range of possible outcomes for the decision using the lottery method if desired. If the utility of outcomes is very different from the simple linear value of outcomes, consider using a utility score to evaluate them.

If the outcomes of a decision can only be described by using several different attributes (for example, cost, reliability, flexibility, delivery time, etc.), then some method must be found taking all the attributes into consideration.

If all the attributes which are used to describe the outcome can:

(a) be quantified,
(b) be expressed in the same unit (money on a 'score' for example) and
(c) be ranked as to their relative importance to the decision,

then it is best to include all attributes in one composite score. If only the last condition applies then use one of the 'separate preference' methods.

# Case Exercise

## Jarlson Office Equipment Limited

Jarlson was a national company which had long been established as a supplier of office equipment. Office furniture, typewriters and copying equipment had been the major part of its trade for many years. More recently, it had also entered the word-processing business. It was through its involvement with word processors that the company was presented with the opportunity to become sole suppliers for an imported make of small business computer. The price and performance of the computer was such that Jarlson was confident of it selling well. However, in order to get the sole agency, guarantees had to be given to the computer manufacturer that it would set up a nationwide service network. This network would repair and maintain the machines which were supplied to customers.

While the deal for supplying the computers was a very good one, the service obligation could cut deeply into the potential profits. One way to offset costs would be to open up the network as a general microcomputer service and repair facility. The company would then offer a repair service for any make of microcomputer.

When the decision to set up a general service organization was taken by the top management of the company, the personnel manager was given the job of recruiting for the new organisation. Three levels of job were envisaged:

1.  A general manager who would be in charge of the whole organization.

2.  Five area managers, each of whom would be based at one of the company's existing regional headquarters.

3.  An initially small number (twenty or thirty) of service technicians who would visit customers and perform repairs. The number of service technicians would grow as the business expanded.

The chief executive of Jarlson had described the requirements of the three jobs to the personnel manager in the following manner:

> The general manager of the service organization is going to have one of the most difficult jobs in the whole company. This deal is particularly important to the future of the company and the general manager can, in effect, make or break it. Not only will he have control over the whole affair but he will also have to fight for resources with the other parts of the company. He should know our business and know how his bit of it fits in. More than anyone else, this person will determine the future shape and overall policy of the organization. Furthermore, he will have to liaise quite closely with our main computer supplier and also tackle the delicate job of maintaining good relationships with the other computer manufacturers whose machines we service. He will have to lead the organization through a difficult and very uncertain time.
>
> The area managers are going to have to be efficient. They are going to have to organize their people so as to give the best possible service at the lowest possible cost to us. If they don't already understand computer technology, then they are going to have to learn it pretty fast. It will be these people who, in effect, determine priorities at an operational level, and so they will have a major influence over how our customers view us. They will also be responsible for generating new customers. They will have to motivate, lead and take a large part in training the local service technicians who will be working for them.
>
> The service technicians need to be good competent engineers. Ideally, they should have experience of repairing this type of equipment. However, it might be possible to recruit general electronic repair people and train them up, though this will take longer. As well as being competent engineers, they will need to be able to make on-the-spot decisions as to whether a machine should be repaired or sent back to base for overhaul. This involves making a spot judgement regarding the importance of the machine to the customer, and weighing this against the company's capability of repairing the machine at any particular point in time. As well as this, they will need to have a friendly and

courteous manner so as to give a good impression to the customer in what looks like being a particularly competitive business.

Back in the office, the personnel manager wondered how on earth she could find such paragons of virtue as the chief executive had described. All the posts would be advertised in the national press, but the personnel manager knew that there would be at least two internal applications for the general manager's job. How was she to weigh up the internal candidates' knowledge of the company against the likelihood that any external applicant would have experience of running a service and repair business in other fields?

There might also be internal applications for the area managers' jobs, but they would certainly have no working technical knowledge of microcomputers. External applications were likely to come from technicians seeking promotion to a managerial position, but they would have no management experience.

Good service technicians with a working knowledge of microcomputers were worth their weight in gold on the labour market. Probably the only way to attract these people would be to pay salaries which would distort existing scales. The alternative of training people up to the job would take longer and was more risky. Even before advertising the positions, the personnel manager would have to decide how she was going to make the decision when all the applications were finally in.

## Questions

1. What broad criteria do you think the company will have to use to select candidates for the three types of job?

2. What circumstances, both inside and outside the company, are likely to influence the relative weightings of these criteria?

3. Where are the major trade-offs between the criteria likely to occur for each job? Try and reflect these trade-offs for one of the jobs by phrasing complex decision criteria as in the 'complex preference' methods described in the text.

## Bibliography

Easton, Allen, *Complex Managerial Decisions Involving Multiple Objectives*, Wiley, 1973. A comprehensive review of the more basic multi-critia decision-making techniques, with many useful and interesting cases.

Fishburn, P.C., *Utility Theory for Decision Making*, Wiley, 1970. A very mathematical treatment of the basis of utility theory. Not to be tackled without a thorough mathematical knowledge.

Gregory, G., *Decision Analysis*, Pitman, 1988. A general decision modelling text, with useful ideas on multi-attribute modelling.

Keeney, R.L. and Raiffa, H. *Decisions with Multiple Objectives: Preferences and value trade-offs*, Wiley, 1976. Another somewhat mathematical treatment of the subject, with a bias towards public decision making.

# References

1. We use the term 'utility' to describe the 'worth' of any decision consequence to the decision maker.
2. Strictly speaking, the term 'utility' should only be used to describe preference under risk, 'value' or 'preference' being used when no risk is present. While this may be of theoretical interest, we shall use the terms interchangeably.
3. We assume that it is the multi-attribute nature of the decision which is pre-eminent. Uncertainty or risk, if present, is considered negligible.
4. Radford, K.J., *Modern Managerial Decision Making*, Reston, 1981.
5. Easton, A., *Complex Managerial Decisions Involving Multiple Objectives*, Wiley, 1973.

# PART IV

## Decision practice

In Parts II and III we presented management decisions as seen from the viewpoint of the behavioural scientist and the mathematical modeller. Part IV continues to draw on these sources, but also includes contributions from other areas, especially strategic planning and the various functional areas of management. Because of this, the 'flavour' of this part is more prescriptive. We do give advice on how to go about decision making, and the topics covered reflect this practical bent. In fact, the chapters approximate to the stage model of the decision process which was introduced in Part I.

CHAPTER 8 — GETTING OBJECTIVES STRAIGHT — deals with an area fundamental to effective decision making: the objectives or ends to which the decision is supposed to be contributing. The various aspects of decision objectives are described, and, more importantly, some characteristics of useful objectives are explored.

CHAPTER 9 — UNDERSTANDING THE PROBLEM — follows the notion of 'expanding' the problem from the 'objective' phase. The chapter provides the broader context and examines a number of approaches and techniques that can help to develop good 'thinking habits' for data collection, analysis and interpretation.

CHAPTER 10 — GENERATING THE OPTIONS — focuses on the development of creative thinking and behaviour, especially in the field of creating alternative possibilities. We look at how the essential quality of imaginative decision making can be integrated with the more obvious analytical skills. The chapter explains the factors which encourage or block creativity and presents a range of operational techniques which have been used to enhance the creative process.

CHAPTER 11 — EVALUATING THE OPTIONS — specifies the attributes of decision options which need to be explored prior to any final choice. We consider issues such as feasibility, acceptability and vulnerability.

CHAPTER 12 — MAKING A CHOICE — moves us on to the decision itself, the point at which we have a view on each of the options and can express preference between them. The various standards against which each option may be compared are described, and the distinction between each option's feasibility and its acceptability is taken further. The particular process of choice is presented as being a function of the extent of agreement in the decision body, with the key issues being the extent of consensus over objectives and over outcomes and consequences.

# 8 Getting objectives straight

## Introduction

Unless you know where you want to go, it is difficult to know if you have arrived. Unless the objectives of a decision are clear and well understood, managers cannot possibly judge how far the preferred option will go towards achieving their objectives. So, without an indication of the extent to which each option fulfils the objectives of the decision, the evaluation process cannot discriminate between options in any useful way. The lack of clear, unambiguous and preferably explicit objectives takes a great deal of value away from the rest of the decision-making process, for in order to understand decisions, we need to understand the direction in which the decision is supposed to be taking us.

### The Hierarchy of Objectives[1]

Stand back from any organization and it is evident that its objectives form a hierarchy determined by how strategic or operational the decision focus is.

#### Primary Objectives

At the most fundamental level, organizations have a set of *things they want to be*. These are their primary objectives. Surviving as an independent entity, being a major presence in the market, maintaining a reputation for integrity, improving the lot of the homeless — all these are primary objectives. They are broad, visionary, fundamental and overriding. They in effect form the decision environment for all the organization's decisions.

Primary objectives are not always made explicit but, especially for strategic decisions, they need to be addressed. Key questions are:

- 'Do we have an explicit statement of our primary objectives — a mission statement perhaps?'

- 'Is there broad agreement over the organization's primary objectives?' If there is no broad agreement within the organization over its fundamental purpose, then decision making is clearly a more difficult process. Not impossible though: overtly political institutions (local government, for example) cope with some degree of permanent disagreement and occasional sharp changes in their mission after elections.

### Strategic Objectives

Strategic objectives guide the organization's long-term direction towards the maintenance of primary objectives. Often primary objectives, by their nature, do not change. Strategic objectives do. As the business environment changes, strategies need to adapt to keep the organization on course. Strategic objectives could include, for example, developing innovative products, keeping a presence in a particular market, funding projects only from internally generated profits and so on.

### Operational Objectives

Operational objectives interpret an organization's strategic objectives into manageable terms for shorter-term decision making. Operational objectives could include such things as controlling costs tightly, giving good delivery, providing a wide range of services and so on.

Operational-level objectives should have been shaped by whatever strategic objectives the firm has adopted. There should, therefore, be a link between strategic objectives and detailed operational objectives. In fact, there must be different layers of such objectives, which will start broad and become more specific as they approach the operational level.

## Contribution and Competitiveness

The logic which binds together the different layers in the organization's hierarchy of objectives is the notion of 'contribution'. This means clarifying how the decision can 'contribute' to the next level up in the objectives hierarchy, by answering the 'So what?' question. For example, if the objectives relate to a civic theatre, we need to keep the artistic, political and local communities satisfied, *so what* does that mean for next season's programme of plays? We have put together this balanced programme of plays, *so what* does that mean for our recruitment of actors to form the company? And so on.

For profit-making organizations this process means ensuring that the notion of 'competitiveness' links the levels in the hierarchy. 'Contribution' means 'contribution to pursuing competitive advantage', so decision objectives should be described in terms of how the decision can contribute to competitiveness (Box 8.1). For example, we want to compete in a particular way, *so what* does that

---

*Box 8.1*

One large UK industrial group makes sure that the issue of competitiveness remains at the forefront of its decision making. Every company within the group is required to submit a 'Competitive Achievement Plan'. This plan is an explicit statement of how the company intends to improve its service to its customers, relative to that provided by its competitors.
This means making clear:

- An overall mission statement for the company.
- Its key strategic objectives.
- The broad business environment.
- The company's opportunities, threats, strengths and weaknesses.
- Customer and market profiles.
- Key factors for serving customers better.

And compared with major competitors:

- Current and future performance.

Further, in more detail:

- The plan to achieve competitive objectives.
- The resources required.
- The risks involved in any change.
- The milestones on the road to achieving competitive advantage.

None of this is original as such. The group's achievement is to build the process into the ongoing decision making of its companies.

---

imply for the way we allocate product groups to sites? We have a particular set of products which compete in such a way, *so what* does that imply for the way in which we set performance targets? We have a particular set of performance targets, *so what* does this mean for the way we run the operation?

## Linking Objectives[2]

Figure 8.1 illustrates the three major checks to ensure effective linking between the different levels of the objectives hierarchy.

### *Appropriateness*

If the aim is to connect different levels in the organization by competitiveness, then above all objectives must be appropriate to each other. In other words,

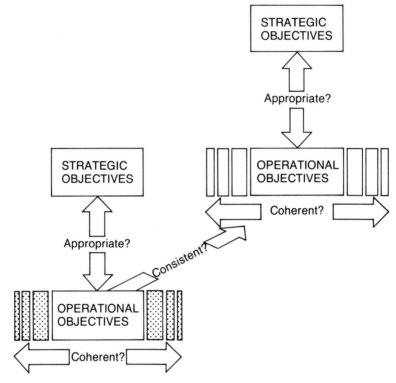

**Figure 8.1**  Objectives should be appropriate for higher objectives, coherent with each other and consistent over time

objectives should move decisions in the direction which on balance is the most likely to provide a performance which best supports the company's competitive strategy.

### Coherence

Linking all parts of an organization to the strategy is a necessary but not sufficient condition for effective decision making. The objectives of each part of the organization must be coherent — they must all point roughly in the same direction. Potential conflicts between the various areas need addressing directly.

### Consistency over Time

While no organization benefits from an overly rigid strategy, the lead time of some decision making means that consistency must be maintained over a reasonable time period. Failing to provide consistency confuses the organization. But, worse, it also leads to cynicism: 'Last year was the year of quality, this year it's keeping costs low, what will be in fashion next year?'

In addition to being useful, any objective must have organizational credibility. An objective which is not regarded as achievable by the organization will not be supported. Its subsequent failure will merely reinforce the perceived futility of the whole decision-making process. Objectives must be seen as feasible to be worth anything.

## Setting Decision Objectives

### Objectives Should be Clear

A sales manager is explaining to the sales force the need to improve their performance:

> Our marketing effort last year was a total write-off! We've dropped a long way behind the competition. If you don't get stuck in this year and get the business, there are going to be some changes around here!

The sales manager clearly has an objective in mind — the sales force must do better. But how much better, and by when — the end of the year, or earlier? The sales manager has a strategic objective here which has something to do with market share, and this provides a starting point for developing operational objectives. Here is another way the same problem might have been presented:

> Our market share has fallen by 10 per cent in the last trading year. We have set ourselves the objective of recovering this drop by the end of next March. OK, can we now get down to discussing ways of achieving this?

At least this way of stating the problem is clearer and sets out a time period (by next March). A clear statement of objectives like this will probably give the sales team a better chance of developing a successful solution to the problem than the exhortation to 'get the business or else!'.

Clarity also implies that a boundary should be drawn between those things which the decision must achieve and those which it need not. It is important at the beginning of the decision process to establish the areas which the decision is not supposed to address, otherwise the exact extent of what the decision *is* supposed to achieve remains uncertain.

Yet uncertainty is no stranger to management decision making, and in practice the boundary of what it is important to achieve will be fuzzy. So if the boundary of a decision's objectives is unclear, it is best to admit it and try to define the extent of the uncertainty (see Figure 8.2). Do this by drawing up three short lists: first, areas in which the decision should have an effect; second, areas which the decision will not be expected to influence; and third, areas which might become important. It is this third area which represents the uncertainty surrounding the

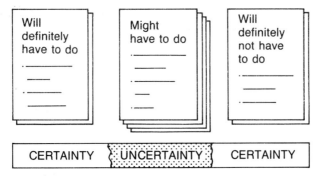

**Figure 8.2** Ideally, what objectives should the decision be addressing?

decision objectives, and which defines the flexibility that should be built into the decision process.

*Example*

A company which rolls aluminium foil for the packaging industry was deciding how to increase its capacity for cutting the wide rolls of foil which it makes, into the narrow rolls which its customers required. The decision involved choosing between several alternative slitting machines (as the technology is called). Objectives were set as (a) improving the finished quality of the product, (b) increasing capacity by at least 20 per cent and (c) doing this with the best return on investment. The company could also define things which the decision was not to achieve. For example, the machine need not be able to cut material above a particular gauge, and it need not be able to 'texture' the foil, which some could do. Other capabilities were less clear. For example, the ease of changing the cutting widths was not particularly important, but could become so if the product or customer base changed. The change-over capability of the alternative machines might become important and so needed to be included in evaluating the options; however, it was treated in a different way from the 'certain' objectives.

## Objectives Should be Agreed

One difficulty in attempting to identify an organization's objectives is determining exactly *who* is chosen to articulate those objectives. Is it the organization's managers who best reflect its goals; and, if so, which managers? Is it the company's board of directors (if it is they who represent the interests of a broader shareholding public)? In practice, there are quite likely to be differences between the objectives of different groups within an organization; or, at least, a different emphasis between groups of objectives.

One study[3] showed considerable differences in emphasis between the objectives of the founders or owners of firms, the managers of firms and the boards of directors. The objectives of the founder or owner were much more likely to be wide ranging, including profit, growth, producing a good product, and personal or company power. Managers, on the other hand, placed more emphasis on profits and less on other goals. Boards of directors were exclusively concerned with profit and company survival.

Practical experience bears this out, especially in setting strategic objectives. The picture of a cosy group of managers from different parts of the organization each contributing his or her piece of the overall picture towards the point where compromises can be struck and consensus reached is somewhat idealized. Sadly, the process is rarely so straightforward. Frequently encountered problems include the following:

1. Different (and conflicting) views of strategic objectives are held by senior managers, e.g. long-term growth in sales volume versus short-term profitability.

2. No formal strategic objectives exist in key functional areas. Some areas of the company may have objectives that are in a form which is not compatible with others: for example, marketing strategies may be framed in terms of 'prime customers', whereas operations have objectives based on technological capabilities.

3. No consensus exists on how the relative importance of overall strategic objectives is developing.

4. There is genuine uncertainty as to how the decision environment (for example, markets and competitors) may change and so change overall strategic objectives.

All these problems do not diminish the need for setting decision objectives, but they do affect the nature of the task. There is no simple process where a few rules translate a statement of competitive objectives into a precise set of operational decision objectives. Rather the process is one of exploration and compromise, often best pursued in a workshop setting and involving all concerned parties. In such a setting, data can be pooled, possible future scenarios debated and common ground defined. The end product, however, must be a ranked set of objectives for the decision.

## Objectives Should be Related

Decision objectives cannot exist in isolation. Reaching one objective is a means of contributing to a higher one. In other words, one person's means is another person's end. For example, the top decision maker in an organization might see one decision objective as increasing the dividend payment to the stockholders of the organization. The means (or one of the means) of attaining this objective is to increase the profits of the company. Slightly below him or her in the organizational hierarchy, the executive in charge of a division of the company will have as his or her decision objective an increase in company profitability. The means of achieving this objective could be many and various. The point is, the *objective* to one decision maker will be the *means* of achieving a higher objective to another decision maker.

Means—ends chains are a useful way of sorting out how objectives connect. See, for example, Figure 8.3. The decision here is how to improve information on how customers perceive the service given by the field service unit of an information technology company. But improving the information of how customers see them is only a means to the end of being able to focus their customer service initiative on the areas which will either improve service to the customer or reduce costs (by eliminating unnecessary elements of the service package). This in turn

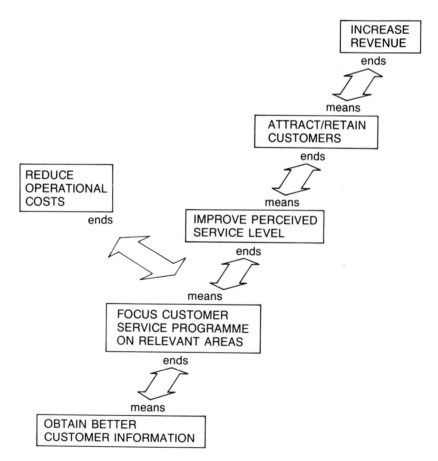

**Figure 8.3** Means—ends chain for decision of how to obtain better customer information

is only a means to the ends of improving perceived service levels and reducing operational costs, and so on.

The value of means−ends chains lies in their ability to 'put the decision in its broader context'. They both clarify the decision's contribution and focus decision makers' attention on overall aims.

## Objectives Should Balance the Long and Short Term

Objectives can differ quite fundamentally depending on whether long-term or short-term needs are being satisfied. Achieving long-term objectives — for example, increased market share and return on investment — can require managerial actions and investments which depress performance — for example, profitability — in the short term.

Take the example of a divisional manager whose sales are down this quarter and are forecast to continue their downward trend into next quarter. The competitors are producing higher-quality and customized products. The manager's company is constrained by old and inflexible technology and cannot hope to produce competitive products. The manager, who is measured by corporate headquarters on return on capital employed, has a dilemma. Should be purchase the new technology, which will allow the division to compete more effectively in the long term but will lower his return on capital employed in the short term (see Box 8.2)?

---

*Box 8.2*

One study[4] of several major companies concentrated specifically on long-term versus short-term decision making at the business level. The study found that product development decisions are often the victim of short-term objectives dominating long-term ones.

*Example 1.* One company in the study frequently delayed small product development projects, so as to maximize short-term profitability objectives, regardless of the effect this had on marketing strategy. Larger projects, however, had more visibility in the corporation and so could not be delayed without the company having to explain the reasons.

*Example 2.* In another company, managerial performance was measured largely on the basis of short-term profits. Because of this the company's history revealed its tendency to 'milk' the current and well-established products rather than invest in future products. The latter would have meant some loss of short-term profits.

*Example 3.* Similar short-term pressures in a third company forced the group to form an entirely new division which was charged with the task of developing and marketing new products. The original division simply could not break out of its short-term habits to invest some present earnings for its future.

Alternatively, should he delay capital expenditure and trim operating costs? This would improve his short-term performance but jeopardize the division in the long-term.

The types of problem illustrated in Box 8.2 can, to some extent, be countered through two approaches:

1. Make all company planning and reporting balance long-term and short-term views, preferably by putting short-term objectives in the context of long-term objectives through clearly linked objective chains (use means–ends chains). The reporting system used by the company in Box 8.1 is an excellent example of this.

2. Reward and remunerate managers by assessing the impact of managerial decisions on long-term objectives as well as measuring quarter-by-quarter results. Short-term assessment is easier, but relying on it alone distorts managerial behaviour.[5]

These two approaches are not independent. Reward systems include the esteem in which a manager is held by his or her peers: in other words, whether the respect of colleagues as 'a worthy manager' is gained. This is governed largely by what is seen as sensible within the value system of the organization, which in turn is shaped, partly at least, by its formal reporting system.

## Objectives Should Include the Intrinsic

Most decision objectives put forward by managers are extrinsic. They are there because they are seen as being effective in reaching the next objective in the objective hierarchy. For example, a company might decide that competition in its market is going to shift even more towards new innovative products with ever-shortening life cycles. It chooses to bolster its product development teams, recruit more development engineers who are experienced in advanced technology developments, and reorganize the functional boundaries to place product development more centrally in the organizational structure. The company does all these things because they are instrumental in achieving its objective of better and faster product development. The justification is rational; the objectives have extrinsic worth.

But the objective of enhancing product development might also have *intrinsic* worth to the company. It may feel personally happier with the 'high-tech' image it gains from these changes, it gets satisfaction from being at the leading edge of product development in its market. The company may even feel it is a 'good thing' to keep ahead of the competition this way, and that the country would be a better place if other companies did likewise. In other words, it gets intrinsic satisfaction because the objective satisfies the company's collective value system.

Do not underrate the importance of the intrinsic worth of decision objectives (see Box 8.3). They often dominate decision making. Take the airline owner who sets his company's objectives as 'to survive as a company, to return profits at a

## Box 8.3

# Down to Earth[6]

Some organizations have particularly strong intrinsic objectives — collectives, for example.

Down to Earth was a retail collective which sold wholefoods to the general public. As well as rice, beans, cereals, dried fruit, etc., they also retailed a limited variety of organically grown vegetables. The collective had been set up some years earlier by three students of the local university. They had provided the capital to start the business and were paid interest on the capital, but had no rights of ownership of the business. Decision-making rights were shared by all members of the collective, which numbered five.

As to the objectives of the collective, one member described her perception as follows:

> The original three people, who set the shop up, saw it as a means of providing themselves with an occupation which would not be too taxing and would be socially useful at the same time. More importantly, though, it was a means of supporting themselves financially without having to work for an organization in an employer/ employee relationship. I guess that we see the business in more or less the same way. It is a pleasant thing to do for a few years after you leave college, and it provides just enough money for us to live on. We all believe in eating the type of food we sell, and we know we are providing a service to other people who want to buy it. I guess there is something evangelical in the way we operate, but not to the point that we constantly preach at customers. Nevertheless, our beliefs do influence all the decisions we take about the business.

The effect of the members' intrinsic objectives can be illustrated by describing one of the business decisions taken since the founding of the shop.

### The Pricing Decision

For the first two years of the business, the prices of the goods sold in the shop had been determined by simple 'cost-plus' calculations. The selling prices were fixed at the percentage over cost which would more or less balance the business's need for cash with its forecast revenue. Although the system worked well (the collective normally had a slight surplus at the end of a period, which it gave to charities), members of the collective came to feel that they were missing an opportunity to reflect their philosophy more accurately in their pricing objective. It was decided to vary the margin on different products.

Margins were set on the basis of how 'staple' the collective considered the products. For example, some products which were considered to form a basic diet, such as beans, lentils, rice and wholemeal flour, had very low margins — sometimes zero. Other products which the collective considered something of a luxury, such as dried fruit and some types of cooking oil, had margins which were considerably higher. Since the change, the system had been working very well. In fact, the collective found that the price changes had very little effect on total demand for the various products.

Both objectives — price in the most straightforward way and price to reflect the collective's philosophy — had identical extrinsic worth, in so much as they both brought in the same amount of revenue. However, the latter objective had considerably more intrinsic worth to the organization, the members of which derived considerable satisfaction from operating things in this manner.

rate comparable with other companies and to grow in the marketplace'. The owner fails to mention that these objectives must be achieved by owning an airline, not an engineering company or a newspaper. He enjoys the flying business and might resist a decision to move into, say, the airport hotel business, even though it would be consistent with his long-term aims. It might have extrinsic worth, but it holds very little intrinsic worth for the owner.

Often there has to be some compromise between the demands of extrinsic and intrinsic pulls on objectives formulation. The airline executive might not want to get into the hotel business, but what if he sees that this is the only way for the airline to compete with its rivals?

## Objectives Should be Comprehensive

Decision objectives need not cover every possible issue no matter how minor, but they do need to be comprehensive enough to highlight the important issues.

Where a large number of objectives are involved, they can either conflict or be compatible with each other. However, even if the objectives do not directly conflict, they can compete when resources are scarce. For example, a company might have the objectives of developing new up-to-date services and also opening a new branch overseas. In themselves, these two objectives do not conflict. But with limited cash available, the company might have insufficient cash both to invest in the research and development programme needed to develop new services and to pay a heavy entry price into the new foreign market. Conflict between objectives cannot always be avoided, but it must be identified and faced.

Even when a decision maker is conscious that a decision involves multiple objectives, he or she may choose not to make all of the objectives explicit. Sometimes being 'too aware' of all the competing and conflicting objectives in a decision can diffuse the decision-making energies within a group, leading to a 'decision paralysis'. For example, an organization considering the introduction of quality improvement teams might be fully aware that it is almost impossible for any group of people to consider quality as an issue independent of other operational problems. But if the group were set up as a general 'performance improvement team', the scope of the decision-making exercise could confuse the decision makers. Concentrating specifically on quality provides a focus for discussions, yet will recognize that decisions made to improve quality levels will have implications elsewhere. So in this case, the single objective of quality improvement provides a useful lead into the consideration of the fulfilment of other objectives.

## Practical Prescriptions

Always set objectives for any decision and, throughout the decision process, relate each of the following back to the original statement of objectives:

1. The problem statement.
2. The decision options.
3. The evaluation process.
4. The choice process.

For any decision, define how its objectives contribute to the overall strategic objectives of the organization.

For any decision in 'for-profit' organizations, define how the objectives of the decision contribute to competitiveness.

Check to make sure that decision objectives are:

1. Appropriate — contribute to higher-level objectives.
2. Coherent — do not conflict with other decisions.
3. Consistent over time — are not always changing.
4. Clear — understandable to all.
5. Agreed — publicly debated.
6. Related — connected through means—end chains.
7. Balanced — long term with short term.
8. Inclusive — of extrinsic and intrinsic objectives.
9. Comprehensive — including all relevant aspects.

---

## Case Exercise

---

### Birmingham Amusement Machines

Birmingham Amusement Machines was a company which manufactured gaming and video-amusement machines. The company sold its products to an operating company which distributed them to bars, country clubs, casinos and pubs. Both companies were started by Bob Greenwood, an engineer who was fascinated by the design of the early mechanical gaming machines. Largely through innovative design the company had grown to be one of the four largest in the market with 30 per cent market share.

Four years ago Bob Greenwood had sold out to a large industrial group, but he was retained as the chief executive of the manufacturing company. The new owners were happy to let Bob indulge his talent for design, especially since the company had entered the video-amusement market. Video-amusement machines did not pay out cash prizes like gaming machines, but allowed the player time on the machine to play a game, usually with a theme drawn from the 'Wild West' or 'Interplanetary Space Warfare'. The company manufactured all parts for the gaming machines and assembled them in its factory. However, many of the components for the video-amusement machines were imported and only assembled into the outer casings in the factories.

Recently, the owners had become dissatisfied with the company's performance.

The market for its goods was still growing, but the company's profitability had failed to match expectations. The owners decided to install a new chief executive and to fire Bob, who was predictably upset at being replaced:

> It's always been the combination of high technology and fashion that's fascinated me about this industry. You have to be first in the field with every advance in technology, especially now video amusements are a big part of our business, but you also have to keep an eye out for the fashionable trends. On average, we've brought out a new product every four months for the last five years. You can't run a company like this by putting an accountant as its boss, you need an innovator.

In fact the owners *had* installed an accountant to be the head of the company. On his first day, the new boss made a tour of the plant, after which he called the manufacturing manager into his office and began to criticize what he had seen of the production set-up:

> It seems to me that the whole plant is totally disorganized. There's part-finished goods everywhere, and no one seems to know exactly what they're going to do next. I found some parts of the plant clearly overworked, and other parts with nothing to do. I am sure, with a bit of tighter management, you could get your unit production costs down dramatically.

The production manager was defensive:

> Of course I'd like to get my unit costs down, and of course I could rearrange the whole plant to make it more efficient. The trouble is, the design department are getting me to change products every few months, so I never really have time to let the production system settle down. At the same time, marketing are wanting me to give them instant delivery on new products, almost as soon as I have the drawings from the design office, and they insist on quality being of the highest standard at all times.

The new boss called in the marketing manager to explain these demands placed on the production system. The marketing manager was equally forthright:

> I couldn't care less about his unit costs. It's not low cost which sells these machines. Look at it this way: in a heavy gambling club one of these gaming machines can pay for itself in less than three months. Under those circumstances, nobody in this industry is competing on price. It's not totally unimportant, but plus or minus 10 per cent isn't going to make much difference to our sales. What sells machines is a new product on the books every few months or so and almost instant delivery — many of the club owners buy on impulse — and an unimpeachable reputation for the highest product reliability.

After listening to the testimony of both his managers, the new boss was a lot less certain on how he should proceed to reshape the business.

## Questions

1. What do you think were Bob Greenwood's objectives when he ran the company?
2. List what you think might now be the priority objectives of:
   (a) the production manager
   (b) the marketing manager

    (c) the new boss.
3. Draw a means—ends chain for what you consider to be the most important elements of the objectives hierarchy.

## Bibliography

Banker, R.L. and Cupta, S.H., 'A process for hierarchical decision making with multiple objectives', *OMEGA* (International Journal of Management Science), vol. 8, no. 2, pp. 137—49. An excellent example of how to cope with multiple objectives in decision making.

Hickson, D.J., Butler, R.J., Cray, D., Mallory, G.R. and Wilson, D.C., *Top Decisions: Strategic decision making in organisations*, Blackwell, 1986.

Jay, A., *Management and Machiavelli* (revised edn), Hutchinson, 1987. A classic on the politics of objectives setting.

Johnson, J. and Scholes, H.K., *Exploring Corporate Strategy* (2nd edn), Prentice Hall, 1989. One of the best books around on strategic decision making.

Porter, M.E., *Competitive Strategy Techniques for Analysing Industries and Competitors*, Free Press, 1980. Another classic on competitive objectives.

## References

1. We use the terms 'objectives', 'goals' and 'ends' interchangeably.
2. Taken from Slack, N., *Achieving a manufacturing advantage*, Mercury Books, 1991.
3. Bilkey, W.J., 'Empirical evidence regarding business goals', in Cochrane, J.L. and Zeleny, M. (eds.), *Multiple Criteria Decision Making*, University of South Carolina Press, 1973.
4. Banks, R.L. and Wheelwright, S.C., 'Operations vs. strategy: trading tomorrow for today', *Harvard Business Review*, May/June 1979, pp. 112—20.
5. Rappaport, A., 'Executive incentives vs. corporate growth', *Harvard Business Review*, July/August 1978, pp. 81—8.
6. Based on the case study 'Down to Earth' by Scholes, H.K., held by the Case Clearing House of Great Britain and Ireland, Cranfield.

# 9 Understanding the problem

## Introduction

The immediate temptation is to skip this stage in the decision process. Objectives have been set and it is natural to start thinking of alternative ways to address them. But even if the decision seems clearly defined, it is worth pausing at least long enough to set it in a broader context. The minimum pay-off will be a better understanding of the reasons for making the decision in the first place. The most likely reward will be that the nature of the decision is redefined so as to target it more accurately on the root cause of the problem.

## Sorting Out the Problem

No organizational process is 'problem free'. We are all surrounded by problems in need of solutions. Some problems though, are more obvious than others. The hidden problem — the problem behind the problem — is often the one on which the decision-making process needs to be focused.

Finding the problem behind the problem is very much facilitated by the use of some relatively simple techniques. In fact, simple techniques are particularly effective in the problem-understanding phase of decision making. Most of this chapter is made up of some of the techniques which are recognized as being particularly helpful.

Problem understanding is also helped by an approach which stresses three particular 'thinking habits':[1]

1. A willingness to question the status quo. The most useful question is 'Why?', and it sometimes needs to be asked even about the most entrenched assumptions and procedures.

2. An ability to see a bigger picture than the one which immediately presents

itself. Understanding problems is very much a contextual process which involves seeing both 'the wood' and 'the trees'.

3. A readiness to look into the future. Spotting problems before they become crises often means that they can be sorted out without the organizational pain they would otherwise cause.

## A Two-Stage Process

Understanding the problem context of a decision involves two types of activity.

First, it is necessary to collect data about the problem area. Some data will be general information, some will be accepted as 'hard fact', and some will be opinions — subjective and even contentious. It all goes to building up a picture of the problem.

Second, the data need analysing or interpreting so as to find the underlying meaning in the picture of the problem. The analysis may be quite simple, like counting how many times a certain event occurs, or more complex, like building a mathematical model. It may be 'mechanical', just presenting data in a different way (e.g. plotting graphs), or more creative — brainstorming for underlying causes. The only requirement is that the process increases our understanding of the problem.

These two stages are not always distinct or totally sequential. We are rarely so dispassionate in our data collection that we exclude all analysis. Nor should we ignore the need for further data which the analysis reveals. But it makes sense to move from data collection to analysis, from information to interpretation, from objective to subjective, from asking 'What?' to asking 'Why?'.

# Data Collection Techniques

## Input—Output Analysis

All organizational activities are operations of some kind. Every department, section, site or division is involved in processing inputs to produce outputs. The inputs can be raw materials, component parts, people, money or information. The outputs can be products, parts, people who have received a service, information, or a mixture of all of these.

Visualizing whole companies or locations as input—process—output systems is commonplace. Less common but just as useful is treating individual parts of organizations in the same way. A prerequisite for understanding any decision or problem area is to understand the context of the input—process—output operation in which it is set.

Three tasks are involved in formulating an input—output model:

1. Identifying the inputs and outputs from the process.

2. Identifying the source of the inputs and the destination of the outputs.

3. Clarifying the requirements of the internal customers who are served by the outputs from the process, and clarifying what requirements the process has for the internal suppliers who provide inputs to the process.

*Identifying Inputs and Outputs*

The procedure here is to list all the inputs to the process. For example:

1. Information necessary for the process.
2. Materials necessary for the process.
3. People who take part in the process.
4. Plant and equipment used in the process.

Next list all the outputs for the process. For example:

1. Physical, tangible products and goods.
2. Information supplied.
3. Anything which has changed as a result of the output.

*Example: Kasgo Pyral Service Limited*

Kasgo Pyral Service Limited (KPS) is the field service division of Kasgo Pyral International, which manufactures and installs gas-fired heating systems. Its sister companies are KP Manufacturing, which makes the systems and spare parts, and KP Contracts, which installs the systems. KPS is organized on a regional basis, the south-eastern region being the largest. This region serves a mixture of customers, mainly owners of large commercial office blocks, but also industrial buildings, schools, colleges and civic buildings. KPS offers a wide range of service contracts to its customers. Each contract specifies the level of preventative maintenance, the times at which the boilers would be made available for preventative maintenance, and the maximum response time in case of an emergency call-out. Originally, KPS serviced only systems manufactured by its own manufacturing company. Recently, as a result of the competitive market, it has started to service systems installed by other manufacturers.

KPS was feeling under pressure in a market which was becoming increasingly competitive. Most competition was coming from independent, often small, third-party service organizations. Not only were they selling themselves as being more 'independent' than KPS, but they were also undercutting KPS's prices. Partly as a response to this, KPS's south-eastern regional manager decided to initiate an improvement programme which would have the brief of improving its competitive position. He decided on a team approach which would include himself, all five service engineers in the unit, the accountant/administrator for the unit and occasionally a trainer from KP group personnel department. They decided as a first step to draw an input—output diagram which would give them a common ground of shared understanding about their operation on which to base further investigations.

They further decided to include only the 'consumable' inputs rather than the permanent parts of their organization. The first category of inputs was information, which came in various forms. First of all there was information on the technical details of the products which they were servicing. Next there was information which came from customers on the way the system had been installed or modified in the customer's building. Finally, there were the requests from customers for service. This could either be to request a change in the existing service schedule or, more often, an emergency call from a customer for service when a system was not working properly. The next class of input was the various types of material which came into the system. There were the spare parts, used to replace defective parts in the customer's systems. Most of these were new, but occasionally the engineers used reconditioned parts from their own workshops. There were also various small items of consumable materials, piping, gas for the blow torches, etc. Also classed as an input was the advice and consultancy which the unit occasionally sought from the personnel of KP Contracts Ltd (the part of the group which was concerned with installing the boiler in the first place). If a problem was particularly serious or of a reccurring nature, the unit would call in a KP Contracts engineer to come along to the customer's site and help diagnose the problem.

The outputs from the system were the regular preventative maintenance type of service, where KP engineers visited a customer's site at regular intervals (this could be anything from monthly to yearly) and carried out a routine programme of cleaning and replacing worn parts, and emergency servicing which involved responding quickly when a customer was having problems. Quickly meant anything from two hours to half an hour depending on the type of contract which the customer had bought. After some discussion the team also decided to include advice and assistance as part of its outputs. Service engineers were often called upon to give advice and assistance to customers on the use of their boilers, to KPS Manufacturing when it found a particular problem with the design of boilers and to KPS Contracts when it found problems with the way in which they had been installed. The team took the view that perhaps they had neglected this part of their output.

### Identifying Sources (Suppliers) and Destinations (Customers)

Information on products and modifications to products usually came directly from KP, and from other heating manufacturers. Information on the individual customer's system should have come mainly from KP Contracts which had installed the system. Frequently, however, the contracting company did not supply sufficient detail and so service engineers and customers also provided informal information. Customer requests for service came primarily through customers phoning up the unit. Occasionally, if the request was non-urgent, they would ask the service engineer performing regular maintenance to take back a particular request to the unit. New spare parts were delivered direct from the manufacturers, while reconditioned parts came mainly from the workshop within the unit but occasionally, if the reconditioning was of a major nature, from the factory. Consumable materials came from a wide variety of suppliers which delivered direct to the depot.

On the output side, regular servicing, emergency servicing and advice on the use of the company's boilers were given to three types of customer — commercial, industrial and civic. Advice and information on design were sent to the manufacturing companies on an informal and irregular basis. Similarly, advice and information to the installation company was fed back to the company as the situation seemed to warrant.

### Defining Input and Output Requirements

On the input side, the requirement for all types of information input was that they must be accurate (error free) and sufficiently comprehensive. In addition, product information should also arrive in time for KPS to make plans to cope with changes in the system's specification. The main requirements for spare parts, whether new or reconditioned, were primarily speed in making them available to the customer, dependability of delivery so that the maintenance visit to the company could be scheduled in advance, and high quality. The requirements for supply of advice from KP Contracts were that engineers should be made available as speedily as possible so as to give good service to the customer, that commitments made to supply a contract engineer should be honoured reliably, that the engineer should have sufficient flexibility in his or her own availability to enable visits to be scheduled when the customer wanted them, and finally that the engineer's diagnostic skills were high.

On the output side, the customers' requirements depended on which sector they came from. Commercial customers were primarily interested in the cost of the service, but also wanted high dependability, speed of response and technical advice. Industrial customers were interested in the ability of the company to schedule preventative maintenance outside of working hours, with speed of response, cost and technical advice also figuring. Civic customers were primarily interested in cost, and also valued the technical advice more highly than other customers; response and dependability could also be important.

The advice and information given to KP Manufacturing regarding the design of the boilers and to KP Contracts on installation procedures were more of a problem. In fact, KPS had never formally asked its sister companies what kind of information they would find useful and whether they wanted it at all. After discussion with both of these companies it was agreed that KP Manufacturing was particularly interested in the frequency of occurrence of problems, and furthermore preferred information to be fed back in such a way as to tie in with its new product development cycles. KP Contracts, on the other hand, was keen to take advantage of the analysis of data on installation problems which KPS could perform.

Figure 9.1 shows an input—output diagram for KPS. The purpose is to reach an agreed understanding of the operational function of whichever part of the

| REQUIREMENTS | SUPPLIERS | INPUTS | | OUTPUT | CUSTOMER | REQUIREMENTS |
|---|---|---|---|---|---|---|
| • Accuracy<br>• Comprehensiveness<br>• Advance notice | • Manufacturers | • Information on systems | | • Preventative maintenance | • Commercial | • Cost<br>• Dependability<br>• Response speed<br>• Advice |
| • Accuracy<br>• Comprehensiveness | • KP Contracts<br>• Customers<br>• Service engineers | • Information on customers | THE KPS SOUTH-EAST REGION FIELD SERVICE UNIT | • Emergency servicing | • Industrial | • Flexibility<br>• Response speed<br>• Cost<br>• Advice |
| • Accuracy<br>• Comprehensiveness | • Customers<br>• Service engineers | • Customer requests | | • Advice on use of system | • Civic | • Cost<br>• Advice<br>• Response speed<br>• Dependability |
| • Response speed<br>• Reliable delivery<br>• Quality | • Manufacturers<br>• KPS workshop | • Spare parts | | • Advice on design | • KP Manufacturing | • Analysis<br>• Co-ordination |
| • Availability<br>• Cost | • Various | • Consumables | | • Advice on installation | • KP Contracts | • Analysis |
| • Responsiveness<br>• Reliability<br>• Flexibility<br>• Skill | • KP Contracts | • KP Contracts engineers | | | | |

**Figure 9.1** Full input–output diagram showing the suppliers and requirements of all inputs and the customers and requirements for all outputs

organization the problem is set in. It is not intended that input—output diagrams give any answers as such. They do, however, provide a useful 'way in' to the problem.

## Flow Charts

Input—output diagrams give a useful overview of the process context of problems. A more detailed technique is the flow chart. Flow charts give a detailed understanding of parts of the process where some sort of flow occurs. They record stages in the passage of information, products, labour or customers — in fact, anything which flows through the operation. They do this by requiring the decision makers to identify each stage in the flow process as either:

- An *action* of some sort — recorded in a rectangular box.
- A *question/decision* — recorded in a diamond-shaped box.

The purpose of this is to ensure that all different stages in the flow processes are included in the problem-solving process, and that these stages are in some kind of logical sequence. The act of recording quickly shows up poorly organized flows. Also the process can clarify the problem and shed further light on the internal mechanics or workings of an operation. Finally, and probably most importantly, it highlights any bottlenecks or problem areas where no procedure exists to cope with particular circumstances.

*Example*

As part of their improvement programme the team at KPS are concerned that customers are not being served well when they phone in with minor queries over the operation of their heating systems. These queries are not usually concerned with serious problems, but often concern minor irritations which can be equally damaging to the customer's perception of KPS's service.

Figure 9.2 shows the flow diagram for this type of customer query. When a customer phones in, the telephonist listens to the nature of the customer query. If the telephonist understands the query, she will divert the call to the relevant engineer. If the telephonist cannot fully understand the nature of the customer's query, she diverts the call through to the manager. If he does not understand the query, he arranges for an engineer to visit. If the manager does understand the nature of the call, he transfers the call to the relevant duty engineer. If the duty engineer cannot answer the query over the phone, he arranges for either himself or another engineer to visit the customer. If the engineer can answer the query over the phone but feels that it would be safer for the customer to receive a visit from a service engineer, again he will organize this. If the duty engineer feels that no further visit is necessary, no further action takes place. If an engineer visits the customer site and can satisfactorily answer the customer query, again no further

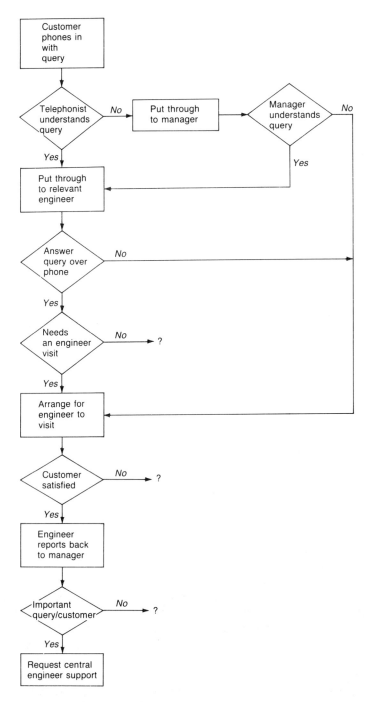

**Figure 9.2** Flow chart for customer query

action takes place. If the customer is still not satisfied, he or she will report back to the manager. The manager then judges whether either the query or the customer is of sufficient importance for central engineering to be brought in. If so, he passes the customer query on to central engineering headquarters and the issue passes out of the regional unit. If the manager decides that the query is trivial, no further action takes place.

The team found this chart illuminating. The procedure had never been formally laid out in this way before, and it showed up three areas where information was not being recorded. These are the three points marked with question marks on the flow chart on Figure 9.2. As a result of this investigation, it was decided to log all customer queries so that analysis could reveal further information on the nature of customer problems.

## Systematic Fact Finding[2]

The key word here is 'systematic'. Too often the problem-understanding phase of decision making is handicapped by skipping over aspects of the problem which at first glance seem trivial, but which lead on to more significant facts. The purpose of the procedure is to generate all significant facts surrounding the general problem area.

Purely factual information is gathered by systematically asking questions which relate to the problem area. The questions are as follows:

1. *What* activities are carried out, and *why*?
2. *How* are things done, and *why*?
3. *Where* are things done, and *why*?
4. *Who* carries out activities, and *why*?
5. *How many* times do things happen, and *why*?

This list of questions can be expanded, shortened or adapted. The important point, though, is that it provides a discipline for systematic questioning, and that the 'why?' follow-up question is used to gather the reasons which are put forward as explaining why things are the way they are. These reasons may be challenged later, of course, but at this stage it is important merely to collect them.

### Example

One infrequent but disruptive service which KPS was obliged by head office to offer was the 'resident engineer' service. This was a service to KP Contracts which could call on the services of one of KPS's engineers to be seconded for a fixed term at the end of an installation contract. KPS engineers would make the final checks and adjustments to the complex control systems as well as give advice to the customers on how best to use the system. Figure 9.3 shows the systematic fact-finding chart which the KPS improvement team used as a starting point of their investigation into how this service ought to be organized.

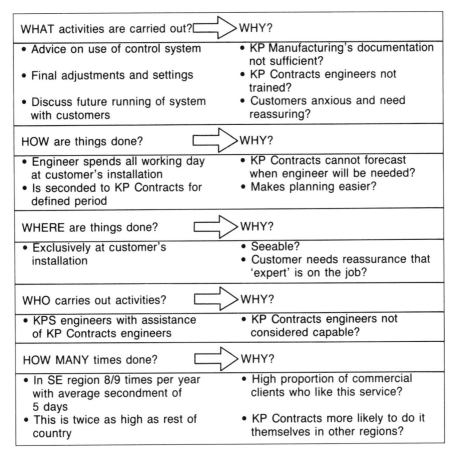

| WHAT activities are carried out? ⟹ WHY? | |
| --- | --- |
| • Advice on use of control system | • KP Manufacturing's documentation not sufficient? |
| • Final adjustments and settings | • KP Contracts engineers not trained? |
| • Discuss future running of system with customers | • Customers anxious and need reassuring? |
| **HOW are things done?** ⟹ **WHY?** | |
| • Engineer spends all working day at customer's installation | • KP Contracts cannot forecast when engineer will be needed? |
| • Is seconded to KP Contracts for defined period | • Makes planning easier? |
| **WHERE are things done?** ⟹ **WHY?** | |
| • Exclusively at customer's installation | • Seeable? |
| | • Customer needs reassurance that 'expert' is on the job? |
| **WHO carries out activities?** ⟹ **WHY?** | |
| • KPS engineers with assistance of KP Contracts engineers | • KP Contracts engineers not considered capable? |
| **HOW MANY times done?** ⟹ **WHY?** | |
| • In SE region 8/9 times per year with average secondment of 5 days | • High proportion of commercial clients who like this service? |
| • This is twice as high as rest of country | • KP Contracts more likely to do it themselves in other regions? |

**Figure 9.3**  Systematic fact finding for resident engineer service

## Analysis and Interpretation Techniques

### Scatter Diagrams

Scatter diagrams are a quick and simple method of identifying whether there seems to be a connection between two sets of data: for example, the time at which you set off for work every morning, and how long the journey to work takes. Plotting each journey on a graph which has departure time on one axis and journey time on the other could give an indication of whether departure time and journey time are related, and if so, how. Figure 9.4 shows the graph for one manager. It would seem to show (a) that there is a relationship between the two sets of data, (b) that the longest journeys were when departures were between 8.15 and 8.30, and (c) that the journey is least predictable when departure is between 8.15 and 8.30.

Scatter diagrams can be treated in a far more sophisticated manner by quantifying

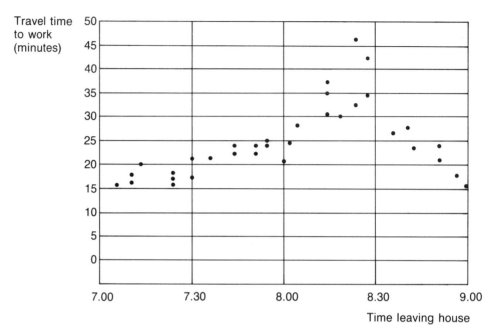

Travel time to work (minutes)

Time leaving house

**Figure 9.4**   Scatter diagram for travel time against departure time

how strong is the relationship between the sets of data. But however sophisticated the approach, we are only identifying a relationship, not necessarily a cause—effect. If the scatter diagram shows a very strong connection between the sets of data, it is important evidence of a cause—effect relationship, but not proof positive. It could be coincidence!

*Example*

The KPS improvement team had completed its first customer satisfaction survey. The survey asked customers to score the service they received from KPS in several ways. For example, it asked customers to score services on a scale of one to ten on promptness, friendliness, level of advice, etc. Scores were then summed to give a 'total satisfaction score' for each customer — the higher the score, the greater the satisfaction.

The spread of satisfaction scores puzzled the team, and they considered what factors might be causing such differences in the way their customers viewed them. Two factors were put forward to explain the differences: (a) the number of times in the past year the customer had received a preventative maintenance visit, and (b) the number of times the customer had called for emergency service. All this data was collected and plotted on scatter diagrams as shown in Figure 9.5.

Figure 9.5 shows that there seems to be a clear relationship between a customer's satisfaction score and the number of times it was visited for regular servicing.

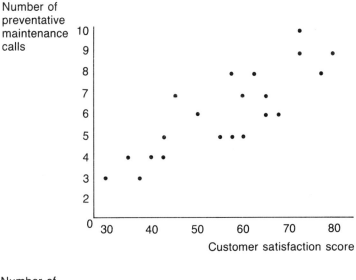

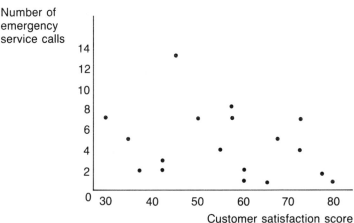

**Figure 9.5** Scatter diagrams for customer satisfaction versus number of preventative maintenance calls and number of emergency service calls

The other scatter diagram is less clear. While all customers which had very high satisfaction scores had made very few emergency calls, so had some customers with low satisfaction scores. As a result of this analysis, the team decided to survey customers' views on its emergency service.

## Cause−Effect Diagrams

Cause−effect diagrams are a particularly effective method of helping to search for the root causes of problems. They do this by asking the what, when, where, how and why questions as before, but this time adding some possible 'answers' in an explicit way. They can also be used to identify areas where further data are needed. Cause–effect diagrams (which are also known as 'fish bone' and 'Ishikawa' diagrams) have become extensively used in quality improvement programmes. Many organizations have found them an effective part of their quality-related problem solving. Figure 9.6 shows the general form of the cause–effect diagram.

The procedure for drawing a cause–effect diagram is as follows:

Step 1. State the problem in the 'effect' box.

Step 2. Identify the main categories for possible causes of the problem. Although any categorization can be used for the main branches of the diagram, there are five categories which are commonly used: machinery; manpower; materials; methods and procedures; money.

Step 3. Use systematic fact finding and group discussion to generate possible causes under these categories. Anything which may result in the effect which is being considered should be put down as a potential cause.

Step 4. Record all potential causes on the diagram under each category, and discuss each item in order to combine and clarify causes.

*Some Tips on Using Cause–Effect Diagrams*

1. Use separate diagrams for each problem. Do not confuse the issue by combining problems on a single diagram.

2. Make sure diagrams are visible to everyone involved. Use large sheets of paper with plenty of space between items.

3. Do not overload diagrams. Use separate diagrams for each major category on the cause–effect master diagram if necessary.

4. Always be prepared to rework, take apart, refine and change categories.

5. Take care not to use vague statements such as 'possible lack of'. Rather

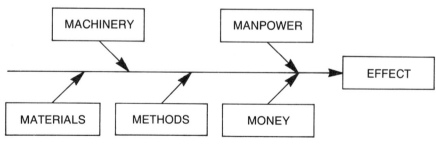

**Figure 9.6**  Cause–effect diagram

Box 9.1

## Problem Identification at Xerox[3]

Like other quality-conscious companies, Xerox uses problem exploration techniques of the type described in this chapter. In an example of quality improvement in their repro-graphics business, they used cause–effect diagrams to classify responses from extensive customer surveys. Figure 9.7 shows some of the reasons for customer dissatisfaction as a cause–effect diagram.

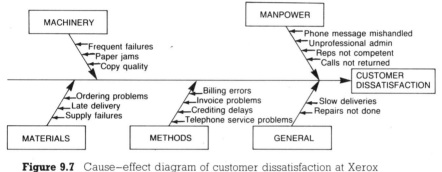

**Figure 9.7** Cause–effect diagram of customer dissatisfaction at Xerox

describe what is actually happening that demonstrates the issues: for example, 'people are not filling out forms properly'.

6. Circle causes which seem to be particularly significant.

*Example*

The improvement team at KPS were working on a particular area which was proving a problem. Whenever a service engineer was called out to perform emergency servicing for a customer, he took with him the spares and equipment which he thought would be necessary to repair the system. Although engineers could never be sure exactly what materials and equipment they would need for a job, they could guess what was likely to be needed and take a range of spares and equipment which would cover most eventualities. Too often, however, the engineer would find that he needed a spare or piece of equipment which he had not brought with him, and therefore he would have to return to the depot in order to collect it. Worse than that, very occasionally the required spare part would not be in stock, and so the customer would have to wait until it was brought from another part of the country. The cause–effect diagram for this particular problem as drawn by the team is shown in Figure 9.8.

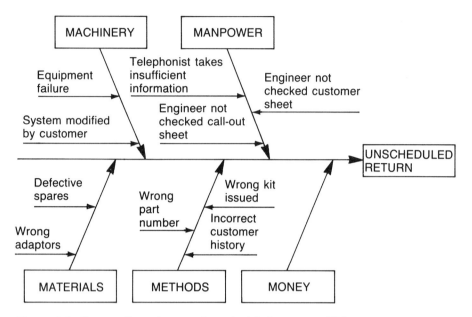

**Figure 9.8** Cause–effect diagram of unscheduled returns at KPS

## Pareto Diagrams

At this stage in the problem-understanding process, it is worthwhile starting to distinguish between what is important and what is less so. The purpose of a Pareto analysis is to distinguish between the 'vital few' issues and the 'trivial many'. It is a relatively straightforward technique which involves arranging information on the types of problem or causes of problem into their order of importance. This can then be used to highlight areas where further decision making will be useful.

Pareto analysis is based on the frequently occurring phenomenon of relatively few causes explaining the majority of effects. So, for example, most revenue for any company is likely to come from relatively few of the company's customers. Similarly, relatively few of a doctor's patients will probably occupy most of his time. The general shape of the curve is shown in Figure 9.9. It is often called the 80–20 rule since typically 80 per cent of problems or resources can be accounted for by 20 per cent of possible causes.

*Example*

The KPS improvement team who were investigating unscheduled returns from emergency servicing (the issue which was described in the cause–effect diagram in Figure 9.8) examined all occasions over the previous twelve months on which

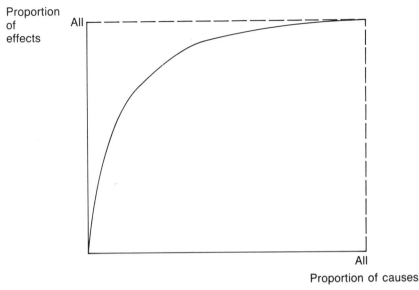

**Figure 9.9** The general Pareto relationship

an unscheduled return had been made. They categorized the reasons for unscheduled returns as follows:

1. Where the wrong part had been taken to a job because, although the information which the engineer received was sound, he had incorrectly predicted the nature of the failure.

2. Where the wrong part had been taken to the job because there was insufficient information given when the call was taken.

3. Where the wrong part had been taken to the job because the system had been modified in some way not recorded on KPS's records.

4. Where the wrong part had been taken to the job because the part had been incorrectly issued to the engineer by stores.

5. Where no part had been taken because the relevant part was out of stock.

6. Where the wrong equipment had been taken for whatever reason.

7. Any other reason.

The relative frequency of occurrence of these causes is shown in Figure 9.10. About a third of all unscheduled returns were due to the first category, and more than half the returns were accounted for by the first and second categories together. It was decided that the problem could best be tackled by concentrating on how

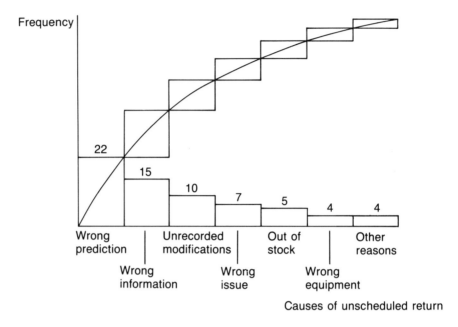

**Figure 9.10** Pareto diagram for causes of unscheduled returns

to get more information to the engineer which would enable him to predict the causes of failure accurately.

## Why–Why Analysis

We finish on another simple but effective technique for helping to understand the reasons for problems occurring. It is an 'expansion' technique which starts by stating the problem and asking *why* that problem has occurred. Once the major reasons for the problem occurring have been identified, each of the major reasons is taken in turn and again the question is asked *why* those reasons have occurred, and so on. This procedure is continued until either a cause seems sufficiently self-contained to be addressed by itself or no more answers to the question 'Why?' can be generated.

Figure 9.12 illustrates the general structure of the why–why analysis for the KPS example discussed previously. In this example the major cause of unscheduled returns was the incorrect prediction of why the customer's system had failed. This is stated as the problem in the why–why analysis. The question is then asked, why was the failure wrongly predicted? Three answers are proposed: first, that the engineers were not trained correctly; second, that they had insufficient knowledge of the particular product installed in the customer's location; and third, that they had insufficient knowledge of the customer's particular system with its

Box 9.2

## Using Pareto Charts

An example of the use of Pareto charts to indicate the priority causes comes out of the Goodyear Tyre and Rubber Company.[4]

The manufacture of solvent-based adhesive involves mixing the product in batches. Each batch should contain (say) 30 per cent solids plus or minus a small percentage. The variation derives from 'deviations' in different parts of the process. The causes of deviations from specification are classified and their frequency of occurrence measured. The data are then put in a Pareto form as shown in Figure 9.11.

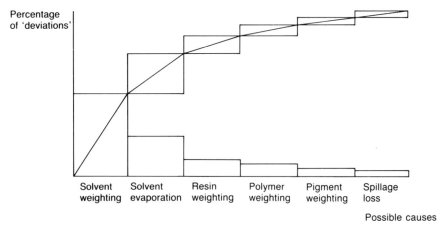

**Figure 9.11**   Pareto chart of reasons for deviation from required percentage of solids in solvent-based adhesives

modifications. Each of these three reasons is taken in turn, and the questions are asked, why is there a lack of training, why is there a lack of product knowledge, and why is there a lack of customer knowledge? And so on.

## Practical Prescriptions

The context of the decision is always worth considering. When the decision area is unclear, it is vital that time and effort are invested in defining the problem. Even when the decision seems clear cut, it is worth pausing to make sure that you are really solving the right problem.

Develop the 'thinking habits' which help define the problem:

1. Questioning the status quo.

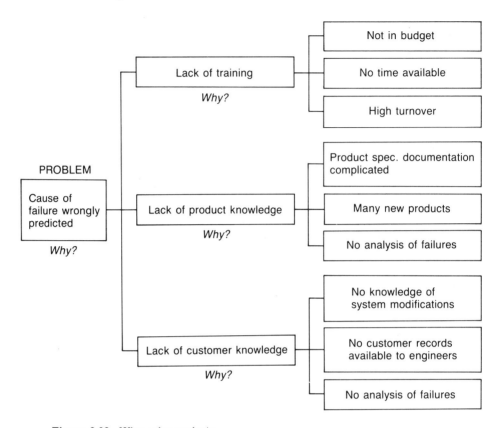

**Figure 9.12** Why–why analysis

2. Visualizing the 'big picture'.
3. Imagining what the future might hold.

Develop an understanding of the problem area in two stages:

1. Data collection.
2. Analysis and interpretation.

Techniques which are useful in data collection include:

1. Input–output analysis.
2. Flow charts.
3. Systematic fact finding.

Analysis and interpretation techniques include:

1. Scatter diagrams.
2. Cause–effect diagrams.

3. Pareto diagrams.
4. Why−why analysis.

## Bibliography

Albrecht, K.G., *Brain Power*, Prentice Hall, 1980. A consistently interesting treatment of the psychology of problem-based thinking.

Dale, B.G. and Plunkett, J.J. (eds.), *Managing Quality*, Prentice Hall, 1990. Contains many examples of problem-solving techniques and case examples in the context of quality improvement.

Heirs, B., *The Professional Decision Thinker*, Grafton, 1989. A stimulating treatment of problem-based thinking.

Stevens, M., *Practical Problem Solving for Managers*, Kogan Page, 1988. A useful and detailed treatment of the more robust problem-solving techniques.

Weisinger, H., *Creative Criticism*, Sidgwick and Jackson, 1989.

## References

1. Albrecht, K.G., *Brain Power*, Prentice Hall, 1980.
2. The basis of this technique comes from work study practitioners. See, for example, Wild, R., *Production and Operations Management* (4th edn), Cassell, 1989.
3. From Ekings, J.D., 'A nine-step quality improvement programme to increase customer satisfaction', European Organization for Quality Control 30th Conference, Stockholm, 1986.
4. From Miller, D.E., 'Statistical process control emphasises zero defects', *Adhesive Age*, July 1987.

# 10 Generating the options

## Introduction

As mentioned in Chapter 2, the process of optimization in decision making depends, among other things, on the ability to consider *all* possible alternatives. While this may not be possible in practice, any improvement, in terms of being able to generate the 'widest possible range' of choice given the resources available, is clearly likely to improve the prospect of making a high-quality decision. After all, we cannot choose a particular option if it is not offered to us for consideration in the first place!

Satisficing, that process of accepting the 'good enough' decision, stops the search for a full range of options. The solution generation process is cut off by the acceptance of the first option that meets the minimum conditions for success. Under such circumstances there is little or no incentive for decision makers to be particularly creative. On the other hand, imagination, breadth of vision and a willingness to link together previously unrelated objects and events are all creative behaviours that will allow the generation of a wider range of alternative solutions, thus allowing us at least the possibility of moving nearer to the optimizing end of the decision-making continuum.

For this reason, therefore, we concentrate in this chapter on the issue of stimulating and encouraging the quality of creativity in decision making. While our emphasis will be on its application in the generation of options, it is important to recognize that creativity plays a wider role in the decision-making process, and for this reason our discussions will start off on a broader footing.

## Creativity in Decision Making

For managers in most work organizations, one of the most desirable and sought-after talents must surely be that of creativity. The need to be involved with innovation and business success, to discover and develop new applications for products and processes, and to be a leader in the field are activities which many managers would rank highly in their list of attributes for organizational success and personal satisfaction. Each of these attributes, in one way or another, is dependent upon creative activity by members of the organization. Yet, while so many highly desirable expressions of organizational creativity abound, while the need for it is so *widespread* in organizational life, most of us would probably regard creativity as *special*, a characteristic of the few rather than the many, a rarity rather than the norm in the organizations in which we work.

Many companies go out of their way to recruit members who are felt to be especially creative. These individuals may then be slotted away into particular roles where 'creative' work is to be carried out. In the meantime, the ordinary 'non-creative' employees can get on with the bulk of 'non-creative' organizational jobs. Perhaps the historical view of creativity as being the perquisite of the few has led to a situation where the opportunity to be creative, at least in the interests of the organization, has been designed out of the majority of jobs.

## Creativity as a Widespread Activity

While it is likely that some people are inherently more creative than others,[1] modern thinking has shifted away from the idea that the situation is one of all-or-nothing, that we are either creative or not creative, towards the notion that the creative process can be stimulated and improved in the majority of people. This is both a crucial and a timely change of approach under circumstances where, for many organizations, creative activity has ceased merely to be a desirable activity and has become an absolute necessity for survival and progress:

> We will also be concerned with the creativity of people like us, rather than the Leonardos, Beethovens and Einsteins. This is no great loss, since most of us have never met a Leonardo, a Beethoven or an Einstein.[2]

The generation of more creative behaviour from a much larger proportion than previously of the organization's human resource, coupled with the provision of the kind of climate and environment where such creativity can flourish, must become a primary objective for managers. This is nowhere more true than in the process of decision making.

## Creativity and Decision Making

Much of the pressure to improve the quality of management decision making has been towards the use of more systematic approaches to problems and towards the development of more useful analytical and evaluative techniques. The role of creativity in problem solving and decision making has largely been ignored,[3] and yet there are at least two key areas in problem solving where a creative approach is vital and where, without it, effectiveness is minimized. These areas are:

- The formulation of the problem itself.
- The generation of a range of alternative solutions from which to choose.

### Formulating the Problem

One of the most difficult stages in problem solving is that transition from a situation where 'something hurts' to one in which we have the problem in sharp focus. Understanding a problem clearly can unfortunately often lead to oversimplification. Our need to know and to understand, coupled with the need to feel in control of a rather ambiguous and uncertain situation (the normal state when we first come across a problem), tends sometimes to lead to a *closure* or simplification of the situation through over-hasty definition. By concentrating on the admittedly crucial need to define problems in a clear and precise way, we may often lose sight of the more basic issue, the process of thinking about and getting an overall impression of the scope and importance of the fundamental problem.

Formulating and 'getting a feel' for the problem is in itself a creative process (or at least it should be!). It can involve a great deal of imaginative and exploratory thinking, a lot of 'what if' questioning, and/or 'pushing outwards' and 'bringing in' of ideas, rather than 'closing down' and 'firming up' on the problem). It is likely that *problem spotting* in itself is a process which can benefit a great deal from creative thinking. Managers who are not very creative may be severely handicapped in that they may not recognize the true nature of certain problems. They may not be able to visualize the likely impact until it is too late, or at least until the only course is remedy rather than prevention. If this is the case, then those who are responsible for organizing decision-making systems and activities are faced with the task of bringing together the creative activity of recognizing and formulating problems with the rather more analytical process of their definition and translation into organizational 'language', so that decisions can then be made as to how much energy to expend in their solution. The setting up of specialist problem-spotting groups is sometimes advocated, and this may indeed be the answer for problems which are concerned with longer-term and strategic matters.[4] However, the need for a link between the creative and the analytical must surely occur so frequently in operational decision making that the two skills could sensibly be developed in the same individual or group.

### The Generation of Alternative Solutions

The formulation of the problem and the ability to come up with innovative solutions are key stages in the total problem-solving process. Indeed, it can reasonably be argued that the fostering of creativity and its successful linking with the other skills that are needed will do as much as anything else to improve the quality of organizational decisions.

## Blocks to Creativity in Organizational Decision Making

If the need for creativity within organizations can so easily be identified, one might ask why it sometimes seems so difficult for decision makers actually to be creative. As is the case with so many other desirable conditions, we can identify a wide variety of factors and conditions which block creative activity or create a climate in which there is little or no incentive for individuals to demonstrate their creative abilities. These blocks range from those which are essentially structural (resulting largely from the process of bureaucratization that seems inevitably to accompany organizational growth), through to those which are much more the result of responses made by people to their organizational circumstances.

### The Development of Control Systems and the Desire for Efficiency

One characteristic of growing organizations is that control over their activity tends to move out of the hands of their originators. With an increase in size and complexity, it is no longer possible for the senior managers or the owners of a company to handle personally everything that occurs. A characteristic of this *loss of control* is the devolution and spread of responsibility for decision making among a wider group of managers and employees. Merton and other writers on bureaucracy[5] argue that a need by the originators to feel that they are still on top of this devolved situation leads to the development of systems and procedures which specify the conditions under which delegated decision-making power may be used by those lower down the organization. Such systems effectively *place limits* on managers in terms of the way they will operate and throw an emphasis on the *means* by which ends will be achieved, rather than on the *ends* themselves.

One consequence of this emphasis is a concentration on *efficiency* judgements rather than on those based on *effectiveness*. (Decision makers are judged on how closely their actions approximate to the prescribed or recommended operating procedures, rather than on whether or not they achieve the required results or goals.) Such efficiency judgements, of course, have a lot going for them in practice. Measurements against established procedures incorporate a great deal of certainty. Effectiveness judgements, on the other hand, are much more difficult to make, involving as they do speculation about what 'might be possible' and thus providing much less certainty about success or failure. Unfortunately, the characteristics of creativity in decision making — imagination, speculation, risk taking, trying out new ideas, and so on — are not the kinds of behaviour that are stimulated by the climate which is usually generated within traditional organization structures with their emphasis on efficiency.

### Creative and Non-Creative Roles

Work roles within organizations vary in the extent to which they are prescribed and defined. Usually, most time and effort is spent in formally prescribing those roles at the bottom of the organizational hierarchy where jobs tend to be more routine and repetitive, with little discretional content allowed the role occupant. A worker on a car assembly line, for example, or a counter assistant in a large department store, will have a closely defined job with little discretion. The assumption that is inherent in tight definition is that jobs at the bottom of the hierarchy do not contain elements where choices have to be made; and, of course, if a job has had the element of choice and discretion designed out of it, then there is not going to be much scope for creativity. Employees occupying such roles are, in a sense, being 'trained' not to be creative. In many companies, special suggestions schemes exist for capturing 'good ideas' from employees. These ideas, far from being regarded as part of normal behaviour, are rewarded by special payments and prizes. The very nature of such schemes assumes that creative behaviour from large sections of the workforce is the exception rather than the rule. When shop-floor workers then get promoted into roles where choice and discretion are required, it should come as no surprise when they are rather less creative than we might like or need.

### Variations in Function

In many organizations, work roles clustered around certain functions are seen as being essentially creative, while others are not. Some managers may feel restricted in the extent to which they try to act creatively because of perceptions about how their particular function or department should operate. Managers in production and financial departments, for example, may see themselves as having little or nothing to do with creative activities, while their counterparts in marketing or product design may see creativity as virtually their *only* concern.

### Status Levels and the Initiation of Ideas

Traditionally, the task of initiating new ideas and of opening up areas for change and development has been seen as the prerogative of senior managers, team leaders or others who have been given the special status of idea generator. This kind of delineation can have two adverse effects. First, it tends to restrict creative output in terms of new ideas from those employees who are not accorded such status. Second, the status holders themselves may feel obligated to deliver particular levels of output in terms of innovative ideas. For some people, but perhaps not many, the stimulus of producing ideas to order, whether self-imposed or not, is a very powerful one. For most, however, it has the opposite effect of restricting creativity. For the organization as a whole, mechanisms which allocate idea generation to a limited number of high-status roles are clearly unproductive. Perhaps a more appropriate expectation of occupants of such roles might be that they should take the lead in *stimulating creativity in others*. In order to encourage the generation of ideas and an interest in problem solving throughout the organization, a climate has to be evolved which spreads the expectation of such behaviour much more evenly through a wide spectrum of work roles.

## Socialization into Non-Creative Activity

The majority of employees within any large-scale enterprise do not usually take part in decision-making activities where they are called upon to exercise discretion. They are usually engaged in carrying out activities that depend on decisions already made by others elsewhere in the organization. If they do themselves exercise choice, then they again do it with little or no discretion. That is to say, the alternative courses of action are already laid out and the decision process really consists of applying whichever best fits the situation.

Under circumstances such as these, the process of socialization works to push the individual into an attitude towards work in which being creative plays little or no part. Such behaviour is rarely required through the formal job description, there is nothing in the pay packet of most employees to reward good ideas, and colleagues and workmates may demonstrate through their behaviour that creativity is the exception rather than the rule.

## Lack of Recognition

Creative behaviour in most large-scale organizations has come to be regarded as something of a bonus, one which cannot be planned in, and which must be seized upon as and when it occurs. As a result, most reward systems are geared towards the measurement of routine rather than of exceptional performances. In this way, the concept of originality and creativity as being extraordinary organizational events is reinforced. The establishment of sytems of rewards and recognition which are based on the exception of creative behaviour from the *majority* of employees, rather than the exceptional few, would go a long way towards creating the kind of climate in which such behaviour can flourish.

# Individual and Organizational Creativity

## The Creative Individual

Having previously put forward the idea that creativity is, or at least can be, characteristic of all individuals, it is only fair to acknowledge that some people are visibly more creative than others. Only a small proportion of employees consistently produce original and worthwhile products and ideas (at least while they are at work!). By looking at the qualities and characteristics of those individuals who are judged to be highly creative, we can get an idea of what might be enhanced or encouraged in others, in order to stimulate creative behaviour throughout a wider population.

### Dissatisfaction

A common finding is that highly creative individuals tend to show considerable dissatisfaction with the current state of affairs. The unknown and the new experience are seen as attractive possibilities, rather than something to be avoided. Change and adaptation are both welcomed and sought after by the creative person.

### Mental Abilities

According to Steiner,[6] 'highs' (highly creative persons) usually outscore 'lows' in tests of conceptual fluency, conceptual flexibility and originality, and in a preference for complexity. Relatively high levels of general intelligence would seem to be associated with creativity, but differences in intelligence within that high level do not appear to be closely linked with differences in creativity.

### Personality and Emotionality

Some writers (Box 10.1) have characterized the creative individual as continuously experiencing conflict in being attracted towards what would normally be thought of as conflicting states: between order and disorder, between rationality and intuition, between conformity and non-conformity. Whereas most people would favour one state rather than the other, highly creative individuals would seem able to accept the virtues of both.

### Self-Awareness

In general, findings about creative individuals seem to emphasize the extent to which they have an awareness of themselves, their acceptance of both good and bad personal characteristics, and, in a sense, the way in which they seem able to turn what to other people would seem weaknesses into strengths.

## The Creative Organization

There is no doubt that many, if not all, organizations of any size contain some highly creative people. This, unfortunately, is no guarantee that the total organization will then show similar signs of creativity. Of course, if these creative individuals occupy strategic positions within the organization, it is possible for them to exert considerable influence on the style adopted throughout the organization as a whole. Generally, though, really creative and innovative organizations are those which are able to make the best possible use of all human talents and resources, rather

Box 10.1

''The more creative personalities show a more rich and turbulent emotional life. Creative males show relatively high scores on femininity tests, whilst creative females show relatively high masculine scores. Creative persons also tend to score high on such measures of pathology as depression, hypochondrias, hysteria, psychopathic deviation and schizophrenia but, contrary to the usual pattern for other persons judged to be psychologically ill, the creative persons tend to have very high ego strength (Barron, 1965; Dellas and Gaier, 1970). The more creative personalities also show higher acceptance of both their desirable and undesirable characteristics than the less creative types.'[7]

Box 10.2

Gary Steiner's view[8] of the creative organization:

- Has ideas people, open communication channels, ideas units, lots of outside contacts.
- Has a policy of heterogenous recruitment, including marginal, unusual types; allows eccentricity.
- Has an objective, fact-founded approach; evaluates ideas and people on merit, not on status.
- Is not over-committed materially and financially to products and policies; invests in basic research; has flexible long-range planning; experiments with new ideas.
- Is decentralized and diversified; has resource slack and a risk-taking ethos; tolerates and expects taking chances.
- Is not run as a tight ship; employees have freedom and have fun.
- Has original and different objectives; is not just trying to be another 'X'.

than leaning excessively on their 'high' creators. It is possible to draw a picture of the highly creative organization in much the same way as we can for the highly creative individual, a picture which points the way for the development of a more creative organizational style (e.g. Box 10.2). As with individuals, creative organizations seem to build on the variety and richness of their members, allowing and even encouraging differences, rather than insisting on prescribed and singular approaches. Allied with this is the need for a structure which is able to capture and to capitalize on this richness, together with a climate that places a high value on creativity and regards it as the norm rather than the exception. In a sense, the characteristics of the creative individual are replicated in the organization, many features of individual creativity having their parallel in the operating mode of the creative organization.

## The Link Between the Individual and the Organization

Organizations which allow their members to display their creative talents are themselves behaving in a creative manner. There would seem to be a number of ways in which individual and organizational creativity are linked or related.

### *Potential Creativity of Organization Members*

The total creativity displayed by an organization is to a very great degree limited by the extent to which its members are capable individually of creative behaviour. It may well be that a particular company may have a rather small reservoir of creative talent; or it may be that the real problem is not that the reservoir is too small, but that the talent is not developed and exploited.

### *The Value Placed in Creativity by the Organization*

The creative talents of organizational members tend to be used in the interests of that organization to the extent that they are seen to be valued. The more a company demonstrates to its employees that certain behaviour is needed and appreciated, the more likely those employees are to demonstrate that behaviour.

### *The Building of 'Creative' Structures and Management Systems*

An impetus to creativity can be provided through the characteristics of the organizational system itself, over and above the potential of its members. Steiner's work shows that creative organizations have distinctive kinds of structure (open and flexible) which allow creative behaviour actually to take place, and distinctive management systems (taking risks, rewarding ideas, eccentricity) which encourage and promote it.

## Recruitment or Development?

One option which is, of course, open to any organization is to seek out and recruit new members who are felt to be especially creative. There is no doubt that, in areas which are often held out as being especially sensitive, this is a very appropriate and rewarding strategy. Specialist functions, such as product design, research and development, or marketing, have traditionally used recruitment to improve their creativity. The major advantage in using this method is that it tends to produce innovative ideas (even old ideas from outside can be very innovative and productive when brought into a new situation!). New entrants to an organization can provide stimulus and challenge to ways of working and to established routines for tackling problems. There are also drawbacks in using recruitment to gain creativity, as well as practical limitations on the extent to which it can be utilized.

*Recruitment Tends to be Most Useful during Periods of Organizational Growth*

Adding new members to an organization is a costly business. When increases in personnel are justified by expansion and growth, then of course it becomes a perfectly feasible and indeed sensible strategy. Many organizations which most need to improve their creativity in decision making are unfortunately not in such a position and their objective is normally to obtain more benefit from fewer resources.

*Recruiting 'Creative' People Tends to Emphasize their Special Status*

The danger here is that organizations will fall back into the trap of regarding creativity as the possession of the few rather than of the many; of assuming that the majority of organizational members are non-creators, which they are not.

*The Problem of Assessing Creativity*

While there have been a number of measures developed which purport to test for and assess creativity,[9] most organizations do not in fact make use of them, preferring instead to look at the record of creative behaviour of potential recruits. The problem here is that performance record often depends on performance opportunity, so that a person who has worked for a 'creative' organization might well be judged to be personally more creative and therefore more desirable than someone who has worked for a non-creative organization. Indeed, a company wishing to improve its own creativity by recruitment from outside might have overlooked or viewed unfavourably its present employees because they have not been given the opportunity to turn creative potential into actuality.

*Recruiting for more than 'just' Creativity*

It is only in very special circumstances that recruiters feel that creativity is the primary quality they are looking for in potential recruits to an organization. Normally it has to take its place on the job specification alongside many other characteristics, many of which take precedence. For instance, a 'creative' engineer is normally recruited from a pool of applicants who are sifted first of all in terms of their engineering competencies. It is unlikely that creativity as such will be the overriding or indeed the decisive factor in most recruitment decisions.

The recruitment of creative individuals is a method which can be used to enlarge or enrich the total pool available to organizations. For the vast majority, however, it must remain essentially a fringe activity. As such, it fits in well with the traditional view of creativity as itself a 'fringe activity' which is carried out by rather special and sometimes rather peculiar people. A move towards its recognition as something that can be expected from a significantly larger proportion of employees, or as an essential part of management activities on a regular basis and in high volume, requires a change in managerial view, together with a different approach to obtaining that creative behaviour.

*The view is:* all organizational members are capable of contributing in a much more creative way than they currently do.

*The approach is:* organizations can encourage and develop creative behaviour through a strategy of 'creative management'.

## The Creative Management Strategy

The turning of potential into actual behaviour which is (relatively) highly creative is a central part of the manager's task, especially in the decision-making situation. Such situations provide an opportunity for the manager to create the kind of organizational climate in which creative behaviour is encouraged, leading to innovative decisions and novel solutions to problems. Such a climate would be characterized by:

1. The free flow of information and open access to it.
2. Encouragement and reward for finding, using and sharing such information.
3. Rewards for the positive acceptance of change and risk taking.[10]

Using these ideas as a basis for the kind of climate which might encourage creative problem solving and decision making, we can identify a managerial strategy for its achievement, or at least for its fostering and encouragement. While the development of any particular climate is not entirely within the hands of the manager, he or she is obviously a key figure whose actions can be particularly influential in 'seeding' the process. Certainly, management style can be very effective in blocking or preventing creativity!

While any successful strategy for 'creativity management' must be tailored to suit particular circumstances, it is possible to identify two key areas:

1. The application of control and reward systems that emphasize creativity and associated activities.
2. The development of a supportive personal style on the part of the manager.

### Control and Reward Systems

This aspect of the strategy is concerned essentially with the development of 'formal' and systematic aspects of management. All employees (managers included) operate within a structure of rules and guidelines which are concerned with relating employee effort to organizational tasks and objectives. Such structures provide a system of *controls*, whereby employee behaviour is channelled and directed towards what are deemed to be the best interests of the organization. The main mechanisms for achieving this are contained within the 'reward system': the means by which formal rewards such as wages and salaries, bonuses, regradings and promotions are determined. Most reward systems evolve in a piecemeal manner as the organization grows, focusing primarily on problems of rewarding for the routine tasks within the organization and on treating employees in a manner which is seen to be equitable. In achieving these goals, reward systems often militate, albeit unintentionally, against creativity. Systems which reward for competence in established procedures can create an atmosphere where the perceived need is *not to fail* rather than to succeed. The following guidelines, if taken into account when designing or modifying the organization's reward system, will encourage and stimulate creative decision-making activity.

### Link Rewards to Task Accomplishment

Focus the attention of your decision makers on the end product, by gearing rewards to success in problem solving and to the accomplishment of organizational objectives, rather than on the minutiae of proper procedures. The emphasis should be on 'getting the job done', rather than on 'doing it the right way'.

### Set High Performance Standards

Performance targets which are set within previously demonstrated capacity are unlikely to encourage creativity and innovation. Employees, knowing that targets are easily achievable, will resort to well-tried procedures and 'satisficing' decision behaviour. Reaching out towards 'unknown territory' is likely to stimulate innovation and lead to new approaches.

### Reward Co-operative Activities

Innovation and creativity can be increased through the sharing and co-operative building up of information and of ideas. Reward systems which focus heavily on personal individual achievement tend to restrict this process. Credit must be given for co-operative as well as for individual performance.

Present moves to encourage co-operation, such as the development and use of 'quality circles',[11] 'cells' and 'task groups', tend to continue to rely heavily on the individual's personal feelings of satisfaction and achievement as the rewards for co-operation. Any formal reward system which is too heavily focused around individual performance will work against and may even negate any potential benefits.

### Encourage Adaptation and Change

Organizational rewards should encourage employees to anticipate and make changes. Too rigid and complex a reward system may generate resistance and slow the adaptation process.

*Reward Risk Taking*

Increasingly, creative decision making brings with it an increase in risk. Not all innovative decisions will be successful. Those making the decisions will be discouraged from taking risks if the penalties for failure outweigh, or are more visible than, the rewards for succeeding.

## A Supportive Personal Style

Reward systems which follow most or all of the five guidelines above will set up the *potential* for increased creativity. The key to turning that potential into reality lies in the hands of management, through the adoption of a style which facilitates creative behaviour in subordinates.

Managers have perhaps traditionally seen their task as being to channel and to control the activities of subordinates in a fairly prescriptive and limiting fashion (see Box 10.3). The key point about ideas like theory Y are that they are judgements about human resources that are *potentially* available to the organization in decision situations. That potential will not be released if it is held in check through a management style which is based on external control and 'assumes the worst' about people. Managers must adopt a *supportive* style, providing and developing the conditions under which those they manage feel able to use the full range of their talents in working on organizational problems and tasks. For some managers, this will require a switch in emphasis that may cause considerable adjustment problems.

The message from writers like McGregor is that creative behaviour is only likely to occur when employees are given the opportunity to meet the higher-order needs of self-actualization and expression within the work situation. If managers want creativity from the people who work for them, they have to take it as part of a package which includes such other factors as involvement, participation and shared responsibility. A manager cannot behave in a directing, controlling manner most of the time and then expect subordinates to produce insights and innovations at the drop of a hat.

The increasing need for creativity requires that subordinates be given the opportunity to develop *self-control* and a high degree of independence of action. The managerial style has to be one of support and encouragement for the individual. It should lead to a reduction in the level of external control, particularly over the determination of the 'means', the way in which organizational goals are to be achieved.

## Management as a Creative Activity

It is certainly true that some decision situations in which managers find themselves are not ones which call for high levels of creative activity, either from themselves or from subordinates. It is equally certain, however, that the number of situations

---

*Box 10.3*

McGregor,[12] labelling the traditional view as 'theory X', argues that managers who see their job as being to direct, control, manipulate and punish have a view of the average employee as being insolent, lazy, lacking in ambition, self-centred and resistant to change. He regards this view, on which traditional management approaches are based, as mistaken, and argues that, while employees might behave in such a way as to support a theory X style, such behaviour represents a learned response to organizational circumstances and forces, to a system which minimizes rather than maximizes human potential. McGregor argues that management should adopt a style which is based on a more accurate picture of human potential, which he has called 'theory Y'.

Some theory Y assumptions are as follows:

- The expenditure of physical and mental effort in work is as natural as play or rest.

- External control and the threat of punishment are not the only means of bringing about effort towards organizational objectives. Human beings will exercise self-direction and self-control in the service of objectives to which they are committed.

- Commitment to objectives is a function of the rewards associated with their achievement.

- Most people learn, under proper conditions, not only to accept but actually to seek responsibility.

- The capacity to exercise a relatively high degree of imagination, ingenuity and creativity in the solution of organizational problems is widely, not narrowly, distributed in the population.

- Under the conditions of modern industrial life, the intellectual potentialities of the average human being are only partially utilized.

---

in which that really is the case is diminishing rapidly. Current conditions of rapid economic and technological change, the scenario of breathtaking political developments in Eastern Europe and throughout the world, and the ever-increasing questioning of the relationship between business and industry and society are combining to push the need for creativity and innovation to the forefront of managerial activity. It would seem imperative, therefore, to modify the traditional view of management's task as being to plan, organize, motivate and control so as to include the need to create and to innovate.

The need for increased creativity and innovation is now widely recognized in companies and work organizations. Knowledge and ideas gained through the behavioural sciences provide guidance as to how to go about encouraging creative behaviour. The achievement of such enhanced levels of creativity in others however, requires that managers themselves be increasingly creative. Subordinates must be recognized as having real worth and the ability to contribute to the understanding and the solution of problems. While such recognition and involvement is, in itself, highly motivating, concern for people and their needs is not enough. Potential creativity must be tapped by allowing employees to contribute actively and genuinely

---

*Box 10.4*

In the short term, supportive management styles have to show themselves in a range of *behaviour and actions* which provides the kind of environment within which decision makers are most likely to feel able to put forward creative and original options.[13] This behaviour might include:

- Giving credit; acknowledging; listening attentively; giving support; showing approval.

- Dealing with others as equals in the generation of ideas.

- Being optimistic; trying to see the value in what is suggested; focusing on the positive aspects of the idea.

- Protecting the vulnerable beginnings of an idea.

- Assuming it can be made to work; taking things on faith; not looking for proof too early.

- Listening to the thrust rather than the detail of the idea.

- Taking the responsibility for understanding; demonstrating that understanding.

---

to the achievement of high-performance objectives. The creative manager is one who recognizes the worth of the human resource, and then uses it to the full in decision making.

Long-term improvements in creative and innovative capacity depend very much on an organization's ability to develop the appropriate control and reward systems discussed earlier, and on the adoption of management styles which encourage innovative approaches to problems (see Box 10.4).

## Techniques for Creative Problem Solving

A number of operational techniques have been developed which are designed to allow individuals and groups to make the most of their present creative capacities in aspects of problem solving and decision making. These techniques are designed primarily to create circumstances under which obstacles to creative action are removed or reduced. As well as having the specific purpose of tackling particular problems, their use is likely to contribute to the gradual development of a climate which is generally supportive of creativity in decision making.

### Basic Rules for Creativity Techniques

All techniques which are designed to foster creativity, whatever their particular emphasis, seem to incorporate two basic rules or elements.

*1.  Separate out Judgement and Evaluation from Idea Generation*

One certain way of drying up the flow of ideas is to pass judgement on specific notions as they are put forward. It has the effect of reducing the contribution individuals may feel like making in the face of negative feedback, and of cutting off an individual's or group's developing pattern and build-up of ideas. Many groups using creativity techniques develop exotic 'penalty systems' which operate when members are felt to be evaluating ideas during the generation phase. 'Separation' here refers specifically to the phases during which idea generation and evaluation are carried out. It does not imply necessarily that different people should be involved in each process. This practice tends to have a restricting effect on creativity.

*2.  Consider All Ideas that are Put Forward*

One particularly non-creative way of treating ideas is to deny them evaluation and consideration. All ideas put forward, even those that are apparently unworkable, must be considered equally and against the same criteria. For this purpose, most techniques include some method of ensuring that all ideas are recorded.

## Conditions which Aid Creativity

It is possible to focus attention and to heighten sensitivity towards the task at hand by structuring the situation in which any particular technique is attempted. Such structural aids, though simple in themselves, go a long way towards improving the chances of success.

*Set a Time Limit on the Exercise Itself*

Although the actual limit must vary from case to case, there is a lot to be gained by limiting the time available and therefore, perhaps, reducing the chances of over-elaboration and evaluation.

*Choose a Private, Secluded Location*

Those working on the problem must be free from distraction and interruption so as to allow them to focus their full attention on the problem before them. Telephone calls are fatal!

*Include Facilities for Writing, Drawing and Display*

Ideas get lost when they are not recorded. Evidence[14] suggests that short-term memory inhibits us in problem solving and idea building because of the limited number of steps and developments that can be held in the mind at any one time. The use of external aids is vital if we are to capture and retain large numbers of ideas. Some people also work best in forming ideas if they are allowed to use visual symbols, to draw pictures, diagrams and maps. External recording also allows ideas to be shared, worked on and developed by others, thus increasing the chances of producing a really good idea.

### Start with Tension-Breaking Exercises

Individuals may well start sessions feeling uncertain, embarrassed or uncomfortable. To this end, it can be useful to start the sessions over a cup of coffee, or to run a preliminary exercise which is designed to help along the loosening-up process. Some groups have used physical exercises and games very successfully in achieving this.

### Give Up When the Energy Goes

Creativity techniques only really work well when those attempting them are enthusiastic and motivated. Techniques are primarily designed to overcome or to reduce the obstacles to creativity. While they may stimulate individual enthusiasm, they cannot substitute for it. When the energy has dropped, move on to the next phase, or finish the exercise.

All creativity techniques rely on two basic approaches:

1. The thorough and systematic analysis of the problem.
2. Attempts to encourage a free flow of ideas and the association of previously unrelated notions.

Some techniques are rooted more in one approach than the other, although many are combinations of both. The difference between the two becomes clear when we look at some examples.

## Analytical Techniques

### Attribute Listing

This technique[15] is essentially very simple and is perhaps most useful in situations where managers might be looking to the development of basic ideas, to spin-off from an existing product or to the extension of a product range. The first stage is to identify and pick out the major attributes of the problem, object or issue under consideration. In the case of a physical product, these might be such factors as size, weight, shape, cost, price and colour. Each of these attributes in turn is then altered in as many ways as possible, each alteration and combination of altered attributes creating a potentially different product or idea. When all the possible combinations have been listed, they can then be subjected to evaluation and judgement against whatever criteria have been chosen.

The idea behind this technique is that, when we think through problem situations in the 'whole', we tend to operate at a high level of generalization. Breaking problems up into their component characteristics allows us to avoid our stereotyped limitations and to recombine our ideas into richer pictures.

---

## Case Exercise 1

---

You have been employed as a consultant by a Christmas novelty company to come up with new ideas for novelty balloons. After discussions with the company, you decide that the major attributes for novelty balloons are: colour; size; shape; price; durability.

1. Establish a range of alternatives (try for at least five) for each attribute.
2. List as many different potential products as you can by combining alternative attributes. Count the total number.
3. Decide which of the potential products you think might be worth taking further as a possible new balloon product.

### Process Analysis [16]

Another way of enriching our understanding of a problem situation is to think about the processes (thoughts, movements, intermediate consequences, etc.) of the actors in the situation, taking it on from the initial scenario. This process will often allow us to make progress towards a solution.

Imagine the following scenario. A party of six male diners enter a crowded restaurant, handing in their coats at reception. When they get up to leave, a helpful waiter hands out coats to each diner without checking to see who owns each one. What is the probability that exactly five diners will be given their own coats? If we think through the process and imagine each diner in turn being given back his coat, it soon becomes apparent that, if five diners have the right coats, then so must the sixth. Therefore the probability of exactly five diners getting the right coat back is zero.

## Techniques for Aiding Creative Thinking

Some techniques are designed to help problem solvers in the process of thinking through and exploring new linkages. The following ideas can help.

*Analogies*

In order to understand and explore situations and gain new insights, it is often helpful to consider analogous circumstances or situations. A variety of analogies are possible:[17]

1. *Personal analogy:* where the decision maker tries to identify personally with elements of the situation, expressing and exploring characteristics through drawing personal parallels.

2. *Direct analogy:* drawing comparisons with parallel situations where more perhaps can be discovered about the direct parallel than can be seen in the immediate problem.

3. *Symbolic analogy:* giving the problem the characteristics of some object such as a tree or an animal. Attempting to describe the problem in terms of those characteristics can allow new insights.

4. *Fantasy analogy:* literally fantasizing about solutions to problems and then developing, in a sense, a 'working model' of that fantastic solution.

*The Intermediate Impossible* [18]

The conventional reaction on discovering that a proposed solution does not work is to give up and try some other route. One way of breaking the evaluative stranglehold is to take a further step forward and to explore ways in which the 'impossible' solution might be turned into a possible one. In terms of our model in Chapter 1, this technique would form part of the recycling process.


Group Techniques

There is considerable evidence that groups, if utilized correctly, can be particularly creative. A number of techniques have been evolved, some of which are outlined below.

*Brainstorming*

Brainstorming[19] is perhaps the most well known of all creativity techniques. Unfortunately, the technique, which has very clear and precise guidelines, has become associated with any generally unstructured ideas session or discussion. Brainstorming would appear to be generally applicable across a wide range of problems, but is perhaps particularly useful in tackling 'how to do it' problems or those where broad direction is needed. It is less effective where groups need to bring together a wide range of different experts who need to make contributions. A small group, preferably not more than about eight people, is presented with the problem. They are then asked to generate as many ideas as possible in a limited time (half an hour is typical) that are designed to resolve that problem. Familiar rules apply in the brainstorming session:

1. Aim for as many ideas as possible.
2. All ideas must be recorded.
3. Building on other people's ideas is encouraged — no judgement or criticism is allowed.

The last rule is particularly important in brainstorming situations, where it is very easy to indicate disapproval by either verbal or non-verbal means. Groups are encouraged to elect a chairperson to keep order and a secretary to make sure that all ideas get recorded. Groups in one company use a small brass ship's bell to 'ring out' anyone caught evaluating.

## Case Exercise 2

You are the manager of an assembly plant putting together electric motors for use in toys and models. Your foreman recently came to you to report that several of his female workers have complained that a fellow worker (male) has been harassing them by continually watching them and staring at them as they work. You have investigated these complaints, and, while the man concerned denies the allegations vehemently, you feel there is some substance to them. The women in the section concerned have threatened to refuse to work with the man unless something is done. What action should you take?

1. Using the brainstorming technique, write down as many actions as possible which you might take (keep going for at least ten minutes). Remember, no evaluation!
2. Go through your list and pick out the ideas you think are pertinent and possibly useful.
3. Select the best idea or combination of ideas for a strategy for action.

A derivation of brainstorming is the technique of *brainwriting*.[20] Here participants write their ideas down on paper, rather than contributing them to a communal list. In the centre of the group is an extra list, containing a few ideas generated by the leader before the group session begins. As soon as a member runs out of ideas, he or she exchanges his or her list with the one from the centre of the group, continuing to generate ideas on the new list. The idea is that participants will be stimulated by ideas they pick up from the centre list and can concentrate on thinking up ideas without being distracted by conversation or influenced by particular individuals in the group.

A further association technique, which has much in common with brainstorming, is the *Gordon technique*.[21] In this case, much the same rules apply but only the group leader knows the precise nature of the problem. This restriction is devised so as to prevent the group from reaching a solution too early. A potential danger of brainstorming is that a participant may well come to believe that an idea that is put forward is the ideal solution to the problem under consideration. That participant is then likely to stop putting forward any more ideas. This cannot happen if only the group leader knows the true nature of the problem. The leader is responsible for starting a general discussion which covers the broad area of the problem and then focuses it down more precisely. Clearly, this technique depends heavily on the personal attributes of the leader for its success.

### Nominal Group Technique

This technique was developed in an attempt to overcome some of the biases that were felt to arise from the social processes within brainstorming groups. It differs from other group techniques in that the evaluation stage is built into the process in a rather more prescribed way. The nominal group technique[22] has the following major stages:

1. Members produce independent lists of ideas in writing.
2. In a group setting, each member describes one idea to the group.
3. Once all ideas have been listed, they are discussed and evaluated by the group.
4. Individuals then vote separately on the ideas in order to arrive at the final decision.

### Forced Relationship Techniques

One group of techniques is based upon the establishment of relationships between normally unrelated objects or ideas. These are clearly techniques based on the association of ideas, but the degree of freedom is limited by the objects under consideration. Objects or ideas are usually chosen arbitrarily, often pushing participants into areas they have never before considered.

*Focused object linking* is a forced relationship technique which is particularly useful in situations where new applications are sought for existing products or services. One object is fixed; the other is chosen completely at random or from a list. Participants are then asked to find as many ways as possible to relate the fixed object with the one chosen at random. The 'forcing' of such relationships can lead to many new and original ideas.

---

## Case Exercise 3

---

You are a manager of a department in a company making computers for the aircraft industry. The rising number of cancellations of orders for new aircraft has placed your future business in jeopardy. Your workforce is highly skilled and versatile. You have been asked to think up new areas in which to diversify your computer application.

1. Your focused object is computers.

2. Ask a colleague or friend to choose a number from 1 to 10. With the number, find an item from the following list:
   (1) Garages and repair shops.
   (2) Schools.
   (3) Bus depots.
   (4) Houses.
   (5) Swimming pools.
   (6) Football grounds.
   (7) Public parks.
   (8) Supermarkets.
   (9) Libraries.
   (10) Garden centres.

3. You now have five minutes to write down as many uses as possible for computers in whatever item has been chosen.

4. Now ask your colleague or friend to pick another number and find that item from the list of uses you have just produced.

5. Write down as many locations or market situations as possible where a computer could be used for the purpose you have just picked out. Again you have five minutes.

This process can be repeated many times, and the number of uses/market situations that can be generated is considerable.

## Individual and Group Techniques

Brainstorming and other association techniques are designed primarily for use in small groups. The obvious advantage is that participants develop and build on ideas through working with colleagues. There is no reason, however, why creativity techniques cannot be adapted and used by individuals.

## Reliance on Techniques

There is considerable danger that managers may see the use of operational creativity techniques as being the 'answer' to the creativity problem. They may be seized upon as a neat and tidy way of structuring in idea generation without having to alter the fabric of structure and culture at all. The dangers of this approach are obvious. First, employees will come to associate creativity with the technique, rather than recognizing the need to be more creative at all times. Second, the techniques will rapidly become part of the routine, something to be endured rather than enjoyed, losing their impact and their effectiveness.

Creativity techniques such as those outlined here must be used against a background of control and reward systems which promote idea generation, and under a management style where innovation and creativity are expected and encouraged. Where this happens, techniques will be used positively and selectively and as deliberate aids to creative expression.

## Practical Prescriptions

Creative thinking plays a valuable role in management decision making. Recognizing and formulating problems, and in particular generating a range of alternative solutions, require a creative approach which must be brought together with the more analytical processes of objective setting and evaluation.

In order to stimulate creative activity, avoid:

1. Overstressing efficiency at the expense of effectiveness.
2. Setting up some roles as being creative and others as not.
3. Teaching staff to be non-creative by having low expectations of them.

Managers can encourage the development of creative behaviour by adopting a supportive personal style and by developing reward and control systems which:

1. Link rewards to task accomplishment.
2. Set high performance standards.
3. Reward co-operative activities.
4. Encourage adaptation and change.

Idea generation techniques generally rely on the two basic principles of (a) separating out judgement and evaluation from the actual process of idea generation and (b) giving equal consideration to all ideas that are generated. Use techniques positively and selectively in order to help solve problems, and at the same time encourage a general move towards more creative behaviour among decision makers.

## Bibliography

Adams, J.L., *The Care and Feeding of Ideas*, Penguin, 1988. A sourcebook of ideas on creative problem solving.

Coopey, J., 'The case for creativity in complex organisations', *Personnel Management*, March 1987, pp. 30–3. An interesting article on the need for the creative organization in today's operating conditions.

Morgan, G., *Creative Organisation Theory*, Sage, 1989. A 'creative' book, full of material which is relevant to this chapter and to decision making in general.

Richard, T., *Stimulating Innovation: A systems approach*, Pinter, 1985.

# References

1. Ribeaux, P. and Poppleton, S., *Psychology and Work*, Macmillan, 1978, pp. 197–200.
2. Adams, J.L., *The Care and Feeding of Ideas*, Penguin, 1988, p. 7.
3. De Bono, E., *Lateral Thinking for Management*, Penguin, 1982, p. 4.
4. In one successful UK manufacturing company, groups of new graduates are brought together to investigate potential problems in a creative and innovative manner, their organizational naivety being felt to contribute to originality. The graduates have to leave the group after twelve months when they have become too familiar with company practice and procedures!
5. For an overview of such views, see Dalton, G.W. and Lawrence, P.R., *Motivation and Control in Organisations*, Irwin Dorsey, 1970, chapter 1.
6. Steiner, G., *The Creative Organisation*, University of Chicago Press, 1965, pp. 6–7.
7. Alderfer, C.P., 'Change processes in organisations', in Dunnette, M.V. (ed.), *Handbook of Social and Organisational Psychology*, Rand-McNally, 1976, pp. 1598–9.
8. Steiner, *op. cit.*, pp. 16–18.
9. Taylor, R.N., *Behavioral Decision Making*, Scott Foresman, 1984, pp. 39–43.
10. Klatt, L.A., Murdick, R. and Schuster, F.E., *Human Resources Management: A behavioral systems approach*, Irwin, 1978, pp. 433–6.
11. For an approach which is very much centred on using people in a co-operative/consultative way, see Collard, R., *Total Quality: Success through people*, Institute of Personnel Management, 1989.
12. McGregor, D., *The Human Side of Enterprise*, McGraw-Hill, 1960, pp. 45–57.
13. These ideas are taken from material by George Prince, reported in Adams, *op. cit.*, p. 185.
14. Evans, J. St.B.T., *Bias in Human Reasoning*, Lawrence Erlbaum Associates, 1989, pp. 28–9.
15. Adams, *op. cit.*, pp. 109–12.
16. Bazerman, M.H., *Judgement in Managerial Decision Making*, Wiley, 1986, pp. 94–7.
17. Summers, I. and White, D.E., 'Creativity techniques: toward improvement of the decision process', in Head, T.C. (ed.), *Organisational Behaviour*, Houghton Mifflin, 1986, p. 164.
18. The notion of the 'intermediate impossible' seems to have been used first by Edward de Bono. See, for instance, De Bono, E., *Practical Thinking*, Jonathan Cape, 1971, chapter 9.
19. Adams, *op. cit.*, pp. 183–4.
20. Gescha, H., Schaude, G.R. and Schicksupp, H., 'Modern techniques for solving problems', *Journal of Chemical Engineering*, August 1973.
21. Gordon, W.J., 'Operational approach to creativity', *Harvard Business Review*, November/December 1956, pp. 41–51.
22. Delbecq, A.L., Van De Ven, A.H. and Gustafson, D., *Group Techniques for Programme Planning*, Scott Foresman, 1975.

# 11 Evaluating the options

## Introduction

Evaluating quite literally means determining the value or worth of things. It involves exploring, understanding and describing the consequences of each option.

Before evaluation, objectives should have been set and workable decision criteria established from them. The problems or context of the decision should be well understood. The alternative options from which the choice will be made should have been identified. The next step is to spell out what it would mean to adopt each option — evaluation.

## Which Factors?

The precise nature of attributes to be evaluated for each option depends on the nature of the decision itself. There will almost certainly be several of them, since very few real decisions can be evaluated in terms of one attribute alone. There is no 'all-purpose' list of attributes to be evaluated, though it is useful to think in terms of three classes of evaluation criteria:

1. The *feasibility* of each option.
2. The *acceptability* of each option.
3. The *vulnerability* of each option.

The 'feasibility' of an option indicates the degree of difficulty in adopting it, and should assess the investment of time, effort and money which it will need. The 'acceptability' of an option is how much it takes us towards our objectives. It is the return we get for choosing that option. The 'vulnerability' of an option indicates the extent to which things could go wrong if it is chosen. It is the risk we run by choosing the option. (See Figure 11.1.)

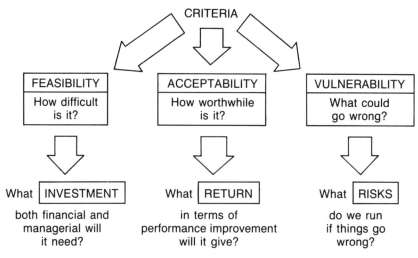

**Figure 11.1** Evaluating options

## Evaluating Feasibility

All decision options have resource implications — even the decision to do nothing frees resources which would otherwise be used. If the resources which are required to implement an option are greater than those which are either available or can be obtained, the option is infeasible. So evaluating the feasibility of an option means finding out how the various types of resource which the option might need match up to what is available.

Three broad questions are relevant when assessing resource requirements:

1. What technical or human skills are required to implement the option?

2. What are the capacity requirements over the evaluation period? (Here 'capacity requirements' means the operational requirements necessary to cope with any increased level of activity.)

3. What are the funding or cash requirements over the evaluation period?

### Assessing Skills Requirements

Every decision option will need a set of skills to be present within the organization, so that it can be successfully implemented. If an option requires a course of action which is very similar to the usual activities of the organization, then it is likely that the necessary skills will already be present. If, however, the option involves the organization in a completely novel set of actions, then it is necessary to identify the required skills and to match these against those existing in the organization.

As an example, consider a small engineering design consultancy partnership which has hitherto specialized in designing port facilities for developing countries. The company is approached by a national government, for which they have worked before, to see whether it would be interested in bidding for the contract for a large petrochemical plant and docks complex. The contract involves the engineering and design of the complex, and also managing the construction itself. The job would be by far the biggest the company had ever undertaken. It would involve hiring more engineers and designers, and also getting involved in project management for the first time.

The first consideration the company will face is, does it have sufficient expertise within the company to cope with this kind of work? The problem lies in identifying the types of skill necessary. As one of the company's managers puts it, 'It's not a matter of hiring the expertise, it's knowing what it is that you want to hire.' After consideration, the company decides to classify the expertise needed for the whole job by the skills necessary in the basic engineering, detailed design and project management of both petrochemical plant work and docks facility work. Figure 11.2 shows the results of the investigation into the existing skills within the company. It illustrates that the company is short of skills in three areas: project management in both docks and petrochemical plant construction, and basic petrochemical plant engineering. The company must now decide how it fills these gaps in its expertise.

## Assessing Capacity Requirements

Determining capacity requirements involves detailing the quantity of resources — people, facilities, space, materials, etc. — required for each option. The number of people and facilities required will depend on the amount of work involved in implementing the option. This in effect means estimating the time necessary to perform whatever tasks are involved.

In the case of the engineering consultancy company, its task is to assess the amount

| EXPERIENCE | Basic engineering | Detailed design | Project management |
|---|---|---|---|
| **Docks facilities** | Plenty of experience in the company | Plenty of experience in the company | No experience |
| **Petrochemical plant** | No experience | Some experience on very similar work | No experience |

**Figure 11.2** Expertise requirements for petrochemical/docks complex

of work which is likely to be involved in the proposed project. It does this by asking its engineers to estimate (as far as is possible with such a novel job) the amount of basic engineering and detailed design work necessary for each part of the job. Work in this case is estimated in terms of 'person weeks' of effort. The company knows the date by which the total project would need to be finished, and so can superimpose the aggregate workload for the proposed project on to its existing work commitment. Figure 11.3 shows how the aggregate workload level would look, up to the end of the project, should it be taken on.

By comparing the aggregate workload (in this case represented by the aggregate number of people required) with the existing capacity, the company can see when fresh capacity will be needed. Here the first twenty months of the project require twice the company's existing capacity for much of the time.

## Assessing Financial Requirements

In many decisions the most important feasibility question is, 'How much cash would the option require, and can we afford it?' For some operational decisions this could mean simply examining a one-off cost, such as the purchase price of a machine. Other, more strategic decisions may need an examination of the effect of each option on the cash requirements of the whole organization. In this type of decision,

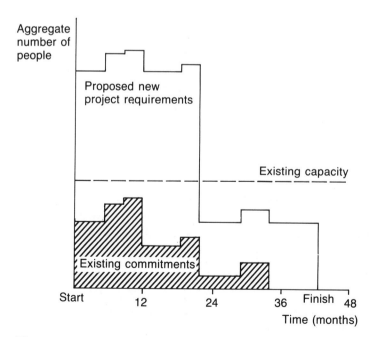

**Figure 11.3** Aggregate workload up to finish of project

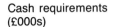

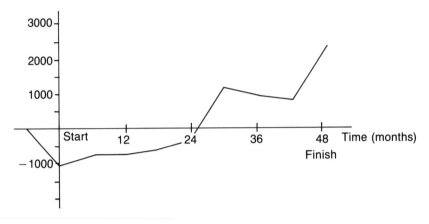

| | Six-month period | | | | | | | |
|---|---|---|---|---|---|---|---|---|
| | **0** | **1** | **2** | **3** | **4** | **5** | **6** | **7** | **8** |
| **Cash inflows** | 0 | 1000 | 1000 | 1000 | 1000 | 2000 | 0 | 0 | 3000 |
| **Cash outflows** | 1050 | 800 | 970 | 950 | 700 | 200 | 200 | 200 | 300 |
| **Net cash flow** | (1050) | 200 | 30 | 50 | 300 | 1800 | (200) | (200) | 1700 |
| **Beginning cash** **without financing** | 0 | (1050) | (850) | (820) | (770) | (470) | 1330 | 1130 | 930 |
| **Ending cash** **without financing** | (1050) | (850) | (820) | (770) | (470) | 1330 | 1130 | 930 | 2630 |

**Figure 11.4**  Cash inflows, outflows and requirements up to the finish of the project (£000s)

it is often worth simulating the organization's cash flow over the period of time being considered. Computing the total inflow of cash over time as it occurs, and subtracting from it the total outflow of cash as it occurs, leaves the net funding requirements for the option.

For example, the engineering consultants first of all find out the proposed schedule of payments from the customers as the work proceeds. They then detail and cost the extra personnel, computing facilities and office space as these costs occur over the project period. The resulting cash requirements are shown in Figure 11.4. A maximum funding requirement of £1 050 000 occurs within the first six months of the project, and diminishes only slowly for two years. After that, the project enjoys a large net inflow of cash. Of course, this analysis does not include the effects of interest payments on cash borrowed. When it is decided how the cash is to be raised, this can be included.

## The Degree of Change in Resource Requirements

We have assessed feasibility in terms of the skills, aggregate operating capacity and funding necessary. Any one of these could render an option infeasible. Yet even if all these resource requirements can quite feasibly be obtained individually by the organization, the degree of change in the total resource position of the company might itself be regarded as infeasible.

So, in the example we have been using throughout, the engineering consultancy company might be able to obtain all the required resources individually. It believes that it can recruit the engineering and management expertise. It can also obtain this expertise in sufficient quantity from the labour market. Furthermore, it believes that it could fund the project until it broke even. Yet the company may still regard the project as infeasible. It may decide that an expansion of its activities, which would more than double in size in six months, would put too great a strain on its own capability of organizing itself. It may want to grow, but may not be able to manage a growth at such a high rate. Thus, it is not the absolute level of resource requirements but the rate of change in resource requirements which is regarded as infeasible.

## Assessing 'Degree of Fit'

Options should not be evaluated in isolation from the normal day-to-day activity of an organization. If an option is eventually chosen, it will have to be implemented alongside existing activities. So an important characteristic of any decision option is its 'degree of fit' with the other activities of the organization. The degree of fit of an option indicates the extent to which any activity implied as a consequence of an option is compatible with the way in which resources are currently organized. This is not the same thing as determining resource requirements. When considering resources, the question was 'Can we do it?'; here is is 'Can we do it without disadvantaging or distracting from our current activities?' Options which have good fit do not detract from, and can even improve, existing activities. Existing skills can be complemented or exploited, and existing capabilities can be more fully utilized. Options which have poor fit detract from normal activities, by requiring either different skills from those currently used or different operating objectives.

The consequences of good or bad fit can be observed in the different functional areas. An option which has good *marketing fit* will fill an obvious gap in the product/service range, use existing distribution channels or require very similar promotion policies to existing products. Options which have poor marketing fit will require marketing activity which is different from, or isolated from, existing activity in such a way that it detracts from existing marketing efforts. For example, suppose a supplier of expensive high-quality shoes is offered a financially attractive bulk deal to purchase cheap imported shoes. No matter how financially attractive the deal may seem in isolation, if the shop tried to sell the shoes through its existing outlets, it would run the danger of its high-quality image being tarnished, which could repel its existing customers. The option, then, although seemingly financially sound in isolation, has very poor marketing fit.

Options which have good *operations fit* require the operations function to operate within its existing set of performance characteristics. Poor operations fit results when an option requires the operations function to perform to more than one set of operational objectives. For example, suppose a factory is producing a narrow range of products at a very high volume and a relatively low cost. Any option which changes the operational objective of cost minimization would fit badly with existing activities. Thus if it is proposed to offer a new product which would compete, say, on variety and delivery rather than cost, the operations function is being required to do dissimilar things with the same facilities.[1]

Often options will have a good fit in one functional area and a bad fit in another. Frequently, such options are proposed by the functional area in the organization which will benefit most from the good fit. The danger is that the benefits in one area will blind the decision makers to the negative consequences in other areas. For example, adding a range of products might be seen to have such beneficial marketing advantages that its negative consequences in other areas (increase in process stocks, new training programmes, production control problems, etc.) are never fully evaluated.

## Evaluating Acceptability

The acceptability of an option is the extent to which it fulfils the decisions objectives, so to some degree acceptability criteria depend on the objectives of the particular decision. Two generalizations can be useful, however:

- The *operational impact* of options should be evaluated.
- The *financial impact* of options should be evaluated.

### Assessing Operational Impact

If all decisions take place in an operational context, they will have operational consequences. So the framework of operational performance objectives described in Chapter 1 should form the basis of assessing each option's operational impact.

1. *Technical specification.* Does the option increase the likelihood that the service or product which the operation gives will be closer to what customers want: for example, better out-patient treatment in a hospital, better products to a manufacturer, better meals in the restaurant chain, and so on?

2. *Quality.* Does the option reduce the chance of errors occurring in the creation of services or products: for example, fewer errors in bank account statements,

less chance of paint scratches on automobiles, fewer errors on dental records, and so on?

3. *Responsiveness.* Does the option shorten the time customers have to wait for their services or products: for example, shorter queues in the supermarket, faster response from consultants, shorter delivery lead time from manufacturers, and so on?

4. *Dependability.* Does the option give an increased chance of things happening when they are supposed to happen: for example, the train arriving on time. the building being completed on time, the service engineer arriving as promised, and so on?

5. *Flexibility.* Does the option increase the flexibility of the operation, either in terms of the range of things which can be done or the speed of changing what can be done: for example, the variety of customer enquiries which can be handled by bank tellers without reference to a specialist, the speed with which an extra shift can be organized in a factory, and so on?

*Spell Out Competitive Benefits*

Assessing the operational impact of each option is especially useful if operational change is viewed in the light of how it contributes to increased competitiveness.[2] It is more useful still if 'competitiveness' includes a comparison of a company's operational performance with that of its competitors. The following nine-point scale can be used to do this.[3] Performance is:

1. Consistently considerably better than our nearest competitor.
2. Consistently clearly better than our nearest competitor.
3. Consistently marginally better than our nearest competitor.
4. Often marginally better than most competitors.
5. About the same as most competitors.
6. Often close to main competitors.
7. Usually marginally worse than main competitors.
8. Usually worse than most competitors.
9. Consistently worse than most competitors.

Figure 11.5 illustrates how this nine-point scale can be used to estimate the competitive effect of a change in operational performance through adopting a particular option.

## Assessing Financial Impact

Financial evaluation involves predicting and analysing the financial costs to which an option would commit the organization, and the financial benefit which might

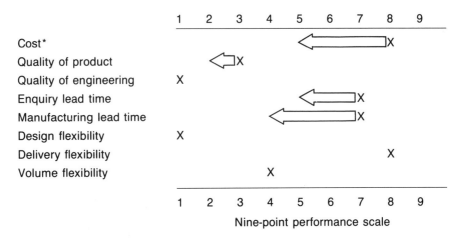

* Estimated.
X = Current performance
◁ = Performance if option is adopted

**Figure 11.5** An example of the competitive effects of operational changes implied by a decision option[4]

accrue from the decision. However, 'cost' must be defined a little more before it becomes a usable concept for decision evaluation.

### Acquisition and Opportunity Costs

Ask an accountant what is meant by cost, and you will get a different answer from that which you would get from an economist. An accountant's view is that the cost of something is whatever you had to pay to acquire it originally. Thus, the cost of investing in a factory to produce a particular product will comprise the acquisition cost of the land, of the factory, of the machinery, of the labour and so forth. An economist, on the other hand, is more likely to define costs in terms of the benefits forgone by not investing the resource elsewhere: that is, the opportunity cost of the resource. Thus, to the economist, the cost of investing in the factory is whatever could be gained by investing equivalent resources in the best feasible alternative investment — a separate decision option perhaps, or somewhere outside the organization, such as a bank.

While opportunity costing has obvious intuitive attractions, and makes a lot of sense in decision analysis, it does depend on what we define as the best feasible alternative use of our resources. The accountant's model of acquisition cost is at least stable — if we paid £1000 for something, then its value is £1000, irrespective of whatever alternative use we might dream up for the money.

*The Life-cycle Cost*

The concept of life-cycle costing is quite simple. It involves accounting for all costs over the life of the decision which are influenced directly by the decision. For example, suppose a company is evaluating two designs for a new integrated manufacturing plant. One of the designs is significantly less expensive to build and seems at first sight to be the less costly of the two options. But what other costs should the company consider apart from the acquisition cost? Each plant would require some initial research and development to remedy outstanding technical problems before construction could begin. The plant would also have to be 'debugged' before operation, but, more importantly, during its years of life the plant will incur operation and maintenance costs which will in part be determined by the original choice of design. Finally, if the company wants to look so far ahead, the disposal value of the plant could also be influenced by its design. Figure 11.6 shows how these costs might occur over the life of the plant.

Life-cycle costing involves identifying and accounting for all the costs which are influenced by the decision over its life. In fact, this is impossible in any absolute sense. The effects of any large decision ripple out waves in a pond, impinging on and influencing many other decisions. Yet it is sensible to include more than the immediate and obvious costs involved in a decision, and a life-cycle approach provides a useful reminder of this.

*The Time Value of Money: Net Present Value*

The life-cycle approach is also a useful reminder that one of the most important factors determining the value of either costs or benefits is *when* they are incurred.

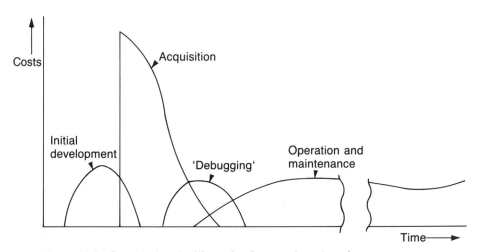

**Figure 11.6** Costs during the life cycle of a manufacturing plant

Money in our hand now is worth more to us than the same money in a year's time. Conversely, paying out a sum in a year's time is preferable to paying it out now. The reason for this has to do with the opportunity cost of money. If we receive money now and invest it (in a bank account or in another project which gives a positive return), then in one year's time we will have our original investment plus whatever interest has been paid for the year. Thus, to compare the alternative merits of receiving £100 now and receiving £100 in a year's time, we should compare £100 with £100 plus one year's interest. Alternatively, we can reverse the process and ask ourselves how much would have to be invested now, in order for that investment to pay £100 in one year's time. This amount (lower than £100) is called the *present value* of receiving £100 in one year's time.

For example, suppose current interest rates are 10 per cent per annum. The amount we would have to invest to receive £100 in one year's time is:

$$£100 \times \frac{1}{1.10} = £90.91$$

So the present value of £100 in one year's time, *discounted for the fact that we do not have it immediately*, is £90.91. In two years' time the amount we would have to invest to receive £100 is:

$$£100 \times \frac{1}{(1.10)} \times \frac{1}{(1.10)} = £100 \times \frac{1}{(1.10)^2} = £82.65$$

The rate of interest assumed (10 per cent in our case) is known as the *discount rate*. More generally, the present value of £x in n years' time, at a discount rate of r per cent is:

$$\frac{x}{(1 + r/100)^n}$$

Figure 11.7 shows the cash flows per annum of a particular investment opportunity. The proposed project requires outlay (negative cash flow) in the first year and thereafter pays benefits (positive cash flow) for the next six years. The total cash flow for the project is the sum of the yearly cash flows and amounts to £1380. However, if we discount the cash flows at an annual rate of 10 per cent, the total discounted cash flow or, as it is more usually known, net present value (NPV) is £816.47. Rather than calculate the discount factor each time it is needed, tables are generally used, such as that in the appendix at the end of this book. Broadly speaking, if the NPV is greater than zero, then the investment is worthwhile from the financial investment point of view.

*The Internal Rate of Return*

The internal rate of return (IRR) of a decision option is the discount rate which, when applied to costs and benefits, results in the net present value of costs being

| | Year | | | | | | | |
|---|---|---|---|---|---|---|---|---|
| | **0** | **1** | **2** | **3** | **4** | **5** | **6** | **7** |
| **Cash flow** (£000s) | − 300 | 30 | 50 | 400 | 400 | 400 | 400 | 0 |
| **Present value** (discounted at 10%) | − 300 | 27.27 | 41.3 | 300.53 | 273.21 | 248.37 | 225.79 | 0 |

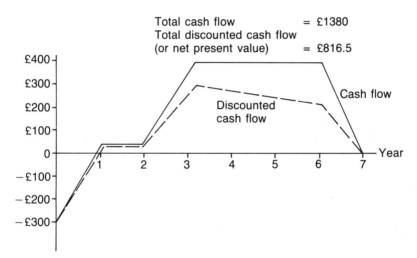

Total cash flow = £1380
Total discounted cash flow
(or net present value) = £816.5

**Figure 11.7**  Cash flow and discounted cash flow

equal to the net present value of benefits. So, for example, examine an option which requires an investment of £1 million and pays £200 000 per year for ten years. Figure 11.8 shows the net present value of the option as the discount rate varies.

When the discount rate is approximately 15 per cent the NPV is zero. This indicates that, at this level, the present value of all benefits is equal to the present value of all costs. Thus the IRR for the option is 15 per cent. The higher the IRR for this type of option, the more we are having to discount the benefits to equal the initial outlay, and therefore the more attractive the option seems.

## The Payback Period

One of the simplest evaluation measures for the type of decision option which involves an initial investment followed by annual cash inflows is the time taken for the undiscounted net cash flow to reach zero; or, put another way, the time

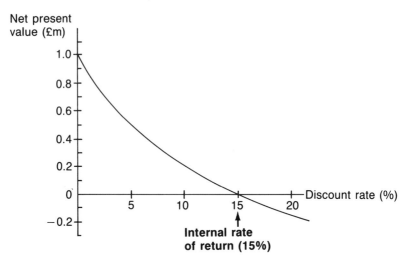

**Figure 11.8** The net present value of a decision option with an investment of £1 million and annual paybacks of £200 000 for ten years

for the initial investment to be paid back. So the previous example of an option requiring £1 million and having annual benefit of £0.2 million has a payback of:

$$\frac{1.0}{0.2} = 5 \text{ years}$$

Here, the shorter the payback period, the more attractive the option seems.

### Comparison of Financial Criteria

Of the measures of financial worth described here — NPV, IRR and payback — the most generally useful is probably NPV. The major reason is that, as an evaluative measure, it has fewer drawbacks than the other criteria. Internal rate of return, in spite of its intuitive attractiveness, can give ambiguous results for options with mixed cash inflows and outflows;[5] payback does not take into account the value of any benefits which might occur after the initial investment has been paid back.

The major problem with NPV lies in choosing the discount rate to apply. Theoretically, the discount rate should reflect the opportunity cost to the decision makers of having money tied up in the investment. This can be interpreted as the current bank or other outside investment interest rate, or the customary return on investment rates for the organization. However, in practice choosing a discount rate is often a little arbitrary, and unfortunately the chosen rate can change the relative merits of alternative options. For example, Figure 11.9 shows the cash flows of two options and their NPVs when discounting at 5 per cent and 10 per cent. At 5 per cent option A is superior to option B, but at 10 per cent their relative positions are reversed.

| | | Year | | | | | | | |
|---|---|---|---|---|---|---|---|---|---|
| | | 0 | 1 | 2 | 3 | 4 | 5 | 6 | 7 |
| **Option A** | **Cash flow (£000s)** | −300 | 50 | 150 | 400 | 400 | 400 | 400 | 0 |
| | **Discounted at 5%** | −300 | 54.5 | 123.9 | 300.5 | 273.2 | 248.4 | 225.8 | 0 |
| | **Discounted at 10%** | −300 | 57.1 | 136.1 | 346.6 | 239.2 | 313.6 | 298.4 | 0 |
| **Option B** | **Cash flow (£000s)** | −300 | 200 | 350 | 300 | 300 | 300 | 300 | 0 |
| | **Discounted at 5%** | −300 | 181.8 | 289.3 | 225.4 | 204.9 | 186.3 | 169.3 | 0 |
| | **Discounted at 10%** | −300 | 190.4 | 317.5 | 258.9 | 246.9 | 235.2 | 223.8 | 0 |

| | | Discount rate | |
|---|---|---|---|
| | | **5%** | **10%** |
| **NPV** | **Option A** | 1181* | 926 |
| | **Option B** | 1173 | 957* |

*Superior NPV

**Figure 11.9**  The net present value of two decision options discounted at 5% and 10%

*Box 11.1*

Conventional financial evaluation of decision options has come under criticism for its inability to include enough relevant factors to give a true picture of complex investments. Nowhere is this more evident than in the case of justifying investment in computer-integrated manufacturing (CIM). With many of its costs and benefits both uncertain and intangible, many CIM investments are justified as an act of 'strategic faith'.

However, arguing for adapting conventional techniques (especially DCF) sensibly rather than abandoning them altogether, Kaplan[6] makes a number of suggestions as to how DCF can be used in a manner sensitive to the attributes of CIM:

- Do not set discount rates too high. Some companies set rates too high in the belief that this makes for high-return projects rather than innovation and competitiveness.

- Evaluate technologies not against current conditions, but against the assumption that competitors may invest in similar technologies.

- Do not underestimate the total costs of technologies — software development, for example.

- Include all benefits deriving from the technology which can be measured in some way. For example, include stock inventory reductions, reduced floor space and increased quality.

- Take account of the intangible benefits such as increased flexibility, shorter manufacturing times and increased learning. Do this not necessarily by estimating the financial benefits directly, but by asking what the cash flows from these intangibles would have to be in order to make the investment attractive, then judging whether such cash flows could reasonably occur. For example, suppose we calculate that the amount of cash flow to bring the NPV of an investment up to zero is £300 000 per year for the next five years. The question then becomes, 'Do we believe that increased flexibility and other benefits which are difficult to measure will give us an extra cash flow of £300 000 per year for the next five years?' If the answer is yes, then the investment is worthwhile.

## Evaluating Vulnerability

The risk inherent in any decision option can be the result of the decision maker's inability to predict or estimate any of the following:

1. The internal effects of an option within the organization.
2. The environmental conditions prevailing after the decision is taken.
3. The reaction of other bodies within the environment to the decision.

Whatever its source, risk is conveniently described by the *range* of possible outcomes. In Chapter 6 we used the 'outcome balance' to illustrate risk where only a limited number of outcomes was possible, and a probability distribution to describe risk where outcomes were measured on a continuous scale.

## Downside Risk

The measures of risk described in Chapter 6 are sometimes too sophisticated, especially for preliminary evaluation. If so, then perhaps the simplest but the most powerful method of evaluating risk is just to assess the worst possible outcome from the option. Then we can ask the question, 'Would we be prepared to accept such a consequence?' This is sometimes called assessing the 'downside' risk of an option. So, if the outcomes of two options A and B are shown in Figure 11.10, then even though option B might be preferred on the basis of expected pay-off, its downside risk could be too great for the company to bear.

## The Risk–Return Diagram

Generally, the most useful measure of the risk of an option is the dispersion or spread of its possible outcomes, and the most convenient measure of dispersion is standard deviation. But this alone is inadequate for evaluation. To say that one option has a standard deviation of £100 and another one of £1000 means nothing without knowing each option's *expected* outcome as well. The standard deviation of £100 could apply to an option which has an expected pay-off of £10, and which is therefore a risky option, whereas the standard deviation of £1000 could apply to an option whose expected pay-off is £1 million. The most satisfactory method of expressing the spread of consequences for evaluation purposes is as a proportion of the expected pay-off. The most common form of such a measure is the coefficient of variation (covar) of a distribution where:

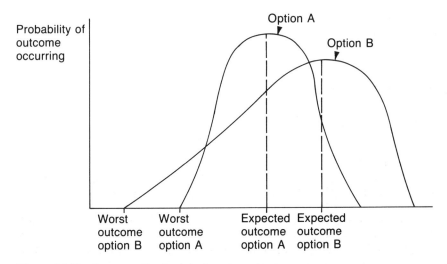

**Figure 11.10**  Outcome distributions for two options

*Box 11.2*

A word of warning about assessing the vulnerability of options. Risk and uncertainty can be a crucial factor in evaluation. But although we stress the importance of assessing and preferably quantifying uncertainty, we do not imply that managers should take a passive view of uncertain events. If evaluation uncovers a potentially negative 'uncertain factor', such as losing a contract or a rise in operating costs, the decision maker is not expected to 'shrug his shoulders and console himself with the thought that even though a bad outcome occurred, he made the correct decision given the information he had at the time'.[7] Most resourceful managers will take whatever actions are needed to try and counter the negative factor or its effects. This is unlikely to eliminate the uncertainty in the decision or the necessity of including it in the evaluation. But it does change the evaluator's question from 'If we chose this option, what would the consequences be if the worst happened?' to 'If we chose this option, what would we have to do to reduce the effects of the worst happening?'

$$\text{Covar} = \frac{\text{Standard deviation}}{\text{Mean}}$$

Any option involving risk can be evaluated in terms of its expected pay-off and its risk, represented by the covar of the distribution of its possible outcomes. Figure 11.11 shows four decision options, A, B, X and Y, plotted on a graph with the coefficient of variation and the expected pay-off as the axes.

The top left-hand part of the graph represents the undesirable area where options have low expected pay-offs, yet run high risks. The bottom right-hand part of the

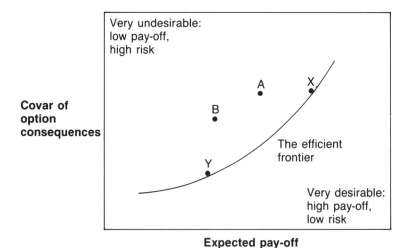

**Figure 11.11** The risk–return diagram

*Box 11.3*

## The Portfolio Approach to Risk

No decision bodies know more about risk than members of the world's stock markets. They look at the risk involved in individual projects mainly in the context of their exposure to risks in their other investments, and it is a useful lesson for all decision makers. An organization which already has several high-risk projects might not want to take on another. Conversely, an organization with safe but low-return investments might look more favourably on the same risky investment. Expressed in the language of the financial investor, the basis of evaluation should be the total portfolio of an organization's investment.

The 'portfolio' of an operation is the accumulation of its recent and active decisions. The risk of the total portfolio is governed by:

- The degree of risk of each decision in the portfolio.

- The amount invested in each decision.

- The degree of correlation or connection between the decisions.

It is this last point which is significant in the portfolio approach.

Suppose two activities are subject in the same way to exactly the same set of uncontrollable factors. If the pay-off from one activity declines, then so will the pay-off from the other — both eggs will be in the same basket. But if the uncontrollable factors in the decision influence the two activities in opposite directions, then a reduction in the pay-off from one activity will be accompanied by an increase in the pay-off from the other. So the effect that any additional investment has on the riskiness of the group of investments will depend on whether the risk derives from the same set of uncontrollable factors in the same way: that is, on the extent to which the risks from investments are correlated. Choosing further options whose risks are similar to existing investments will increase the risk of the total portfolio. But choosing options which benefit from the things which threaten existing investments will decrease the portfolio's total risk.

graph includes the extremely attractive options which give a high pay-off, but involve little risk. Somewhere between these two extremes will lie a line representing combinations of risk and pay-off which are the best that can be hoped for in a particular decision. Options X and Y are contained in this set — sometimes called the *efficient frontier*. Any option which is positioned on the line is said to *dominate* any other option which lies towards the top left-hand part of the graph. So option X dominates option A (X gives a better pay-off for the same risk) and option Y dominates option B (Y gives a better pay-off for the same risk).

## Assessing Future Flexibility[8]

Another way in which decisions influence other decisions is by constraining the range of options or 'room for manoeuvre' in future decisions. For example, if a construction manager purchases a special piece of equipment which is capable of doing one currently important and frequent task (but few other tasks) with great efficiency, the ability of the operation to cope with a totally different mix of tasks will be seriously impaired. This does not mean that the decision to buy the special-purpose equipment was necessarily the wrong one, but it does limit one's future options. If there is an alternative option which does not limit what can be done in the future (especially if uncertainty is high), then trading off short-term efficiency for long-term flexibility should be considered.

Take a production investment example. Suppose a specialist machining company is considering replacing ten of its oldest machines. The market for its products, however, is likely to change quite drastically in the next few years, so it is not entirely clear whether all the machines will be needed. Since the company does not want to renew machines which are unlikely to be useful in the future, it engages in an exercise to try and determine the five most likely 'product-mix scenarios', and to decide which machines would be needed under these five possible futures. The machines to be replaced are labelled A–J, and the requirements for these machines are shown for each alternative scenario in Figure 11.12.

Machine C is mentioned five times, and so will be needed no matter which of the alternative scenarios materializes. At the other end of the scale, machine F is only mentioned once. So if we choose to replace machine C as our first decision, we are not constraining our future actions, whereas if we choose machine F, it would inevitably have an effect on our future decisions. To maintain maximum future flexibility, machine C should be renewed first. Note that, if we choose machine F, it does not mean to say that we have 'damned' ourselves if scenario 5 does not occur. We can generally undo our decision — but at a cost. Note also that we are not taking into account factors such as the likelihood of each scenario

| Scenario | Machine requirements |
|---|---|
| 1 | C A E I |
| 2 | A E C D G H |
| 3 | D G J I   H E C |
| 4 | C G H E B |
| 5 | A F G C J B |

Number of times machine mentioned: A = 3
B = 2
C = 5
D = 2
E = 4
F = 1
G = 4
H = 3
I = 2
J = 2

**Figure 11.12**  Machine requirements for five alternative demand patterns

to occur, the cost of each machine replacement, or the capacity needs of the company. Beware of too great an emphasis on future flexibility. It can lead to a reluctance to take any decision at all, on the grounds that delay will not commit us to any future which might not occur — the vacillator's ideal excuse! But be sure to assess future flexibility either where uncertainty is very high, and therefore putting probabilities on future events becomes very difficult or meaningless, or where the cost of redressing a 'wrong' decision is high, and so the total cost of a series of decisions is very sensitive to the initial decisions in the series.

## Practical Prescriptions

Put together a picture of what each decision option would mean by considering:

1. Its feasibility.
2. Its acceptability.
3. Its vulnerability.

Evaluate the feasibility of each option by considering:

1. The skills required to implement it.
2. The effect it would have on the capacity of the operation.
3. The financial requirements over time of the option.
4. The proportional change in the resources of the operation implied by the option.
5. The 'degree of fit' of the option with existing activities.

Evaluate the acceptability of each option by considering its operational impact on:

1. The technical specification of services and products.
2. The quality of services and products.
3. The responsiveness of the operation.
4. The dependability of the operation.
5. The flexibility of the operation.

Spell out the competitive benefits of changes in operational performance by comparing performance with competitors.

Financial evaluation should take into account the total life-cycle costs of the option and the time value of expenditure and benefit.

Evaluate the vulnerability of each option to risk by:

1. Assessing its downside risk.
2. Considering risk and return together.
3. Considering the causes of risk in a portfolio approach.
4. Assessing its future flexibility.

# Case Exercise

### Buxton Transport Company

The management of Buxton Transport Company were making decisions in circumstances which were totally new for them. In the ten years of its existence, the growth of the company had been phenomenal. Starting with his own truck, Andy Buxton had built the company into one of the largest independent transportation groups within the food and drinks industry. Three months ago the position changed dramatically. The start of a recession in the economy had coincided with the bankruptcy of one of the company's major customers. The result of this for Buxton Transport was a 20 per cent drop in business.

The last few months had been taken up with coping with this drop in demand. Some drivers had been made redundant, and a few of the vehicles sold. Other vehicles which were not being used had been garaged in the company's main depot. The small management team which ran the company were meeting to consider what to do next. The company's business manager had spent the last few weeks trying to find new business and was due to report back to the meeting that day.

First of all, Andy Buxton sketched out the company's financial position:

> Our retrenchment exercise of the last couple of months has been reasonably successful. We have reduced our costs to the point where, at current levels of business, we are slightly better than breaking even. Largely because of this the bank are being most sympathetic and are encouraging us to invest in new activities which will enable us to grow again. I guess that given our current assets and operating forecasts we could probably borrow up to £½ million for new projects.

The business manager spoke next:

> There is still very little business about. Nevertheless, our reputation in the industry is high, and of the several possibilities which I have been discussing with potential customers, three seem particularly interesting. I have called these proposals A, B and C, and you will find in front of you a very brief synopsis of each.

### Proposal A

This is by far the largest of the three proposals. A large supermarket chain is closing down its own distribution network and intends to contract out all its transport operations. I believe that if we bid for this proposal we would almost certainly get this business. It would fit in well with our existing system and is right in the area where we have the most experience. Furthermore, the business would be almost guaranteed for many years. The major problem is the size of the proposal — it would require at least £450 000 investment. Coupled with that, transportation rates are depressed at the moment and are likely to be for at least another couple of years.

This means that I doubt whether we would get a total operating profit from this contract of much more than £70 000 per year, and at present bank interest rates that isn't very attractive. But it is a big deal — if we decide to go for this one it will be the single biggest bit of business we have, and will increase our turnover to a good 30 per cent above what it was a year ago.

## Proposal B

This proposal is a development of an existing contract we have with a particular customer. We already transport this customer's goods from his factory to his regional warehouses. From the warehouses the goods are then distributed to the retailers by another company. Our customer has become increasingly dissatisfied with the service which he gets from this company, and is willing to let us take over the final part of the distribution chain. This would mean buying a small fleet of smaller vehicles, but we could use the drivers to whom we have just given notice to quit. Short-haul daily deliveries are not at all popular with long-distance drivers, but at least it would be a job for them. I calculate the investment for this proposal at around £150 000, and the yearly operating profit as about £30 000. The contract would be on a yearly basis, but the company is unlikely to change contracts after only a couple of years. After all, they have only disposed of their previous contractors after several years of poor service.

## Proposal C

This is the most unusual of the proposals. It concerns the import, transportation and, most importantly, packaging of frozen meat products. It would be quite a different sort of business for us, for two reasons. First, we would have to invest in refrigerated transportation units. Second, we would get involved in a packaging operation, although it would be a relatively simple one. The investment would be about £350 000 (we could quite easily lease the packaging facilities). It is difficult, however, to put a precise figure on the operating profit from such a venture since this depends on the size of the market for the product. According to the market forecasts of the producers, we should be shipping enough in the first year to break even, in the second year to make about £70 000, and in third and subsequent years to be making about £170 000 a year operating profit.

## Questions

1. What are the decision options between which the company must choose?
2. Set out a list of the attributes of each option which could be used as evaluation criteria.
3. List the most important four or five bits of extra information you think you would need before starting to advise the company.

# Bibliography

Bridge, J., *Managerial Decisions with the Micro Computer*, Philip Allan, 1989. A good introduction to a useful topic.

Houston, B., *Avoiding Adversity*, David and Charles, 1989. A pro-active approach to future risks.

Moodie, P.E., *Decision Making: Proven methods for better decisions*, McGraw-Hill, 1983.

Rosenhead, J., 'Planning under uncertainty II: a methodology for robustness analysis', *Journal of the Operational Research Society*, vol. 31, 1980, pp. 331–41. A very good introduction to the concept of robustness which is closely linked to future flexibility.

Van Horn, J.C., *Financial Management and Policy* (5th edn), Prentice Hall, 1980. For more advanced financial analysis and portfolio approaches to risk.

Vause, R. and Woodward, N., *Finance for Management*, Macmillan, 1981. One of the clearest introductory texts on the basics of finance.

# References

1. Skinner, W., *Manufacturing: The formidable competitive weapon*, Wiley, 1985.
2. This obviously applies to 'for-profit' operations, but it can be adapted for 'not-for-profit' operations. Instead of using competitiveness as a measure, use the extent to which options bring the operation in line with overall strategic goals.
3. For a fuller explanation, see Slack, N., *Achieving a Manufacturing Advantage*, Mercury Books, 1991.
4. Adapted from Slack, N., *op. cit.*
5. For an explanation of this effect, see De Neufville, R. and Stafford, J.H., *Systems Analysis for Engineers and Managers*, McGraw-Hill, 1971.
6. Kaplan, R.S., 'Must CIM be justified by faith alone?' *Harvard Business Review*, March/April 1986, pp. 87–95.
7. See this and similar points in Kaplan, R.S., 'Quantitative models for management accounting in today's production environment', Harvard Business School Working Paper 9-785-037, 1985.
8. A good introduction to the concept of robustness which is linked to future flexibility is Rosenhead, J., 'Planning under uncertainty II: a methodology for robustness analysis', *Journal of the Operational Research Society*, vol. 31, 1980, pp. 331–41.

# 12 Making a choice

## Introduction

The evaluation phase will have taken us to the point in the decision-making process where, as far as possible, the consequence of each decision option will have been investigated, clarified and made explicit. This brings us to the stage where a choice must be made. The choice phase involves forming a view, or opinion, on the decision options, expressing preferences between them, and eventually deciding on the option to be implemented.

### Evaluation and Choice Merge

The distinction between the two phases of evaluation and choice are rarely clearly defined. It is not easy to exclude consideration of the choice phase when evaluating the options. Nor should any decision maker ignore the way in which evaluation influences choice. For example, suppose a choice has to be made between several investment options. In deciding which attributes of each opportunity to evaluate formally (investment, riskiness, return, etc.), some consideration must be given to which of these attributes are going to be regarded as the more important when it comes to choice. Also, each party involved during the choice phase will probably be very careful to ensure that the manner in which the attributes of each option have been measured and presented do not give bias against his or her preferred option.

### Decidophobia

The choice itself is by our definition very short. All it involves is the act of commitment to one particular course of action; the choice of one decision option. Also it is the point in the decision-making process at which any advisers leave responsibility to the decision makers themselves.

The process may be short, but it is often far from easy. What is sometimes called 'decidophobia'[1] is a recognition that making a choice is a commitment to an action which involves some degree of risk. There is, after all, a possibility that we may finish up worse than when we started. To overcome decidophobia remember:

1. Choice is not the big moment it is sometimes made out to be; it is only the beginning of the implementation task.

2. Being 'right' in a choice is rather a theoretical concept — who is to know how the other options would have worked out?

3. If two or more options are close in terms of their desirability, the choice between the best options is not as crucial as when options exhibit big differences.

4. Sometimes consistency in making choices which do not interfere with each other is more important than being 'right'.

5. Once chosen, many options can be made to work by effort and skill in their implementation.

All this does not mean that careful, thorough analysis is unimportant. On the contrary, without systematic analysis we would not recognize the truth of these points or even perhaps have the confidence for rational choice. It simply means that analysis without the courage to act is a waste of the effort put into the whole decision process.

## Better Than What?

The evaluation phase described each option's consequences, but generally was not concerned with the worth of each option in an absolute sense. To consider this it is necessary to compare the consequence of each option against some reference standard, or datum point. This can be a useful first step in putting value on the consequences of each option. Decision makers will, of course, want to compare options against each other, and it is this comparison which is likely to be the deciding factor in making the choice. However, it is likely that the decision makers will want to fix this ranked list of options against some point or reference scale. The value of this is that the relative merits of the options are put in some kind of meaningful context. There is a big difference between saying 'This option is the best of those we have considered' and saying 'This is the best option, but it is still well below what we feel we ought to be achieving, or what we have achieved in the past.' The first statement may go some way towards making the choice, but the second one tells you whether the choice is worth making in the first place.
Reference standards can be:

1. Derived from past performance — a *historical standard.*

2. Derived from the performance of similar organizations elsewhere — an *external standard*.

3. Derived from some notion of what is ideal — an *absolute standard*.

4. Derived from a notion of what would happen if no decision were taken — so-called *do-nothing standard*.

## Historical Standards

Historical standards are derived from previous performance levels, and look back to conditions within the organization as they were. So the usefulness of such standards will depend on the relevance of previous conditions to present or future conditions. For example, suppose we say that a particular option is a good one because its consequences will ensure a better state of affairs than used to be the case. The statement has some relevance if conditions are broadly similar before and after the decision. Then improvement is a good thing, and is likely to be welcomed. But suppose conditions in the future are such that merely to improve on past performance is not in itself sufficient. It may be that a considerably higher standard than existed previously will be necessary to ensure the survival of the company. Also, some things which at one time were important might, because conditions change, cease to be relevant. Conversely, measures once unimportant may become relevant. For example, a company which in the past has judged its options on the basis of how they affected operating costs might be moving into a future where some other measure, such as technical superiority or quality, is more relevant.

## External Standards

When trying to judge how well we are doing, it is a natural reaction to look round and compare ourselves with similar people or organizations. Indeed, this is probably a sensible thing to do, especially if we are in direct competition with those against whom we compare ourselves. In the same way, the consequences of decision options may be compared against the reported performance of other similar organizations. Again, the standard is used to put the decision options in perspective. For example, there is a difference between saying 'This option is the best one' and saying 'This is the best one, but even the worst of all the options we considered will give us a better performance than any of our competitors.'

There are, however, difficulties in using standards which derive from outside our organization. The first problem is that all the criticisms of using historical standards will probably still apply. Using external standards is merely using other people's history, rather than our own. There is no certainty that what was reasonable for *them* in the past will be reasonable for *us* in the future. The second problem is that we have far less opportunity to check the veracity of the standards. Even if other people's performance is reported faithfully, there are probably aggregations and assumptions about which we are ignorant. Nevertheless the various published standards which do exist from government, industry and inter-firm comparison companies indicate that organizations find external standards useful in judging their own performance.

## Absolute Standards

All comparison against standards is an attempt at calibrating the options. Using absolute standards is the ultimate in calibration. In effect it is saying 'At the very best, what would circumstances be, and how does the option compare to this ideal state?' For example, suppose the effect of an option on the operational performance of some company had been evaluated. How does the resulting quality compare with perfect quality — zero defects? How does the resulting responsiveness compare with instant response — zero waiting? How does the resulting dependability compare with absolute dependability — zero lateness? All these standards are absolutes. They cannot be improved upon.

Absolute standards are perhaps never achievable, but they do show how far we could go in devising better options.

## The Do-Nothing Standard

A standard which is used particularly in strategic decision making relates to what would happen if no decision were made. In a way this is introducing a dummy option, the do-nothing option. Sometimes, of course, this may lead to the dummy option being chosen. We could say, 'This particular option is the best of those which were originally evaluated, but even that is no better than we believe could have been achieved by doing nothing.' In such a case, we probably would be better to do nothing.

This type of standard becomes particularly significant where the effect of options on future flexibility is important. For example, suppose that a supermarket chain is considering two possible new sites. Each site has different advantages and disadvantages, but if either site is bought, the company would be unable to fund further expansion for one or two years. Although one of the two sites is preferred, the company believes that several more sites might become available in the next few months. So, even though both existing site options are adequate, and one is preferred, the option of doing nothing for the time being offers the chance of adopting an even better (if as yet unspecified) option.

In the example above, the do-nothing option turned out potentially better than the options being considered. This was because the decision was what was termed in Chapter 1 an *opportunity* decision:[2] we do not have to make the decision, but there may be potential benefit if we do. At the other end of the scale were *crisis* decisions: where we are taking the decision to avoid some possible calamitous occurrence. Here the do-nothing standard is likely to be the base standard, with all the options providing potential improvement. So the usefulness of the do-nothing standard derives from more than merely providing a reference point for the decision options. It in effect tells us the benefits which derive from making the decision itself. It shows us the difference between what *would* happen and what *can* happen.

## Which Standard?

It will have become clear that an option might be evaluated quite differently against different reference standards. Suppose we are again judging an investment opportunity. It might give a return which is very good when compared with our previous investments, only adequate when compared with the return that other companies in the same business are getting, relatively poor when compared with what we believe is reasonable and possible in the circumstances, but considerably better than the return we would get if we did not make the investment at all.

Different reference standards will be appropriate for different types of decision. For example, suppose an airline is about to begin a major investment programme which will totally change the mix of aircraft it operates. The decision concerns choosing between alternative methods of organizing its maintenance crews which overhaul the aircraft. If the major factor being considered is the 'turn-round' time for the crew to overhaul the aircraft and get it back into service, the reference standard could be any of the following:

1. The average turn-round time taken for similar operations over the previous year (historical standard).

2. The turn-round time taken by similar, but rival, concerns (external standard).

3. The turn-round time equal to the sum of only specified work with no wasted or ineffective time (absolute standard).

4. The turn-round time that it is believed the existing arrangements would achieve under the new conditions (do-nothing standard).

If the decision is concerned with the rate of productivity change in the organization, then past performance may be a reasonable basis for a standard. If the decision concerns continuous operational improvement, then absolute standards will be appropriate. If the decision concerns whether it is worthwhile to change at all, then the do-nothing standard might be appropriate.

This may sound as if managers have to choose one particular reference standard, but this is not so. In most decisions it is helpful to use more than one standard. Suppose a company is making a decision where Figure 12.1 shows the forecast performance of two decision options, A and B. These are compared against four

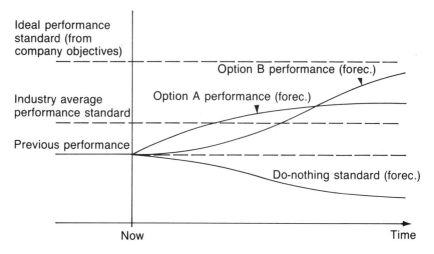

**Figure 12.1** Comparing options against several preference standards

reference standards. The base standard, representing the future state of affairs which the company wishes to avoid, is the do-nothing standard. The upper standard is the level of performance derived from the company's stated objectives, and represents an ideal or target performance level. In between them are the average industry performance level, which reflects the state of competitive companies, and the previous performance standard, which indicates the degree of change in performance. As we can see, both options are forecast eventually to attain performance levels lower than the ideal standard but better than all the other standards. The eventual decision between A and B is likely to be based on the utility of different performance levels between the upper and lower standards, and on whether a short- or long-term view of the decision is taken. But again, the role of the reference standards is to set the options in as full and useful a context as possible.

## How Feasible? How Acceptable?

As well as comparing options against reference standards, decision makers will want to compare options against each other. In the evaluation phase we identified several general attributes of decision options which could be used to establish a uniform basis for comparison. We also distinguished between those things which shape our view of the degree of *acceptability* of each option, and those which determine each option's *feasibility*.

The acceptability of an option means the extent to which the option satisfies all the objectives of the decision. At one extreme lie options which meet fully all the objectives, and at the other lie options which meet none. Between the two extremes, options may satisfy different objectives to different extents. It is in this middle range that decision makers face all the problems of assigning preference to multi-attribute options which were described in Chapter 7. At some point in this continuum there may be an identifiable notion of the 'minimum degree of acceptability' to the decision body. This notion will probably not be represented by a single point on the continuum which will divide acceptable from non-acceptable; rather it will be a range, within which lie various ideas of minimum acceptability.

The feasibility of an option reflects the likelihood that the organization has, or can acquire, the necessary resources to implement the option. Again there is a continuum between, at one extreme, those options whose requirements are well within the organization's existing resources, and at the other, those options which would require resources which the organization has no chance of obtaining. As with acceptability, there will probably be no clear divide between feasibility and infeasibility. But unlike the acceptability scale, it is not the multi-attribute problem which causes the difficulty — for an option to be feasible *all* the required resources must be obtainable. Here the problem is uncertainty, which comes from two sources. First, the decision body will probably be unsure as to the type of resources required and how many will be needed. Second, the decision body might not be certain that it can obtain all the required resources in the time available.

Figure 12.2 illustrates these two dimensions. Any options which are both clearly

| | | | ACCEPTABILITY TO DECISION BODY | | |
|---|---|---|---|---|---|
| | | | Acceptable | Minimum acceptability range | Not acceptable |
| | | | Very acceptable | | Totally unacceptable |
| RESOURCE FEASIBILITY | Feasible | Well within available resources | Consider any options in this area | Relaxation of objectives? | ↑ |
| | May be feasible | | Resources from other areas? | | │ |
| | Unfeasible | Totally unfeasible | ← | | Reject any options in → these areas ↓ |

Figure 12.2 Degrees of acceptability and feasibility

acceptable and feasible should be considered further, and any option which is neither acceptable nor feasible should be dropped from consideration. Similarly, options which are feasible but not acceptable, or acceptable but not feasible, should be dropped — although this is not as easy as it may seem. An option which is particularly acceptable to the decision body may prove so attractive that problems of resource feasibility are played down or 'wished away'. Similarly, options whose resource requirements are particularly light may be adopted, even though they do not really meet the objectives of the decision. Unfortunately, there are usually rather a lot of options generated in these two areas of the diagram. We would all find it relatively easy to think of very acceptable options, given no resource constraints; and easily feasible options, given no acceptability criteria to meet.

More difficult to handle are the options which, although clearly feasible, are on the boundary of acceptability, or those which, although very acceptable, might be only just feasible. This is especially true when the only options which are being considered lie in these two areas. Where an option is barely acceptable, it may be that the decision body can relax or reshape the priorities of its objectives in some way. Where an option is in the area between clear feasibility and infeasibility, the organization will have to take resources from other areas of its activities, or accept some risk that it may not be able to implement the option because of lack of resources, or do both of these things.

## Confidence and Consensus

### Confidence in the Evaluation

Implicit in all discussion so far has been the assumption that the evaluation of an option really can describe its consequences. Often, though, we have less than total control over how an option will affect performance. We may choose an option, but we can only guess at the consequences since they are beyond our experience, or partly out of our control, or both. Under these circumstances it is not surprising if different members of the decision body hold different views on the options' likely consequences. For example, suppose we are deciding whether to adopt a radical new organizational structure for part of our organization. The evaluation shows that the impact on performance is likely to be high. Yet the reorganization is a complex affair involving many other people in the organization who may not either agree with or understand the purpose and details of the reorganization. We can try to educate, inform and motivate, of course, but the fact remains that the implementation of the option is substantially out of our control. The question is, how should we trade off the lack of control against the potential benefits of the option?

One simple technique for at least exposing the trade off is the *priority matrix*.

| | | IMPACT ON BENEFITS OR OBJECTIVES | | |
|---|---|---|---|---|
| | | Low | Medium | High |
| DEGREE OF CONTROL | Type 1 | Low | Medium | Very high |
| | Type 2 | Low | Medium | High |
| | Type 3 | Low | Medium | Low |

**Figure 12.3** Priority matrix

It involves categorizing each option by the degree of control the decision makers have over it and its impact on the objectives. Degree of control is categorized as:

Type 1: largely under own control.
Type 2: partially under own control.
Type 3: little or no control.

Impact on objectives is categorized as:

Low: little benefit.
Medium: reasonable benefit.
High: major benefit.

The priority given to the option is then determined by its place on the priority matrix shown in Figure 12.3.

## Consensus on Objectives

Decision bodies are not composed of totally like-minded individuals. It is a longstanding source of surprise and irritation that members of decision bodies, who are essentially of good will and who might well agree on the details of the decision, cannot agree on the 'correct' option to choose. It is in this area that differences in the values held by members of the decision body, especially where they themselves represent the varied interests of stakeholder groups, can cause particular problems. There is, of course, a fundamental difference between expressed public agreement over objectives and true consensus and conviction among the members of the decision body. Assuming consensus where it does not really exist can lead to difficulties in implementation and commitment to the chosen option.

Of course, it may be that the degree of consensus within the group is very high. If so, the multi-decision maker problem is reduced in effect to a single-decision maker one. However, if the degree of consensus on the actual objectives of the decision is low, then some thought must be given as to how the choice process itself is managed.

## The Choice Process[3]

Two factors have a considerable influence on how the choice process should be managed:

- The amount of confidence the decision body has regarding the consequences of the options it is considering.
- The amount of consensus on the decision objectives.

The less confidence we have in our estimates of what will happen if particular options are chosen, the more the experience and judgement in the organization must be tapped. The less agreement there is over decision objectives, the more the process becomes one of negotiation. If we have neither confidence in what would happen should we make a particular choice, nor consensus about what ends we should be pursuing, the choice process is particularly difficult to manage. (See Figure 12.4.)

### Choice by Computation

Agreement over both the consequences of each option (or at least the probability of several alternative consequences occurring) and the objectives or preference scale to be applied is an underlying assumption made by decision models of the type described in Part III of this book. And, as we have argued in previous chapters, that may not be an unreasonable starting point. If such conditions do in fact exist,

| | | CONSENSUS ABOUT DECISION OBJECTIVES | |
|---|---|---|---|
| | | Agreement | Disagreement |
| CONFIDENCE IN ESTIMATES OF THE CONSEQUENCES OF DECISION OPTIONS | High | Decision by computation | Decision by negotiation |
| | Low | Decision by judgement | Decision by creative 'inspiration' |

**Figure 12.4** Confidence and consensus in the choice process. (Based on Thompson and Tuden, *op. cit.* In fact, they use the term 'causation' rather than 'consequences', since it includes future and present states. Within the scope of this book, 'consequences' is clearer.)

then, providing that the model is adequate, the model will 'make the choice' and the decision is really one of computation. But even if the choice circumstances are more complex, make some assumptions, use the model as a starting point and test out the effects of relaxing the assumptions. At least the model will structure the decision for you.

Two particular classes of decision model were explained in some detail in Part III: uncertainty models (mainly decision trees) in Chapter 6 and preference models (multi-attribute models) in Chapter 7. As the choice situation strays away from the very top left-hand corner of Figure 12.4, these two types of model become particularly useful. Moving downwards towards the 'judgement' part of the matrix, the degree of uncertainty in the choice situation increases. Under conditions like this, decision tree and decision matrix type models could be used. Moving rightwards towards the 'negotiation' part of the matrix, argument centres on the relative importance of the various consequences of options. Multi-attribute models at least analyse decisions in this way, even if they do not necessarily achieve any compromise.

## Impact Analysis

If the choice is not a particularly complex one, a relatively simple choice technique is probably appropriate. Impact analysis is such a technique. It presents the advantages and disadvantages of options in a simple visual manner which allows their overall impact to be assessed. The steps in impact analysis are as follows for each option:

Step 1. Identify the 'positive forces' which the option would give to the problem. These are the strengths, benefits or other advantages associated with the option.

Step 2. Score all these positive forces on a scale from 5 to 1, where 5 indicates a major impact on achieving the objectives of the decision process, and 1 indicates only a minor impact.

Step 3. Identify the 'negative forces' which are associated with the option. These are its disadvantages, shortcomings or weaknesses, including unwanted side-effects, implementation problems or resource implications.

Step 4. Score all these negative forces in a similar way to step 2. A score of 5 indicates a major disadvantage, a score of 1 a minor one.

Step 5. Bring all the positive and negative forces together on a force diagram. An illustration of a force diagram is given in Figure 12.5. It relates to a decision whether to adopt a new type of packing for a food product. Here the positive forces are stronger than the negative forces.

Step 6. Use the force diagram to present the choice to the decision body.

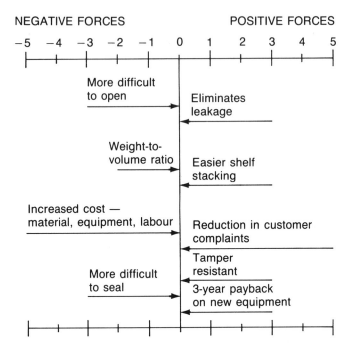

NEGATIVE FORCES

POSITIVE FORCES

-5   -4   -3   -2   -1   0   1   2   3   4   5

More difficult
to open

Eliminates
leakage

Weight-to-
volume ratio

Easier shelf
stacking

Increased cost —
material, equipment, labour

Reduction in customer
complaints

Tamper
resistant

More difficult
to seal

3-year payback
on new equipment

**Figure 12.5** Example of impact analysis used to decide whether to adopt a new type of packing for a food product

## Choice by Judgement

If all the members of the decision body agree on what outcomes are preferred but disagree as to what the outcomes are likely to be for each option (or what the relative chances of several outcomes are), then a judgement must be made. It has been suggested that a 'collegium' is an appropriate choice process for these circumstances.[4] This means that the individuals' judgements should be pooled in such a way as to make sure that:

1. The group always bears in mind its (agreed) objectives.
2. Every member of the group participates.
3. All relevant information is made available to every member of the group.
4. Every member's views carry equal weight.
5. A majority vote determines the ultimate choice.

In the academic world, for example, where subject and specialist differences are encouraged but where collective decisions over matters of common concern have to be taken, the collegium system is traditionally adopted.

The approach is, of course, designed to ensure that factors other than those contained within the immediate decision situation do not impinge on the choice process. It is not, however, uncommon for historical 'residues' to produce coalitions

*Box 12.1*

## Voting

In terms of gathering collected judgements, voting has its drawbacks. Even in simple choices it does not necessarily reflect the degree of opposition to an idea. For example, if a decision maker favours option A to option B and votes accordingly, this could mean that the decision maker is almost indifferent between the two options, but marginally prefers option A. On the other hand, he or she could be very much in favour of option A and violently opposed to option B. So if ten members of a decision body, after much careful consideration, all decide that they marginally prefer option A to option B and vote accordingly, option A would have 10–0 majority. On the other hand, if six members of the group are strongly in favour of option A and violently opposed to option B and vote accordingly — and four members of the group are marginally in favour of option B and vote accordingly — then option A would have a 6–4 majority and would 'win' again.

Yet these two votes do not totally reflect the nature of the group preference. The 10–0 vote in A's favour was, in fact, the result of the two options being regarded as very close; the group probably would not mind too much if option B were the final decision. But in the 6–4 vote the opposition to B being chosen is likely to be considerable, in spite of the seemingly close vote.

Furthermore, simple majority voting can be paradoxical. The following example is often quoted to demonstrate the illogicality of simple majority voting. A three-person decision body is voting on three proposals, A, B and C.

Group member 1 prefers A to B, B to C, and therefore A to C.
Group member 2 prefers B to C, C to A, and therefore B to A.
Group member 3 prefers C to A, A to B, and therefore C to B.

In the contest between A and B, group members 1 and 3 prefer A, and therefore, by majority rule, A is preferred to B.

In the contest between C and B, group members 1 and 2 prefer B, and therefore, by majority rule, B is preferred to C.

In the contest between A and C, group members 2 and 3 prefer C, and therefore C is preferred to A.

This means that, on a simple majority voting system, the group prefers A to B, B to C, but C to A — which by rational standards is illogical!

or antagonisms within decision bodies, leading to choices being made other than on the strict merits of the case. Clearly, such a collegium system of judgement has to be highly valued and supported in its own right by participants in order for decay not to set in fairly swiftly.

Of course, the choice situation may only be in the 'judgement' part of the matrix because the members of this particular decision body have little confidence in how the options will perform. It could be that another decision body, whose experience is wider or just more appropriate, would not see any problem in understanding the consequences of each option. So if a choice is being made in this part of the matrix, the questions to be addressed are:

1. Is there expertise or experience within the organization which could help the decision body to form its judgement?

2. Is there expertise or experience within other organizations which could help and which could be accessed? Perhaps consultants or other organizations with similar problems should be brought in to provide expertise.

3. Is this decision going to be taken in a similar form again in the future? If so, what are we doing to make sure that we capture the learning and experience in making the decision so that next time the decision is easier to take?

## Choice by Negotiation

In this type of choice situation the dilemma is stark. If one group's preferences are satisfied, another's are denied. Choice then involves negotiation and compromise. At least some members of the decision body will not have all they want.

This need not be 'unfair' as such. Some compromises may even be 'efficient' in their own way. Consider the idea of *Pareto optimality*, which states that an option is Pareto optimal if no single member of the decision group can increase his or her own benefit without simultaneously decreasing the benefit of another member of the decision body. So, generally, we should reject any alternative that is not Pareto optimal, since at least one person's utility could be increased without any loss of utility to any other member of the group.

Figure 12.6 illustrates this effect for a two-person decision body. The Pareto optimal set of alternatives form the boundary between what is achievable and what is not achievable. So options $X$ and $Y$, although having different benefits to group members A and B, can only be changed at the expense of someone's utility. But option $Z$ is inferior to both A and Y, since, by moving in the direction of the arrow to any point on the boundary between $Z_1$ and $Z_2$, both A and B's utility is increased.

One danger in resorting to choice by negotiation is that the aspect of 'winning/losing' tends to mean that choices get made as part of some longer-term sequence where an underlying (although often unstated) principle seems to be that the parties to the process are treated equitably over a period of time. 'Losses' in one situation are recovered in another, and so on. We can often see this happening in companies in rounds of wage bargaining, or in the process of annual bidding for capital allocation.

## Choice by Creative 'Inspiration'

When agreement within the decision body cannot be reached either over what objectives we should be pursuing, or over the most likely consequences of adopting

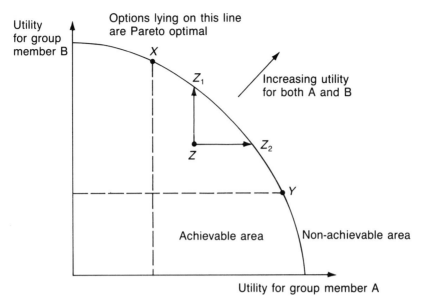

**Figure 12.6** Pareto optimality — an option is Pareto optimal if no person's utility can be increased without reducing the utility of another member of the group

---

*Box 12.2*

When consensus is not total, organizations often see an outside authority as a way of bringing in expertise, structuring a complex issue and, perhaps most importantly, neutralizing the decision — partially at least.

For example, investment in information technology can be hugely expensive, and with budgets of millions of pounds at stake, companies often call in one of the management consultancy firms which have specialists in choosing computer systems. One large consultancy uses a complex weighted ranking technique very similar to those described in Chapter 7. It starts by interviewing relevant users and internal 'customers' of the prospective system. This provides a 'shopping list' of capabilities which the system should possess, as well as a 'secondary list' of capabilities on which there is less consensus but which might prove useful. These lists of objectives include both the strategic ('How will the system enable us to gain competitive advantage?') and the operational ('How long does sales order processing take?'). After defining objectives, the alternative suppliers of systems are evaluated. Those with uncertain futures or those whose systems fall down on one of the important criteria are eliminated. Before reaching a final conclusion, it is common to examine and question some of the original assumptions. As one consultant puts it, 'When we are near a conclusion we stand back and consider the constraints. In certain cases where we have been given a mandate to buy from, say, IBM, we ask ourselves whether, if we were to relax it, it would make a difference to our decision.'

options, the choice process is particularly difficult to manage. Many organizations when faced with this type of choice attempt to avoid the choice altogether!

It may be difficult but it is not impossible to manage choice under these circumstances. The following points help:

1. More than any other situation this one calls for inspired leadership. A leader who takes on responsibility for the process as well as the decision itself, who understands the views, interests and values of all parties in the decision body, and who gains the trust of all involved, is the greatest asset for this type of choice.

2. Do not forget that you are in this choice situation only within the frame of the options currently being considered. There may be another 'solution' — an option around which more consensus can be engineered or which finds more certainty among the decision body. So consider cycling back to generating further alternatives.

3. The difficulty in managing this type of choice comes when lack of consensus and lack of confidence occur at the same time. So work to reduce either lack of confidence or lack of consensus, but not necessarily both at the same time.

## Practical Prescriptions

The distinction between the two phases of evaluation and choice is hard to define, and indeed the way in which evaluation is carried out sometimes means that the choice is made along the way. On the other hand, actually 'making' a choice can sometimes appear to be impossibly difficult. Remember:

1. The moment of choice is really just the start of the implementation phase, not the end of solving the problem.

2. Very few choices are absolutely right.

3. Complementarity in choice may be more important than making the 'right' choice.

4. Once chosen, many options can be made to work. (This does not mean that anything will do!)

It is important to establish appropriate reference standards against which to judge our evaluated options. These standards can be historical, external or absolute. The do-nothing standard is an important one in relating all options to the status quo. In setting reference standards:

1. Ensure the appropriateness of the chosen standard type for your particular decision situation.

2. Where appropriate, use more than one type of reference standard in order to provide as full and useful a context as possible.

The mechanism of choice depends on two factors:

1. The degree of confidence we have in our understanding of the consequences of any option (how clear we are about what will happen).

2. The degree of consensus about what our objectives should be (what we actually *want* to happen).
    (a) Where there is consensus over consequences and objectives, make the choice by computation.
    (b) Where there is consensus over objectives but not over consequences, make the choice by judgement.
    (c) Where there is consensus over consequences but not over objectives, make the choice by negotiation.
    (d) Where there is no consensus about anything, find an inspired leader, or change the problem!

## Bibliography

Boddy, D., McCalman, J. and Buchanan, D.A., *The New Management Challenge*, Croom Helm, 1988.

Moodie, P.E., *Decision Making: Proven methods for better decisions*, McGraw-Hill, 1983. A lively and entertaining approach.

## References

1. Albrecht, K.G., *Brain Power*, Prentice Hall, 1980.
2. The 'opportunity–crisis' continuum in Chapter 1 is adapted from Mintzberg, H., Raisinghani, D. and Theoret, A., 'The structure of unstructured decision processes', McGill University Working Paper, 1973.
3. This way of looking at the choice process is based on Thompson, J.D. and Tuden, A., 'Strategies, structures and processes of organisational decision', in *Comparative Studies in Administration*, University of Pittsburgh Press, 1959.
4. *Ibid*.

# Appendix

## Discounting Factors

| Year | 1% | 5% | 10% | 15% | 20% |
|------|------|------|------|------|------|
| 1 | 0.990 | 0.952 | 0.909 | 0.870 | 0.833 |
| 2 | 0.980 | 0.907 | 0.827 | 0.756 | 0.694 |
| 3 | 0.971 | 0.864 | 0.751 | 0.658 | 0.579 |
| 4 | 0.961 | 0.823 | 0.683 | 0.572 | 0.482 |
| 5 | 0.952 | 0.784 | 0.621 | 0.497 | 0.402 |
| 6 | 0.942 | 0.746 | 0.565 | 0.432 | 0.335 |
| 7 | 0.933 | 0.711 | 0.513 | 0.376 | 0.279 |
| 8 | 0.924 | 0.677 | 0.467 | 0.327 | 0.233 |
| 9 | 0.914 | 0.645 | 0.424 | 0.284 | 0.194 |
| 10 | 0.905 | 0.614 | 0.386 | 0.247 | 0.162 |
| 11 | 0.896 | 0.585 | 0.351 | 0.215 | 0.135 |
| 12 | 0.888 | 0.557 | 0.319 | 0.187 | 0.112 |
| 13 | 0.879 | 0.530 | 0.290 | 0.163 | 0.094 |
| 14 | 0.870 | 0.505 | 0.263 | 0.141 | 0.078 |
| 15 | 0.861 | 0.481 | 0.239 | 0.123 | 0.065 |
| 16 | 0.853 | 0.458 | 0.218 | 0.107 | 0.054 |
| 17 | 0.844 | 0.436 | 0.198 | 0.093 | 0.045 |
| 18 | 0.836 | 0.416 | 0.180 | 0.081 | 0.038 |
| 19 | 0.828 | 0.396 | 0.164 | 0.070 | 0.031 |
| 20 | 0.820 | 0.377 | 0.141 | 0.061 | 0.026 |

# Author Index

# Subject Index